THE TIP OF THE PYRAMID

To Darelle, a champion of freedom speech.

THE TIP OF THE
PYRAMID

Cultivating Community Cultural Capital

by TONY DIAZ,
EL LIBROTRAFICANTE

Tony D, El Librotraficante Ally + thats #Hic Oct 9, 2022

UNIVERSITY OF NEW ORLEANS PRESS

ISBN: 978-1-60801-240-4

Cover photograph provided by author.

Cover and book design by Alex Dimeff.

Library of Congress Cataloging-in-Publication Data

Names: Diaz, Tony, 1968- author.
Title: The Tip of The Pyramid : cultivating community cultural capital / by
  Tony Diaz.
Description: First edition. | New Orleans, Louisiana : University of New
  Orleans Press, [2022]
Identifiers: LCCN 2022016021 (print) | LCCN 2022016022 (ebook) | ISBN
  9781608012404 (paperback) | ISBN 9781608012855 (ebook)
Subjects: LCSH: Mexican Americans. | Mexican Americans--Ethnic identity. |
  Mexican Americans--Intellectual life.
Classification: LCC E184.M5 D527 2022 (print) | LCC E184.M5 (ebook) | DDC
  305.868/72073--dc23/eng/20220509
LC record available at https://lccn.loc.gov/2022016021
LC ebook record available at https://lccn.loc.gov/2022016022

First edition
Printed in the United States of America on acid-free paper.

UNIVERSITY OF NEW ORLEANS PRESS
2000 Lakeshore Drive
New Orleans, Louisiana 70148
unopress.org

CONTENTS

AztecMuse:
Preface on the Precipice

I stood on The Pyramid at Teotihuacan.

The Tip of The Pyramid is concrete proof of Mi Gente's brilliant Art, History, and Culture.

Looking up from the base, I felt pride. But as I ascended, I broke out of that.

At The Tip of The Pyramid, I eclipsed the names branded on my great past by the kings english and the kings spanish. the kings money is designed to make a buck, to reduce the experience to a tourist trap, an exchange of trinkets. It is more than a symbol for math, the shape on the dollar bill, the logo for clandestine groups, the nickname for schemes that rip off people.

I felt The Pyramid in the infinite present.

During Our forever, it summons from around the world and broadcasts Our place in the universe, coding Our Art, History, and Culture into its base, its slopes, The Tip of The Pyramid. Clearly, the kings spanish morphed into the kings english morphed into corporate english is designed to keep Us from this vista.

There are three pictures of me there, captured narratives framing experience.

Two of those pics were taken on my phone by a Columbian writer who indulged me. The first photo consists of me snarling, my fist up in the air, representing Chicano Power at the base of the Mexica Pyramid, Our Pyramid.

The second shot I requested was taken about halfway to the top. I'm sitting, staring down the camera phone and daring anyone watching.

Adriana, a visual artist from Argentina, took the last shot of me. Adriana is a writer by trade, a photographer by vocation. She brought her high-powered camera with a telescopic lens. She was not interested in my clichés about myself. She had her own images of me, the gringo from America who spoke Spanish, who was audacious, who was smart, who was delivered to the American Dream and then came back to hear the Mexican Dream's rebuttal.

So she directed me.

Adriana put a blazer on me. She told me to open my arms. She told me to look up. She told me to yell. Shout. Then smile. She shot me, arms open, ready to fly, bursting off The Tip of The Pyramid, a conversation with the cosmos charted in green grass, hills, and brown dirt on the horizon below me. I'm smiling like a guru.

AztecMuse took me there.

Standing on the testament to My Community's vision, I knew the right words were impending.

I was reminded of how I felt during my first job as a kid: translating the outside world into Spanish for my mother and father. In those moments, I didn't feel as if I had the right words, but I had to act. I needed and wished I had more time to ruminate. I figured that was what school was for. That was what reading was for. And it was soon evident that even the adults weren't sure of what words profoundly meant. That was what education was for. But on the South Side of Chicago, on the butcher's floor or arguing with the clerk at Spiegel's department store, I had to pick the right words to survive the fight of words, to get my folks the best deal possible, and to push Us towards the next day.

There, an hour's bus ride from Mexico City—as it's known in the kings english—I no longer trusted the words conveyed by the kings hand.

The spanish pirates razed my people's temples, Libraries, and Works of Art. They plundered the gold, the silver, the copper, and enslaved the people. The spanish marauders didn't spare this Pyramid for historical purposes. If The Pyramid had been made of gold, it would have been melted and sent to the king after his minions skimmed their cut off the top.

There, looking as far as my eyes could see around that spot in the universe, my gaze is shaped by the architects who envisioned, planned, and beautified—not just half a century before when the Mexica government collapsed, but over half a millennium before that. In other words, and beyond the words of corporate english, The Pyramid was built by the Aztecs of the Aztecs. I can see clearly that the raiders let stand these monuments because they were told that within was something even more valuable than all the gold, all the silver, all the copper. And that is the truth, and I have unearthed it. The Tip of The Pyramid is its own proof.

Yet it has been erased from the words, the history, the books I have been taught as I received one of the best educations on the planet. There are forces in language that separate Us and make Us sign user agreements all day long enforcing, creating, or accepting borders. the kings spanish gives way to the kings english, which gives way to corporate english—all of which obscure My People.

South Side Chicago child interpreter rule number one: you are fighting with words. And to win, you have to land. You need something concrete. You need to land with a brick. Don't hit someone with an actual brick 'cause you will go to jail, or that dude ya hit will come back with his boyz. Instead, boggle his mind with an intellectual brick. It might not be perfect, it might not fit the rules, but it works. It has to work. If not, you lose. This is not a game. This is money, this is the roof over your head, this is your family's freedom, the food on your family's table.

The Tip of The Pyramid is concrete.

AztecMuse is not concrete.

AztecMuse got me to The Tip of The Pyramid. Figuratively. Literally. Spiritually. Financially. I was there on the Mexican government's dime.

My folks never talked about the American Dream with reverence. It was alluded to as the cliché quoted by people from the USA. Instead, my family uttered the spell of "El Norte." A literal translation into corporate english reduces the vision to simply a direction: "The North." If you're in Minnesota, it makes no sense to dream of going north . . . to Canada? There is no Canadian Dream. I grew up on the South Side of Chicago, located on the edge of Lake Michigan: the border of El Norte. In other words, the end of El Norte. Clearly, this was a racket where my folks were destined to always be on the South Side of El Norte.

My family fled Mexico during the 1910 revolution. There was no border patrol. They walked into Texas. They became migrant workers. I am the last child of nine that my parents raised. I am the only one who did not pick crops. My family followed the industrial revolution to Chicago, where my father worked for Conrail, el camino de fiero, as the Mexicans called it—the steel road. That paved the way for me to study once my family had a permanent address, regular meals, union jobs with benefits, and extra money to pay for school. We were not rich, but my dad had worked himself up to lower middle class from off the radar.

AztecMuse was the name of the magazine I founded. My parents once fled Mexico in poverty. The Mexican government was now paying for me to fly to Mexico City, putting me up in a hotel, paying for my meals, and giving me a per diem.

I crossed into Mexico City because I am a Cultural Accelerator (CA).

I was a writer, an activist, a Community organizer, the first Chicano to earn an MFA from the UH Creative Writing Program, and the founder of the nonprofit organization Nuestra Palabra: Latino Writers Having Their Say.

But the kings spanish did not care about Community Work.

AztecMuse was the name I gave to the magazine I founded to appeal to upper-middle-class Mexican Americans in the fourth largest city in America. They were the potential donors who We needed to unite with grassroots groups.

Meanwhile, Mexico wanted writers, journalists, publishers, and media from all over the world to visit to get a fresh view of the country. Of course, this was during the rise of the cartel wars.

There were stories, rumors, and news reports of violence escalating. And still, there was the poverty. My mother was proud to be Mexicana, but she made me swear to never return to Mexico because it was corrupt and the poverty was overwhelming. She had passed away about a decade earlier. Otherwise, I might not have been on that trip.

Felipe Calderón was the president of Mexico. Barack Obama was the president of the US—the first Black president of the nation. It would be easy to be smug, to chalk up that win to the American Day Dream over the Mexican Day Dream. But time levels.

One year later, right-wing republicans in Arizona would ban Mexican American Studies, and then a few short years after that, America would elect donald trump president.

I would ask the Mexican officials about the violence and the cartels, and they would reply that I was safe. I was. Were others? Were the people who lived here? Were the Mexican journalists?

At night, the cabs I rode would speed, stay in touch via walkie-talkies, blow through red lights, and when I asked about their tactics, they would tell me I was safe.

By day, I was shuttled in buses with journalists, writers, and media folks from around the world. I hung out with writers and photographers from Argentina and Columbia, staying at the same five-star hotel.

The rest of this Book is to indict, call out the kings spanish for its crimes. To put it on trial. But at the same time, it's like having someone in your family who is doing or has done time: they are still family. They are part of you, and you are part of them. I am spain, too. The tongue—a literal translation of the word for "language" from the kings spanish to the kings english—is not bad or good. Right now, I'll tell you the good it's done, because it has also done so much bad and continues that sinister work.

I hit it off with the Argentinians and Columbians because they were my age, they were intellectuals, they were visual artists, travel writers, and editors, so they also got shit done. We loved each others' dialects of Spanish, and they thought America was super cool, but, of course, as screwed up as any other nation. They had all been to America: New York, Chicago, Miami, San Francisco, and yes, even Houston.

We were CAs. We defied borders.

And, We spoke the universal language of partying, dancing, drinking, joking non-stop, from bachatas to merengue to US pop songs that they could sing without knowing exactly the words or, if they did, not exactly what the words meant. That is Us: Use the words. Don't let the words use Us, because finally, even when We think We really understand the meaning of the words, that is sometimes when they fail Us the most.

United by Spanish, by the language of my mother and father, my grandmother, my brothers, sisters, my neighbors, and My Community. United by the food, the music, and something else, the ineffable: 3 a.m., in a club, singing Britney Spears songs, finding more booze but still waking up on time for the tour that meant so much to me: Teotihuacan.

There was a crew of six of Us. Two of the women joined me for the trip to Teotihuacan. It was not part of the travelog they might write, not the shot they take and publish in dozens of magazines online and on newsstands throughout Argentina, Columbia, Chile, El Salvador, Guatemala, and yes, Mexico, with traffic from the US. I also didn't try to sell them on the idea.

America dressed my Pyramid companions. They wore blue jeans—showed off their midriffs. Adriana had light hair tied in a ponytail and loved repeating whatever I might say in english. They were clever, irreverent, gifted, and strapped for cash. When they ran out of stipends and free drinks, I would spring—a gringo partying on Mexican prices. I was loaded in Mexico.

I also had the elegance (or audacity) of a gringo, an American, without the loud, tacky shirt, the loud english, and tacky lack of Spanish. Ugly Americans go to Mexico to invest their supremacy, liquidate their privilege, and leverage the exchange rate to export exoticism and erasure. Their capital turns Teotihuacan into trinkets.

I was not an Ugly American. At the time, I simply thought that meant I looked good. I wore a light blue Guayabera with a tight, slim fit, not like the old men wear. I wore white pants, badass tan shoes, handmade in Italy, that I bought from Lucho, a clothier owned by Héctor Villarreal, a Mexican American former weatherman, and Patricia Sturion, a Brazilian designer, two bon vivants of Houston. How much did they cost? You mean in capital? Capital buys the least. Cultural Capital moves more.

Of course, We need capital. The electric company flows electricity to my house, to this computer, because I pay their bills. Capital, cash, is basic, like food, a roof overhead, and/or supplies. But the kings english is forged on barriers to keep Us from capital, to starve Us into working to make capital for their maximum wage while We fight for minimum wage. Capital is good for the minimum to survive. If We want to thrive, Our Communities need to understand the power of Community Cultural Capital (CCC).

Some people who try to use the kings english against Us are alarmed that Our Term CCC has the word "capital" in it. I suppose they think that makes Us capitalists.

Nah.

the kings english oppresses as much as capital oppresses.

the kings spanish oppresses as much as capital oppresses.

So shall We not use capital? Shall We not use english? Shall We not use spanish?

Instead of discarding, CAs co-opt capital, the kings english, the kings spanish, and corporate english.

In Mexico City, on Teotihuacan, I was unearthing the power of CCC without the precise words dawning on me. Now, years later, I must liberate english to rise to this task.

I translate the phrase "Cultural Capital" into corporate english as assets like skills, networks, and knowledge, as well as literal capital that Our Community Members possess. Our Community is aware of these assets, and We put them into practice, but We don't always realize their power or value. For example, CCC helps Us stretch capital—or, as We called it on my block, money—to make ends meet. When my parents were short on capital, which in Our house We called dinero, my mom had a recipe for tamales that she could invest in to make dozens of the delicious iconic food that folks from, around, or who knew Our Community would buy.

AztecMuse ads materialized my clothes through promotions, trade, patrons of the arts, and yes, even boring capital whose price is never fixed and always on the fix. *AztecMuse* had a fashion designer. I had New York City-level, European-imported clothes at Houston, Texas prices, styling in Mexico City. Screw borders.

I followed The AztecMuse to shatter borders. That much was clear to me then. I return to these moments because now I have The Words.

AztecMuse was the name of the magazine I founded. But it is also the term I have for that state I felt while on Teothihuacan.

Note, *AztecMuse* is not the title of this Book. That is the title of this section, which is, according to the kings english, not part of the work. It is the preface, as in that which comes before.

AztecMuse brings together words that were not born together. It crosses a lot of borders. Aztecs is the name of the Mexica in the kings english.

The muses are the kings english version of the greek metaphor for inspiration. Are they goddesses, spirits, literal, or figurative?

They are branded as feminine.

Are the Aztecs masculine? This question forces another question. The Mexica are not humanized in english. They have the wrong name, just as Indigenous peoples are called the wrong name of "Indians" taught in grammar schools across this continent and europe. They are genderless because they are body-less. The spanish pirates dehumanized to plunder land, gold, silver, and people.

AztecMuse is built on two words that do not go together in corporate english. That plurality was always there, but I could not put my finger on it. Or, better said, I was not being graded on it. In fact, some people have bothered to tell me that the word is wrong. Such critics are versed in supremacist ways that deny Us Our Power to create—anything. To be experts on Ourselves, to speak for Ourselves. To voice.

Yet I see the AztecMuse clearly, right now, revealing the path for this Book, but defying capture.

Do We use language, or does language use Us? There, on The Tip of The Pyramid, I thought I had coined a term. And that term was AztecMuse. That word still defies me, stays just out of reach. Within the pages of its magazine incarnation existed the word "Librotraficante." I thought it was cool, but it was not quite catching on yet. On the other hand, AztecMuse had brought me to The Tip of The Pyramid.

Or was I summoned?

AztecMuse was the state of mind edifying my self-determination, there, closer to the cosmos, in conversation with celestial bodies, above the calendar, corporate language, barriers, free.

I collected myself to buttress my determination to strike a balance, so I could be of use to myself, my family, and then my Community.

That state of mind, that balance, that freedom is a threat to some.

Eventually, I would have to come down. And on the ground, "Librotraficante" would help navigate Us through an attack on Our People—the following year, Arizona right-wing republicans would ban Mexican American Studies. And We would flaunt the term Librotraficante as We organized a six-city caravan to smuggle back into Arizona the Books on the outlawed Curriculum.

*   *   *

The AztecMuse helped me come to terms with translating this Book. I am translating this work from the kings english into Our english.

The title is concrete: *The Tip of The Pyramid.* That is the title for this Book, with a capital "B." "book" with a lowercase "b" refers to simply a product, wood pulp shaped to fit corporate publishing templates and sales forecasts. This Book is infused with CCC to create more Culture. How can I dare to challenge grammatical dictates? Because We decide grammar. If you need to see my license, my papers, I just pointed to the MFA on my wall. I mastered the kings english, but I rejected masters. I hacked the kings english, fixed it, and now I'm giving it back.

corporate english reduces the "Tip of The Pyramid" to the clichés of a "goal" or the cliché of a "north star," definitions that give the illusion of truth. Those clichés roughly, barely describe.

My Culture, my Art, and my History are solid when conveyed in metaphors over five hundred years old.

I write this five hundred years after the Mexica leaders surrendered their governance to the spanish pirates. If kings named mariners who stole *ships* pirates, then I name spanish mariners who stole *land* pirates, too.

This Book is published ten years after Arizona right-wing republicans enforced a ban on Mexican American Studies.

I write this ten years after I co-founded the Librotraficante Caravan.

I write this as We prepare for the twenty-fifth anniversary of the Nuestra Palabra: Latino Writers Having Their Say, the nonprofit group I founded to promote and defend Latino literature, literacy, and culture because the fourth-largest city in America did not have a regular reading series for Mi Gente, even though We formed almost half of the city's population.

I couldn't put all of that into words myself.

I, We, conjured *AztecMuse*.

The AztecMuse unearthed Our power. Our Leaders. Our Roots. Our Unity.

I was ready to spread the magazine to San Antonio, Austin, Dallas, and Corpus Christi.

There in Mexico City, with drinks in hand, governments bowing for Us, an abundance of two nations twisting the immigration laws to Our benefit, I did not know The AztecMuse was preparing me for an attack on Our Gente. It prepared me by revealing Our Power at The Tip of The Pyramid.

Of course, I suspected. In the back of Our Minds, We always suspect.

How would I have reacted if a nonprofit prophet had stopped me on that Pyramid, or in that hotel bar, or in a Mexico City antro, and warned me that in the near future my History and Culture would be banned?

How do *you* react now that I tell you that in the near past, it happened? How do you react when I tell you that on Our watch, during Our lifetime, Our People's History and Culture was banned in the United States of America?

Do you doubt me? I'll give you all the legal, media, and historical receipts in this Book.

What if I told you that it was Our Own Gente who united to contain and overturn the racist law?

We had the Power. And We still have it. Why is that erased from Our History?

What if, instead of warning you about the past, I am here to reveal Our Power? I am here to reveal CAs. And We must reveal Ourselves right now, We must Unite, and We must Act—or intellectual freedom, freedom of speech, and civil liberties are doomed for everyone. Cultural sovereignty is doomed for everyone.

The AztecMuse is helping me to put all these signs into words into sentences, so We will not be sentenced, but liberated.

Only Art can save Us.

But let me give you something concrete:

Whether or not you are a CA, you must find Your Voice.

Start writing right now.

Write one paragraph, write one page, write two. Your enemy is the blank page. An entire generation of Our Youth has been conned into believing that reading and writing don't matter. That is the generational racket created by the rulers who create the rules to maintain their rule. And they pass the most powerful of those rules in writing. The fewer of Us who excel at reading and writing, the fewer of Us there are to read the constant flow of user agreements that trick, numb, cajole, threaten, or wear Us down to sign every day.

There are forces at work to silence you.

You gain Your Power by Writing. By Reading. By Thinking.

If I reduce this Book to one sentence, in the kings english, coded by AztecMuse: This Book will reveal Your Power, reveal the Work of CAs, and inspire Us to unite to Cultivate CCC.

At The Tip of The Pyramid I edify my self-determination, honed my vision. It cleared me of the supremacy, the castes, the rackets to see the plurality We can achieve, Together.

The Tip of The Pyramid is an intersection of influences.

The Tip of The Pyramid represents Our Art, History, Culture, beyond the five hundred years of the kings spanish imposed on this land. It becomes a metaphor.

The Tip of The Pyramid is not a tip. It is a plateau.

If you stand there, it is because of all the steps leading there. You can simply climb up and then down. Or you can consider the science, the astrology, the urban planning, the labor, the art that raised it, raised you. Is the tip a tip, a plateau or a top?

Did you rise there on your own?

Is the top separate from the base?

Is the tip one spot independent of every bit of stone, rock, sand, brought to together to rise from the ground?

As We organize, The Tip of The Pyramid becomes a metaphor for an outcome vetted by Our Community. Once the campaign towards this vision manifests, the advocates, the champions for this cause also embody The Tip of The Pyramid. Additional symbols gain meaning in the process. This is the power of language. We create meaning.

The closer We are to The Tip of The Pyramid, the more certain We are of Our People's Art, History, Culture. the kings english strives to pull Us away from it.

Now, when I am far from the literal proof of Teotihuacan, I see how The Tip of The Pyramid shapes me. This empowers me to understand that I count. This empowers me to count my CCC. This empowers me to play a role in edifying My Community by keeping Our Art, Culture, and History alive, or by manifesting it anew through Art.

*　　　　　*　　　　　*

There are three facets that shape the forms of the Books in this Series. These facets also shape the work of Community Organizing. In other words, these same concepts apply to individuals and also to the form of this Book. This is the first Book in the Series, and its purpose is in the subtitle: Cultivating Community Cultural Capital. I am not going to focus on devising Fair Exchanges in this Book, as that could be its own Book. I don't want readers to experience how the kings english squirmed for those of Us who grew up translating. So, I'll spell out some aspects of the form of this Book. I'll review these three forces in terms of how they influence Us as individuals and break down how they shape this Book. After that, the Book takes flight off the precipice. The Book itself puts into practice, dramatizes these approaches.

These forces are:

1) Cultural Acceleration

2) Cultivating Community Cultural Capital

3) Quantifying Community Cultural Capital

Cultural Acceleration occurs when a CA quickly moves CCC towards The Tip of The Pyramid. The way power works in America, this happens the fastest on a "level playing field" like national corporate media, for example a nationwide broadcast.

Cultivating CCC refers to planting the seeds of culture. This requires investing time, energy, and resources for effects that are long-term/in the future.

Quantifying CCC involves taking stock and counting Cultural Assets. This can be an inventory of Cultural Value.

We are always at a disadvantage because We have to define Our Terms using corporate english which ignores Us on some days and on others erases Us. It's challenging to sum up my identity in one word. It's even harder to define "white," but "white" does not have to define itself because it is the default setting.

That's the same racket that creates the phrase "The American Dream" without ever having to truly define it.

A Cultural Accelerator (CA) is a person who has achieved self-determination. They choose to learn more about their Culture. This does not happen in school. They must look for that on their Own time, using their Own energy. This could also mean consulting and believing in elders. This involves seeking more wisdom, more wise people.

There is no license for this or a major in college, so the safe bet is to embrace the delineated paths of occupations to occupy your mind. This leads to living within one business card: Certified Public Accountant, VP, Bank Pres., Esq., Partner, CEO, CFO.

This is neither good nor bad.

Someone might possess all the traits of a CA; however, they might not believe they are one. This is because they have only one business card: immigration attorney, partner at a firm, for example.

In the past, a single business card formed the border. Others worked without that business card, which is equivalent to working in the shadows, in the margins. They too might not consider themselves CAs.

With this Book, those of Us who are overtly, loudly, clearly CAs can build, shine a light on, replicate, chart, and repeat strategies, so that undocumented CAs can now more clearly and deliberately unite with their Community. We will all see how these traits count. We see how We count. Culture adds up to Us, and We add to Our Culture. This is how a person thrives, and then a family thrives, friends thrive, a neighborhood, a network, a Community, a nation.

We, as CAs individually must profoundly *Quantify* Our CCC in order to understand what We can and can't do, what We need help with, what We can help others with, and We must also tell others what We expect, want, or need. CAs Accelerate CCC when they are in tune with those aspects and adjust them for working with more and more CAs. But first, We have to get more of Us into the Community.

These forces shape this Book in several ways, including finding and creating an audience. corporate education, as I received in graduate school, frowns on writers talking directly about an intended audience. We're graded by some mysterious universal aesthetic, never fully explained by the lords of the ivory tower.

But, there is always an intended audience.

When the intended audience is not stated, the intended audience is the default setting of culture, which means it is not Us. I am putting into words, finally, those transactions, moments, memories where you sensed you were coming up against something, but it was not clear what it was. And if it is invisible, by default, it is hard to talk about because everyone else just respects the border, loves the border.

the kings english wants to limit My Community.

Claiming to write, follow, or impose a universal aesthetic is a supremacist tendency forged from centuries of caste systems and intellectual rackets. It stems from the kings english and the kings spanish since monarchs are the ultimate supremacists, and by ultimate, I mean last. If you were good at school, you were accustomed to groping around in the dark of the ivory tower, feeling for the edges of these unspoken universal rules. In that intellectual caste system, Our Voice is never the omnipotent voice of god. Our Voice disrupts the narrative.

Not here.

Art shatters borders, transmits Culture, codes Our experiences. These issues are not often enough directly talked about, especially in books.

Novels, short story collections, poetry collections code them.

Textbooks are still products of corporate publishers for corporate education.

We talk about this among each other as We re-invent the wheel often. We begin again, from scratch.

The forms for books, novels, nonfiction are shaped by corporate publishers, corporate bookstores, corporate media, corporate english, so that they not only are not conducive to Our questions, they do not provide forms that We can use to take these issues head on.

I take these issues head on in this Preface.

I take them head on in the Book by bringing them to life.

In other words, We are rewarded for not bringing up these issues. We are given good grades for ignoring Our Culture and repeating the facts teachers and textbooks test Us on.

If We can adjust to this omission, We are rewarded by being called well-behaved students. We pass. We are moved to the next gradation.

There is a default setting for school. The default Culture never has to be explained. It is the source of all facts, all importance, all important dates, history, art, of which We are not. You are tested on the cultural shrapnel of bits and bytes and data points that add up to the perspectives you must adopt to get a good grade.

Finding The Tip of The Pyramid is more like finding a frequency. A CA must be in tune with their Community.

The Tip of The Pyramid is not "charted" in "corporate time." A goal that is set by The Community does not need to be achieved by, for example, the clock of corporate education in one semester, or the clock of corporate business in one quarter or one fiscal year. A profound Tip of The Pyramid might be achieved over the span of a lifetime, several lifetimes, a generation.

The term "Acceleration" does not refer to reaching, achieving, or experiencing The Tip of The Pyramid quickly.

A Book aimed at Cultural Acceleration alone would not explain what I am explaining. This Book is not geared towards reaching Cultural Acceleration. When We are in the middle of Activism, We Act. We won't, as this Book will do, stop and explain strategies, tactics, or metaphors. Cultural Acceleration pushes metaphors (and people and resources) to their limits.

Instead, this Book is shaped to Cultivate CCC.

The tactics in this Book examine several moments when We as a Community have accomplished in a short time that which was not accomplished before in decades, and which therefore seemed impossible. For example, several generations of activists advocated for Ethnic Studies before curricula were ever approved. During this modern era of the Ethnic Studies Movement, We have seen Ethnic Studies courses devised, approved, and taught. Not every generation gets to see the fruits of its labor.

This Book plants the seeds for more CAs to organize their Community and for their friends, family, neighbors, and allies, to help them. This Book also will inspire readers to recognize CAs who might not know they are CAs, or reveal to folks that they are CAs, or push them to lay the groundwork to unite with other CAs or to lean into the Work they are doing already.

This Work is not clear-cut. This Work does not pay a lot of money, but this Work creates a lot of CCC which is powerful.

This Book is not intended to Quantify CCC, either. That would entail breaking down even more aspects, explaining even more terms, and adopting a strategy similar to the style of scholars or academics who employ the Modern Language Association guidelines to cite other scholars and academics.

This Book is intended not for academics, but for CAs and those folks who love them.

This Art works. This Book functions in the real world. It thrives off the page via radio, TV, social media platforms, livestreams, and live and remote events.

The Community chooses The Tip of The Pyramid, a vision, an objective to which We will rise. A CA furthers Our Progress towards that. Inevitably, that course will intersect with a so-called Level Playing Field. As oppressed people, We do not get to choose the site for a battle on The Level Playing Field; those battles are determined by the systems and institutions that surround Us. However, We *do* choose where and how The Tip of The Pyramid will pierce through a Level Playing Field—how Our path as a Community will rupture the status quo. This means that the CA competing on The Level Playing Field is not alone. They represent Us. They are empowered by The Community. They advance The Community. They have the resources of CCC.

And, as this Book addresses, if a CA is fighting on The Level Playing Field of the court, The Community also broadens the fight to the Court of Public Opinion and pools its other CCC, including capital—straight-up money when needed—to win the fight. This process, which We repeat in endless combinations of Pyramid Tips and shattered Playing Fields, is how We rise, survive, and thrive.

A Community Goal or Vision achieved becomes a step towards a new Tip of The Pyramid.

Each Tip of The Pyramid forms the foundation for a next Tip of The Pyramid. When We, as a Community, achieve a Tip of The Pyramid, We have to embrace it, archive it, acknowledge it, so that We build on it.

This empowers Us to progress. This allows Us to compete on the The Level Playing Field of society and culture.

The Level Playing Field is more accurately the *myth of* The Level Playing Field. It is not level. It is a racket. This refers to a space created by, for example, a power broker, such as corporate education, to conduct its business in public in order to define and maintain its power, under Our noses. This "field" can be a court, it can be a university, it can be national news or an art scene or politics.

Americans are told the courts are Level Playing Fields, sites of colorblind, impartial justice; however, most folks know that if you have the money and connections to secure the best lawyers, your justice improves. Worse, when donald trump was president, he went out of his way to create a republican supreme court—which was the story he pushed from the white house, even though the SUPREME court of the land is supposed to be impartial.

The only reason that the illusion of "level" or "fairness" can be invoked is because the proceedings of these fields are in public, and the rules created by the rulers who maintain their rule are often skewed slightly so that one out of millions of Us might make it to compete on that terrain. That one person out of a million is then held up as the exception that "proves" the rule of the field's fairness, hiding its actual unfairness and sidelining the question of why so few of Us actually make it to the field.

Our Community does not have the generational wealth or power to compete on The Level Playing Field when one of Us winds up in that court.

The Tip of The Pyramid changes this discourse.

*   *   *

From 2002 to 2007, the crew of Nuestra Palabra: Latino Writers Having Their Say (NP for short) organized the largest Book fairs in Houston, and the largest in Texas at the time, drawing 30,000 attendees to the George R. Brown Convention Center. This is notable because Latinos are perceived or stereotyped as not caring about reading or writing. NP was only four years old when it shattered these stereotypes by organizing this massive event with limited funding, but a potent flex of CCC. With the Book Fair, NP Accelerated CCC.

Nuestra Palabra was a Tip of The Pyramid first. NP submitted to being documented as a 501(c)(3) nonprofit by the IRS, but We were way more than that corporate definition. We gained meaning as a movement for Our Gente. That led to the next Tip of The Pyramid—an FM Radio Show. Once that became a reality, that led to Our massive Book fair. And then We built on that.

If this Book were Accelerating CCC, these words would simply thrill. I would not explain terms.

If this Book were Quantifying CCC for scholars, the rules, shaped by corporate education, would demand that I produce a handbook about Our decades of work. I will—in the future of this Series, but not here.

For an individual, Quantifying CCC takes on a different nature. That is not the work of explaining something to many. In the course of the life of a CA, they must, for themselves, profoundly understand the facets of Culture that have shaped and will shape them. They must count their CCC. This sounds easy. However, as CAs understand deeply, you can't count CCC if you don't believe that *you* count. This means that members of Our Community achieve self-determination before they profoundly understand that they count, their voice counts, their family counts, their neighborhood counts. QCCC means one thing for this Book aimed at many people, versus what it means for a single person shaping their experience, their life, their time, their energy.

For The Community, QCCC can also mean saving Our History. This ranges from sharing oral histories and family stories, to archiving them, to writing them down, to putting them together for a book. The most formal version of QCCC accepted by the kings english is the least accessible and interesting, at this time, to Our Community: writing in the code of the ivory tower, using their rules to quote experts they consecrate, based on the evidence they see fit, for books no one wants to publish or read, so as to advance half a step up the corporate ivory tower ladder.

That doesn't mean the ivory tower is never compatible with Our work. There is a brilliant example of this approach co-opted for The Cabrera Report, which I discuss in this Book. That academic research was used as evidence at the Arizona Supreme Court case to overturn the banning of Mexican American Studies.

corporate education, along with corporate media and corporate entertainment, et al., want to stay illiterate about Our Community. There are a ton of works that exist that fit their molds (and a ton more that do not), written by CAs that they don't care about. If they were really interested in reading Us, they would bring attention to the attacks on Our Art, History, and Culture.

Activism is important. But activism without a larger plan—in this case, the vision shaped by The Tip of The Pyramid—could become an individual act that dissipates over time, or does not directly add up to a larger movement. Likewise, there are members of Our Community who do achieve self-determination but do not stay in touch with CCC. This Book argues that those very folks are lured away from CCC on a regular basis, to their own and Our peril.

CAs are those individuals who achieve self-determination, are expert in their field, and most likely several fields, and also stay in profound touch with The Community.

This Books is not directly about achieving Self-Determination.

If someone wants to truly understand Self-Determination in Our Community, Our Elders are the first great source. Another great source are any of the over eighty works from the Mexican American Studies curriculum banned by right-wing republican legislators in Arizona. If someone does not read a dozen of those works before asking a CA about Self-Determination or which label identity is the right one for all of Us, they are just playing.

On that note, this Book does not feed into the clickbait topic of which identity label corporate media, corporate government, corporate politics, or corporate marketing wants all of Us to fall into at a given time. This is not to dismiss the work begun by activists to achieve representation for Us, which peaked in 1970 when the census bureau under Nixon added the lines for Us, grouped under the phrase "persons of Spanish origin," to the constitutionally mandated survey. However, that was in 1970! To rehash an ancient approach without updating it, without taking into consideration Our profound thoughts, without treating Us as the experts on Us— all this not only enables a system that is illiterate about Us to *remain* illiterate about Us, but also feeds into their myth that they know Us better than We know Us.

*   *   *

In the past, Our Community stayed in the shadows for different reasons. Some of Us were not documented, some of Us were not fluent in education, some of Us were simply being worked to death. Those same folks worked like mad because it was clear that their children would have a better life as a result. That was the mantra my parents repeated, and I lived. That better life was often made possible through education.

Well, that is not so clear anymore.

As I write this, it is getting harder and harder for the next generation to do better than their parents did. Today, I hear news stories, even on "progressive" outlets, about how college is not for everyone. This is nonsense. In 2019, over fifty rich white parents were busted in a scandal for bribing college officials, college coaches, and test supervisers to make sure that their kids got into college. If college does not matter, why are rich white parents bribing people to make sure their kids to get into the right college?

By the way, one of the targeted schools for the felonious affluent was the University of Texas at Austin, which is in Tejas, and which Texas high school students who graduate in the top seven percent of their class are automatically admitted into. Tejanos don't always realize how valuable what We have is until others covet it. Rich white parents went to jail for access to a school mandated to Texas kids.

But that mandate is in danger right now.

College tuition is insane. Students accrue too much debt. And worse, Our Gente's intellectual advancement is seen as a threat to others.

This is the main thrust of this Book:

Your edification is a threat.

Your Child's Self-Determination is a threat.

This was made clear to me when Arizona right-wing republican officials banned Mexican American History. Legislators feared Chicanas and Chicanos reading books about Our History and Culture.

Let me repeat that: In Our lifetimes, a state in the union banned Our History and Culture. And it happened right in front of Us.

If I have to explain to you how this is a travesty, I do not have time for you.

*   *   *

When I held *AztecMuse* in my hands as the magazine, I believed I grasped the metaphor by grabbing the hard copy. But I did not.

At the time, it was so much work to forge the pages that created a lattice for The AztecMuse that I lost sight of the brutal honesty of the metaphor of a magazine—as a place to hold still ideas, to store them, display them for Us to digest, taste, experience, at that moment, as meaning, reality, culture moving along a long road. A magazine might testify to the spirit of AztecMuse, but it can never be synonymous with it.

These years later, AztecMuse still has not clearly revealed itself to me. But it does revisit me, taps at the window of my memory. It whispers that it loaded in that magazine the term "Librotraficante," waiting to coin itself in the real world, ready to fire at the moment when Our History and Culture would be banned, so We could act, furiously, splendidly.

Acceleration.

Now, what does AztecMuse ask of Us?

PART I:
SHATTERING THE MYTH
OF THE LEVEL PLAYING FIELD

Arizona Banned Our History and Culture. We Decided to Make More.

During Our lifetime, just a few years ago, Arizona republican legislators banned Mexican American Studies.

Whether or not you know this reveals a lot about American History. This is not ancient history. This is erased history about the erasure of Our History. If you knew about this and perhaps even defied the ban, ask yourself if mainstream media, textbooks, or curriculums have allowed this direct attack on Our community to fade. If you have never heard about this attack, ask yourself why.

This oppression revealed to me that there are forces at work in this nation to sabotage Our intellectual growth. This is not a conspiracy theory, this happened. I was sitting in the courtroom at the Ninth Circuit Court of Appeals in San Francisco when a federal judge said to the lawyer for the state of Arizona: If a curriculum is proven to help minorities succeed academically, and you ban it, how is that not an example of discriminatory animus?

That sentence freed me from sentences.

In that courtroom I profoundly understood the power of Self-Determination and CCC, and that there were people threatened by Our intellectual advancement.

The Librotraficantes were uniting with scholars and educators from Tucson and across the southwest and the entire country, leading legal minds, all of Us shaping national media, indy media, social media, and history. Yet, my first time visiting the Ninth Circuit Court of Appeals, a Legal Playing Field of the courts, was to watch the state of Arizona attack teenage Chicanos for reading about their Culture and History. Our Crew mounted a public relations campaign that would rival anything the corporate world could sell Us. Yet, no news outlet profoundly understood that this attack was clearly intended to debilitate Our CCC for generations.

This attack also revealed that there are forces at work that are threatened by Our intellectual progress—which is part of Our basic humanity. Yet corporate media insisted on reducing Our plight to a discussion about the existence of a course. That is the system Librotraficantes had to hack to Accelerate Our campaign. The rest of the cultural shrapnel We would have to sift through in the wake of Our success. If We did not win, We would be occupied with the shrapnel forever. For that reason, at that time, The Tip of The Pyramid was overturning Arizona's ban of Mexican American Studies. We knew this would involve raising awareness and support so that the brilliant legal team assembled by Chicano civil rights lawyer Richard Martinez could overturn the discriminatory law. These were the goals that We Librotraficantes needed to broadcast to Our Gente via social media, indy media, mainstream media, and one Mexican at a time. Policy change was The Tip of The Pyramid as Our Community united across state lines to thwart the ban of Our History and Culture.

We were expert at that, because We had been practicing those skills since 1998 through Nuestra Palabra: Latino Writers Having Their Say. We didn't have time to pause and explain too much. We had to unite Our CCC and Accelerate the resources We counted on to build Our voice to defend Our voice.

I began Our revolution by first summoning the poets:

Mind Altering Pros

Only Art Can Save Us.
Our Terms on Our Terms.
Mind-altering prose fuels Cultural Acceleration.
Legal terms sentence Us.
legal english undocuments Us.
Metaphors are forced confessions.

Now, well past the urgency of that moment of Cultural Acceleration, I am pausing to explain some of the tactics We employed and
provide some behind the scenes information, so that more CAs
can unite to address newer challenges. That is the purpose of this
Book that is not merely a book.

This Book is the Tip of The next Pyramid.

And CCC is still and will always be the base.

On the ten-year anniversary of the 2012 Librotraficante Caravan,
as this movement grows, I have the words, the time, the audience,
and the platforms to break down what happened.

I also have the advantage of knowing I was right. Our truth has
come to pass. Arizona right-wingers knew We would not overthrow
the government through violence, We would overthrow them by
voting them out of office. And this has come to pass. The main
characters of that racist attack on Our History were either voted
out of office or they dropped out.

Of course, corporate media, politicians, and entertainment have
ignored, erased, or whitewashed all of Our History, so We must
also archive it, as We dramatize is, as We spread it.

This Book is about *Cultivating* CCC, by documenting some of the
essential tactics, approaches, and histories CAs employ to empower
Our Community. These words will add up to a Book, bills, policy
change, more CCC. And more CCC. And more . . .

This cycle, this investment in CCC, is a direct fortification of Our
Community, Our Culture. By attacking Our History and Culture,
right-wing politicians revealed what they feared most: intellectuals
from Our Community, the edification of CCC, The People Uniting.

If this crisis in Tucson had not erupted, I would have probably
never crossed the borders of Texas to unite with my familia of writers, scholars, and activists in New Mexico and Arizona. We Houstonians barely knew what Our brothers and sisters in San Antonio and
El Paso were up to. The 2012 Librotraficante Caravan to smuggle
back into Tucson the books banned by Arizona changed that. We
crossed borders, We opened underground libraries, We flagrantly
trafficked contraband prose and created more contraband pros.

Once Our brothers and sisters were attacked, We became Librotraficantes to fight back, because AZ officials were attacking Us, too. Let me be clear. This was state violence against Chicanos. The people of Tucson suffered the brunt of it. Their CCC was attacked and harmed. Their Community cultivated the Chicana and Chicano educators and scholars to create the leading Ethnic Studies Program in the nation. Instead of extolling it, Arizona right-wing legislators attacked. Arizona officials maligned, fired, and sued the very educators they should have celebrated. Our CCC was destabilized and traumatized. However, the people of Tucson stood up to this oppression.

The people of Tucson are inspiring. We were blessed to meet them, work with them, learn from them. They were courageous in the face of racist attacks from the state and those in power. They inspired Us Tejanos to join them and to stand up to Our own oppressors as well. Texas has its own history of politicians erasing Our History. The Librotraficantes began writing Our own chapters.

This Book is one of Our campaigns for changes in policy. This Tip of The Pyramid will reveal the next Tip of The Pyramid. Those specific actions, or initiatives for change, which shatter barriers and continue to work as guided, fueled, and inspired by CCC, are profound examples of Cultural Acceleration. The 2012 Librotraficante Caravan is a powerful example of how thrilling Cultural Acceleration toward The Tip of The Pyramid can be—and, in 2012, The Tip of The Pyramid, the point of focus for all Our Acceleration and Cultivation, consisted not just of overturning the Arizona law, but also making sure it didn't spread to other states. At the time of the Ninth Circuit trial, Texas right-wing officials were already copying parts of the law, testing it.

I'll ruin the ending for you: Our Community united to overturn Arizona's right-wing, racist law banning Mexica American Studies. We thwarted that.

In response, Ethnic Studies campaigns were re-ignited or inspired in states throughout the nation. The Librotraficantes returned to

Tejas to focus on reviving and re-energizing the struggle for Ethnic Studies in the second most right-wing state in the Union at the time.

The Librotraficantes captured the American Imagination and rocketed to national and international notoriety. However, that Cultural Acceleration was possible only because of the organization it grew out of—Nuestra Palabra, a wellspring of Our CCC.

As a writer, I literally graph, chart, Our CCC. I talk to leaders, other artists, elders, the youth, to get their thoughts on what may be the next Tip of The Pyramid, or what may be the steps to reach that goal, point, organization, once Our Community agrees on its importance. In the vernacular of the children of the computer era, We writers code these visions into novels, short stories, plays, poems, songs, and even broadcasts, radio shows, TV shows, podcasts, memes. NP Cultivated these skills, Cultivated CCC for fourteen years before Arizona right-wingers banned Our Culture.

The Librotraficante Movement was The Tip of The Pyramid. Nuestra Palabra: Latino Writers Having Their Say was the base. This Book is about the fundamental connection between CCC and Change.

The Myth of The Level Playing Field

I go back to that moment in the courtroom of the Ninth Circuit Court of Appeals in San Francisco January 12, 2015, for "Maya Arce v. John Huppenthal Oral Argument."

Our cultural lives were at stake. There was no time to explain. If these battles were lost, there would be no one to explain it to. There would be no voices left to speak. It would be too devastating to keep writing. We would have had to push Our Cultural Acceleration even harder, and We were already at an amazing capacity.

The judge warned the state of Arizona of its discriminatory animus. This animated me. We were not crazy: the ban of Our History and Culture was racist. Up to that point, there were policies, laws, and rulings that said otherwise.

Long before "Maya Arce v. John Huppenthal," a generation of Arizona republican elected officials, state representatives and state senators crafted the law over several years and several tries, with former Arizona Superintendent of Education John Huppenthal at the helm. Then-governor Janet Napolitano would veto the law every time it got to her desk. Then Arizona republican legislators would try again.

In the meantime, Chicano and Chicana educators at Tucson High School in the Tucson Unified School District continued to refine and conduct the gold standard of Ethnic Studies programs. The curriculum they designed was based on over eighty works by Chicana, Chicano, Latinx, Black, and Indigenous writers. Chicana and Chicano scholars would later develop the research that would prove, beyond the shadow of a doubt—even under cross-examination at the Arizona Supreme Court, from the only expert witness Arizona hired—that this curriculum raised Tucson High's graduation rate to ninety-eight percent and increased student performance and engagement across the board. Of course, the student body was predominantly Mexican American.

And still, Arizona republican legislators dedicated their time, energy, and resources, year after year, to stop the threat of Chicano students reading, writing, and graduating.

Of course, that was not the message they spread to scare voters into supporting, or at least not defying, their attack on Our History and Culture. Several Arizona heads of education instead would use the stereotypes of Mexican Americans as violent, telling the media and their constituents that the program promoted the overthrow of the US government. If you are sitting in your living room watching TV in a suburb of Arizona and the only Mexicans you have ever seen or imagine are gangbangers in films, rapists on TV, and criminals on the news, you would be terrified to hear a REPORT that La Raza instructors are teaching gangbanger-age Mexicans to overthrow the government.

After it bolstered the campaign to ban Mexican American Studies, this stereotype actually made it into the letter of the racist law, forming one of the four prongs designed to prohibit Ethnic Studies curricula by "[p]rohibit[ing] courses that promote the overthrow of the government."

America has overlooked this disgusting detail. In Our lifetime, there was a law on the books that institutionalized the racist trope that Mexican Americans are prone to violence.

It further dehumanized Us by using this racist trope to attack, vilify, and outlaw a program that was helping foster Chicana and Chicano intellectuals; high school graduates who would go on to earn college degrees, advanced degrees, who would run for office. Elected officials fought to maintain this stereotype, to codify it— even as Our Community is conned on a daily basis into believing that elections don't matter.

For years, Governor Napolitano would veto the law banning Our History and Culture when it got to her desk. However, when President Obama was elected he named Napolitano to head Homeland Security. The next governor of Arizona was jan brewer, who would become the posterchild for the far-right. She would sign into law S.B. 1070—Arizona's "Show me your papers" law—to further vilify immigrants and push the anti-immigrant movement into high gear. She was aided and abetted by many, including sheriff joe arpaio, who oversaw Arizona's Tent City, cited around the world as a humanitarian travesty. He would become a convicted racist whose conviction was later pardoned by donald trump.

After villainizing immigrants with one law in 2010, jan brewer was more than happy to sign the 2012 legislation banning Mexican American Studies. After jan brewer attacked Our bodies with one law, she then moved on to attacking Our minds. Additional bodies aided and abetted: The Tucson Unified School District voted to enforce the law. The Arizona Supreme Court, the first time around, upheld the law. Media reported the case as Arizona simply "managing a curriculum," or else focused on instances of the youth and Community protesting as indications that perhaps it *was* true: they *were* being trained to overthrow the government! At any rate, mainstream media was careful not to call this update of censorship a "ban." The System became apologists for tyrants.

In Houston, the Librotraficantes acted. If Arizona officials were going to ban Our History and Culture, We would simply make more.

The Librotraficante Movement was founded by me and four veteran members of Nuestra Palabra: Latino Writers Having Their Say: Liana Lopez (Librotraficante Lilo), Bryan Parras (Librotraficante High Tech Aztec), Laura Acosta (Librotraficante La Laura), and Lupe Mendez (Librotraficante Lips Mendez). In eight weeks, We organized a six-city tour, opening four Librotraficante Under Ground Libraries along the way and donating over $20,000 in books. We fueled a movement across the Southwest and then the entire nation, to draw attention to Arizona's campaign against Our minds and imaginations.

I was a fiction writer at the time. I am the first Chicano to earn a Master of Fine Arts from the University of Houston Creative

Writing Program. I wrote the novel *The Aztec Love God*, and I was working on another novel as this ban broke loose. When I heard what was going down, I abandoned fiction—I could not make up this shit. Instead I decided to use my skills as a writer, radio host, Community organizer, educator, translator, comedian, and intellectual to defy this attack on Our Gente.

Our campaign took off like a rocket.

That is the beauty and power of Cultural Acceleration.

At the time, We had to push that Acceleration to defy all the powerbrokers who were trying to break Our power. We also knew the costs of losing this battle.

Arizona's ban of Mexican American Studies was intended to eradicate Our CCC. Worse, it was happening right before Our eyes, using time-proven tactics to disempower Us. In this case, this was a wreck of several Level Playing Fields converging:

1. The educators, scholars, and Community organizers of Tucson created the leading Ethnic Studies program in the nation for The Level Playing Field of education.

2. That program worked so well for six years that Arizona right-wingers wrote an actual law—via The Level Playing Field of politics—to ban the curriculum.

3. The Chicano Community then had to sue Arizona on The Level Playing Field of the court system. And this would all be reported, but mostly ignored, via the corporate media that traditionally ignores Us or reduces Us to generalizations, myths, or stereotypes.

The ill logics of these Level Playing Fields converge to create illogic.

The cost of admission to any single one of those fields is exorbitant because these Level Playing Fields are created by the rules the rulers create to maintain their rule. This is true even when We manage entrance onto the fields, such as the Tucson scholars, who had PhDs and decades of experience teaching. Our Familia de Tucson also had the deep CCC to succeed beyond expectations on The Level Playing Field of Education for six years. They succeeded so well that Arizona right-wingers noticed, and smashed their work.

Civil rights lawyer Richard Martinez cultivated a powerful base of Legal Capital to withstand this struggle across several levels of US law. And the Gente of Tucson had the profoundly deep CCC to organize and engage students, families, and activists around the Tucson Unified School District (TUSD) Mexican American Studies (MAS) program, thrive with it—and then to stand up to the attack with protests, marches, and lawsuits.

corporate media reduced this generational struggle to the sound bites and stereotypes that AZ officials broadcast on The Level Playing Field of corporate media, using the press secretaries they knew, the friends of friends of sponsors, the talking heads that average Arizonans were used to hearing, to put racist lies into the voters' brains.

Of course, you need the right scholars, students, lawyers, and more to combat this—but to LEVEL their racket of The Level Playing Field, you need Librotraficantes to hack it.

Metaphors Are Forced Confessions

On the more level playing field of education in Houston Community College, I'm expert at professing both rhetorical analysis and Mexican American Literature. My campus is reported to be over 40 percent Latino. This statistic on any given day looks like an under count.

As a CA, I am privileged to not only have advocated for Mexican American History, but to also teach it and create it. One way or another, or another, I bring Ethnic Studies into the classroom.

The laws being the laws, currently every college student in Texas must successfully complete Composition I Rhetorical Analysis. The handbooks explain that the course teaches students to understand how words and forms work. I tell students I am helping them earn a black belt in language.

We fought to get Mexican American Literature into Texas classrooms. Currently, it is an elective. So, as of this writing, British Literature is more prevalent in Texas colleges and in dual credit high schools programs, where students earn credit towards their high school diploma and an associate's degree at the same time. Of course, British Literature may be prevalent, but British students are not. I have never even had a British student. In all, I have had three white students total in my classes in the year I've been at my new campus.

Of course, 53 percent of Texas's over 5.2 million students are Latino. If you teach in a public school or a community college in Houston, the majority of your students are Brown and Black: African American, Mexican American, Mexican, Salvadoran, Guatemalan, Costa Rican. The news might call Us Latinos. Old Texans might say Hispanics. Young folks might say Latinx. Us.

Naturally, in my classes I inform students that Arizona officials once banned Mexican American Studies.

They had never heard about it. They are pissed off. They want to know more. I tell them We are going to study all about it. The proceedings are now of official record. They are documented in writing and on television for the nation, the world, including on C-SPAN, the broadcast version of The Level the Playing Field of the court, broadcast on The Level Playing Field of corporate media, where Our Community usually gets played.

This exercise is typically the first time the students have watched C-SPAN. Some are stunned that We are going to watch a court case. Some worry they won't understand. I tell them I was once the same way.

Before I got involved in the movement to overturn the racist ban of Mexican American Studies, I imagined this nation's laws as the height of ethics, a testament to Our civilization. I imagined the proceedings in a high court as regal, refined, erudite.

Boy was I wrong.

I tell my students, *Don't worry, you will understand what is going on. You will be surprised. You may be shocked. You may even be stunned.*

When I was in the courtroom, I went through all of those emotions in real time. I will talk more about it at the end.

But to make you feel at ease, yes, there is some technical legal language that may lose you for a bit—but I promise you, there will be plenty you understand.

As you watch, for a quiz grade, you need to simply write down three words, phrases, or sentences that catch your attention. Write that down and you will earn a 100%.

I'd like you to keep writing after that so that We can discuss between testimonies. There are examples of logic and reasoning—kind of. Back then I assumed, silly me, that I would be privy to a discourse of the highest form of logos. Nahhhh.

Look for emotions. There will be pathos throughout.

Look for values at work, either stated directly or indirectly.

The entire case is forty-five minutes long. Each side gets twenty minutes. The plaintiff reserved five minutes in the end for rebuttal.

I will resist chiming in. We will watch the opening arguments by the plaintiffs, lawyer Erwin Chemerinsky, who represents Maya Arce, the student from Tucson suing Arizona for banning Mexican American Studies. At the time she was a seventeen-year-old Chicana, about your ages now. She had to be a current student to be eligible to sue the state.

I guess that's progress: At seventeen, my father was picking crops. I was in high school and working as a petroleum allocator. Maya was suing Arizona.

*   *   *

Before I became a Librotraficante, I had never been in a courtroom.

I thought becoming a writer, a professor, an intellectual would save me from run-ins with the law. Instead, I unleashed a generation of pros at contraband prose.

Before Arizona's ban of Mexican American Studies, before that state sanctioned violence on Our Gente, I drew my epiphanies from fiction—short stories, novels.

Once I became a Librotraficante, I lived epiphanies.

On January 12, 2015, in downtown San Francisco, California, in the hallowed halls of the US Ninth Circuit Court of Appeals, I experienced multiple epiphanies. I could not write about them at the time because We were Accelerating CCC. Now, the backdrop of the case provides the perfect chalkboard to demonstrate the myth of The Level Playing Field and the power of The Tip of The Pyramid.

english is brutally honest about its oppression. We are forced to buy metaphors without understanding the cost. Gen Z must live with this even more profoundly because it is raised on user agreements signed without being read, only to find out later what We have given up. We are starved, bullied, or lynched into internalizing the metaphors. Stereotypes, generalizations, myths become facts. We are hit with these metaphors all day, every day.

Librotraficantes hit back. During CA, Art breaks barriers.

Cultivating Cultural Capital requires visiting those boundaries and creating more Culture from the shrapnel. Additionally, We can learn from the processes the Mexica used, building greater and greater pyramids on the foundations of previous ones.

You can watch Our History and Culture fought over on C-SPAN. You can watch the play by play on *Level The Playing Field*, where We convened to figure out if Chicanos are violent and want to overthrow Western Civilization. This is not the exact phrasing of the law, but its spirit.

As I repeated in interview after interview, speech after speech, essay after essay, Community charla after Community charla, one of the books on the outlawed curriculum was *The House on Mango Street* by Sandra Cisneros. The words "overthrow" and "government" don't even appear in the book.

However, the exact line "Chicanos promote the overthrow of Western Civilization" would appear again a few years later, when a right-wing former Texas State Board of Education representative would submit a history textbook for implementation in Texas high schools. Though it bore the misleading title *Mexican American Heritage*, it was written by all white folks. Not one of them was an expert on Our Culture. That racist textbook included that line as the definition for Chicanos: people who want to overthrow Western Civilization.

On The Level Playing Field of the court, the phrase "promote the overthrow of the government" was addressed. However, the fact that those words made sense to only those who dehumanize Us was never addressed. And worse, it was "clearly" not the place to address that, on The Level Playing Field. That phrase could only be repeated, again and again, never properly rebuked.

That aspect of the law was the only part struck down by the Arizona Supreme Court's Judge Takashima as "too broad" the first time he reviewed the case. The rest of the law, thus the law, was upheld, each line gaining its meaning from an entirely different set of stereotypes.

Another judge tried to fathom the logic dictated by the law. He asked Arizona: How can you design a course for a group of people without mentioning the group of people? Why would you want to do that?

Arizona stuttered.

This was a good day for The Level Playing Field.

However, I was joyous and still in despair.

I was sitting in the courtroom. Maya Arce and her family, including her father Sean Arce, who designed the curriculum, were one aisle over and in the first row. Also in the audience were many of the original Mexican American Studies teachers who had designed and conducted the curriculum: Curtis Acosta, Jose Gonzales, and his wife Melissa Gonzalez. The other original plantiff, Korina Lopez and her father, one of the original instructors, were also in attendance.

None of these names of Our CCC appear or are archived on The Level Playing Field. That is the cost of admission to this game. This is the only way to gain your forty minutes to fight for justice, against blatant oppression, so that the next case of oppression in line starts on time.

C-SPAN does not cover CCC.

However, at that moment the power of Our CCC dawned on me.

Librotraficantes were in the house. We were, right then, Accelerating Cultural Capital.

So I screen the case's oral arguments in my classes. However, because I am an expert, a pro about Us, I teach not just the myth of The Level Playing Field; I pierce that pale pale with The Tip of The Pyramid, and I unearth the CCC that got Us to victory.

When you watch the link, you will watch history in action. The players on the field are white. The stars of The Level Playing Field are white, always.

The force to be reckoned with is old white men.

I teach CCC at the base. I thrive there. I Accelerate CCC. I shatter myths, pales, and planes. It's disturbing. It's upheaval. It's thrilling.

When I teach, I am also always learning. I study how Our CCC grows, evolves, flows, updates, stays the same; how it is is traumatized, grows numb, thrives.

The way I screen C-SPAN's Level Playing Field tears up the field.

Of course, C-SPAN only tells part of the story, I am sure to tell my students. *The court tackles only part of the problem. I'll fill you in on the rest afterwards.*

I sit behind the students. They won't read my language or reactions, because even years later, I still get stirred up.

I let them settle in.

I turn off the lights.

I point the remote, and the generic white voice of God says, let it be C-SPAN.

On The Level Playing Field of court, history, TV, cable, here is what state violence against Us is reduced to as C-SPAN crams Our plight into a caption. That is what the kings english does—reduce Us, contract Us, border Us:

Maya Arce v. John Huppenthal Oral Argument

A three-judge panel at the Ninth Circuit Court of Appeals heard oral argument in Maya Arce v. John Huppenthal, on the constitutionality of Arizona's ban on ethnic studies programs in public schools. The ban led to a dismantling of a Mexican-American studies program in the Tucson Unified School District. A group of students sued, arguing the law was overly broad, discriminatory, and violated free speech.

The Arizona ban, passed in 2010, prohibited a course or class that "promotes the overthrow of the US government, promotes resentment toward a race or class of people and is designed for pupils of a particular ethnic group."

Press play.

My students watch the three old white judges stroll in, dressed in their long black robes, all white, white, white, with gray hair.

My students laugh. I don't tell them to; I try not to. We watch The Level Playing Field unfurl the way it has for generations.

The three old white judges are perfect for Court TV. Even when it is not made-for-tv, The Level Playing Field is made for TV, and a classroom of Houston students can't contain themselves.

We quiet down to hear the court.

This is an indictment of The Level Playing Field, how the span of generational oppression is reduced to the captions, angles, and perspective of C-SPAN—The Level Playing Field of media.

The Level Playing Field of education is distorted by the lawyers for Arizona.

The Level Playing Field reduces the plight of Our Gente to forty minutes to be judged by three old white men, appointed by older white men, elected on the Level Playing Field of politics.

And this is actually the more progressive court. Even if it is the Liberal Ninth Circuit Court in San Francisco, which saved the law upholding Same Sex Marriage that same week, the optics belie the myth of The Level Playing Field that We have been forced to watch for generations.

Of course, the judges are addressing and are on the verge of overturning the racist law banning Mexican American Studies. That is a great thing which We don't know yet. However, the myth must be pierced for Us to survive and thrive.

For forty minutes they will discuss a law whose intention, it will not be said, was to destabilize if not destroy Our CCC and to destabilize Us for generations. For forty minutes they will discuss this law.

The only Spanish surname that appears on screen is the name of Maya Arce at the beginning; she does not appear. No other Mexican Americans appear at all in the battle on The Level Playing Field for Our History and Culture.

Even more telling, the only glimpse of Our CCC that does appear on screen is the back of Richard Martinez's head.

If you watch, near the bottom of the center, you will see a shock of white hair. That is the back of the head of Chicano civil rights lawyer Richard Martinez. He began the case. His son was one of the original Chicano educators who started the program. His son was sued by Arizona.

What has not been discussed, until now, is the fact that he had to hand off the case to a white lawyer, the brilliant and capable Erwin Chemerinsky.

I don't say this to slight Chemerinsky in any way. He was brilliant. However, the case made it clear to me that no Chicano, not even the brilliant Richard Martinez—not even the handsome actor Antonio Banderas who should play him in the movie version of this fight for Ethnic Studies which should be produced—could compete on The Level Playing Field of American politics, and win.

I want to stress that the way the plaintiff's team did its work is profoundly based on interracial CCC. Richard Martinez is brilliant for understanding this and assembling the legal eagle dream team along several levels of court to fight this, donating millions of legal services in-kind. And Chemerinsky and the Seattle School of Law are champions of justice and freedom of speech. These are leaders, visionaries, experts who fight to defend CCC.

The non-Chicano lawyers' contributions are powerful because their whiteness enabled them to simply pursue more capital, as in money—that is the way the nation is set up. They leveraged the privilege of their whiteness and invested in La Gente's CCC. The Level Playing Field says nothing about the possibility of true allyship.

The price of admission to The Level Playing Field is capital and not just capital, but also power, but not just power, generations of wealth and power. Bodies infused with that, raised with it, so they can muster the elegance of indifference, affront, shock with a glance, a gesture, a word.

We cannot.

If We do appear as a dot on The Level Playing Field, We do not have the generational wealth and power to compete a sustained pitch battle.

Every time I watch the oral arguments, two instances during the testimony bring home the fact that only a white lawyer could be a true contender on that Level Playing Field. I will cross the border of this essay into the next to pinpoint those points.

Look it up, Foo.

english.

Seems so easy.

Just speak english.

We have to speak english to compete on The Level Playing Field. But not just any english—the right english. Which english is that? Exactly.

Look it up in the dictionary.

Part of the case proving Arizona's discriminatory campaign was focused on a former Secretary of Education telling his constituents, during campaigns, that he was going after "La Raza." This is what got folks elected in Arizona at the time. This is what elected officials said about their job, especially John Huppenthal. This is what consumed their time, energy, and intelligence: "going after La Raza."

I watched several news clips of this. And of course, Huppenthal said it with an accent to make clear the words were not fit for his mouth, did not deserve to be properly pronounced. This too is a trope Americans are used to. Distort the word. That is the biggest giveaway that their definition is being distorted, too. Yet, this went on.

This also demonstrates that no matter how perfectly We speak the kings english or its bastard son corporate english, even win awards for it, We still are prevented from competing on The Level Playing Field.

First, there is the irony that the court case was based on banning a curriculum of over eighty works—written in english and published by the gamut of Community Publishing and corporate publishing, thereby updating the standard for the kings english—by almost that many Chicana, Chicano, and Latino writers, some of whom having received the highest awards offered in the nation: the MacArthur Fellowships, PEN/Faulkner Fiction awards, Guggenheims, American Book Awards, Pushcart Prizes, Primo Quinto Sol, etc., etc., etc. Their work formed the curriculum. Yet not one of their names made it to The Level Playing Field of the Ninth Circuit courtroom. An entire generation of genius contracted, reduced to one headline, and thrown out of the classroom. Part of Our work was to humanize them and in doing so humanize Us. Those works, those writers, are proof that We have a Voice, We have a story, a history, intelligence. We have to fight for this on a daily basis. Otherwise, even those who stand up for Us must also constrict Our efforts in order to make their case against those who want to completely erase Us.

Our Community risks starvation and homelessness to carve time out from work and life to write. Some of Our stories survive to be conveyed through publication. Some of those works fight their way to the classroom. The TUSD MAS Course existed due to even earlier civil rights legislation. And then Chicana and Chicano scholars rose through the education system that pushes Us to achieve degrees, advanced degrees, and then become educators and experts just to form a curriculum that conveyed Us. A Community embraced the work, the educators, the school, the works. After generations of work, Our Art, History, and Culture was centralized and organized on The Level Playing Field of education, and it worked.

It worked so well right-wing republicans attacked it.

Oppressors have convened to erase Us, again.

Erased from the court case, Our Curriculum erased from the school district's offerings all the names of the Chicana and Chicano writers, erased from the school; Our Art, Culture, and History erased by and from corporate media. Our erasure is standard and further institutionalized right before Our eyes. Alone, Our skill and knowledge are not enough to stop this.

This was made clear during a moment that involved the lawyer Erwin Chemerinsky getting cocky with one of the judges. The oldest of the three white judges was a reagan appointee and was the most conservative, if not the least impressive, of the three. The fellow spoke slowly with age, or with privilege, generations and generations of being right because he utters. He was the one who interrupted discussions to pose the most questions.

And, when Chemerinsky questioned John Huppenthal's racist campaign promise in court, he was the judge who replied, "Are you sure that was what the Secretary of Education [Huppenthal] meant by 'La Raza?'"

Okay, part of that was badass—it was great to hear "La Raza" uttered out loud in the US Ninth Circuit Court of Appeals on C-SPAN. The most chill Chicano students in my classes get a kick out of it, too. They shout at the screen, "Eso!" We, La Raza, are listening to the judge repeat what the Arizona head of Education said: "La Raza."

And I also laugh, because to me, to Us, to La Raza, it's like a first grader asking a cute question like "Why is the sky blue?" or "Can you turn on the dark?" Yet, here We are. A judge asking, to Us, the most basic question: What the fuck is La Raza?

Us staring back at the screen—there. We are La Raza. Presente.

On the other hand, it is also an existential moment, through no brilliance of the judge who resembled the old actor made famous in toxic genre films, Clint Eastwood. It's a flip of the script that reveals how the script is rigged.

After all, what is La Raza? Who are We? Are We? Will We? Will We continue? Cease?

Any student studying the prohibited curriculum would not only know what "La Raza" refers to, they would understand how the term evolved, and they would have been familiar with the thinkers, its context.

Translating is always an art, never fact. What is not brought up in court is the fact that translating requires moving words from the kings spanish, which forged a very real caste system, to the kings english, which forged an informal caste system. english-speaking haters reveal their supremacist tendencies by dubbing the phrase as "The Race." Librotraficantes smashing caste systems understand the term means "The People."

The students who did know this information could not speak in court to defend the knowledge that made that question so basic.

We as Chicanos in the room watching laugh and look at each other—but then We have to move on because that is not the end of it. The best part comes next, when Chemerinsky, lawyer for Maya Arce, smirks at the old man.

With that look, that gesture, he throws some serious shade. He is voicing with his face and body language what the fuck We are all thinking.

But a Chicano could not look at a white judge that way.

Chemerinsky then says the funniest line of the day: "Generally, when We don't understand the meaning of words, We look them up."

Damn.

Homeboy schooled the old guy. He just told him, "Look it up, foo."

We were flying towards The Tip of The Pyramid—all of a sudden it seemed clear to me. We were going to get there. Martinez picked a lawyer who could do that. They needed to be a bare-knuckle legal brawler.

Some of my students turn to look at me, bemused; some laugh, but try to fight it, as if they are in the courtroom, too. They are not sure if they can laugh, should laugh.

I resist, just as I did in court that day, standing up, and yelling, yes! Put him in his place!

Of course, I can't. Not only could I not say that out loud that day in real time, but a Chicano lawyer could not say what Chemerinsky said to an elder white reagan-appointed judge. That just would not happen. It should not happen if We want to win the case, and if We don't want to be charged with contempt of court.

If you Cultivate CCC, you know what I mean. Part of the cultivation means picking your battles, Once they are revealed, Our progress towards The Tip of The Pyramid leads to pushback, conflict, resistance. CAs blazing that trail have to figure out if We must react, and they have to decide that quickly. At the time of the trial, We were in peak Cultural Acceleration. But I will slow down here to Quantify CCC, as this moment deserves documenting, analysis, and time, in order to Cultivate CCC.

I have proof that a Chicano Civil Rights Lawyer could not get away with saying the same thing to a white judge.

Let's focus on The Level Playing Field of elections. There is the myth that anyone can be president. That is not true. In this day and age, a Latino can't be president. I hope one day this sentence will be defied with a sitting Chicana president. This sentence reveals that We are relegated to second-class citizenship, and We are oppressed. We are allowed to prosper but not rule.

You need only look at what transpired on The Level Playing Field of the 2020 presidential election Democratic primary.

First of all, the only Latino candidate did not make it on stage for the first debate. There were, as always, arbitrary numbers branded into Our central nervous system.

Forced facts:

The Democrats creating the rules of this racket decided to require that candidates have 2 percent in national polls to get on the debate stage in the first place. (Of course, the folks making money off polls don't know what to call Us, so they don't know how to quantify Us.)

For candidates to appear on national TV on the debate stage, Dems decided to base eligibility on the amount of cash donated by those already quantified. The official requirement: "One percent support in three national polls or polls of early primary states, or raise money from a minimum of sixty-five thousand donors from twenty states, including at least two hundred unique donors per state."

So it's expensive to get on the primary stage, yet staying off it might tank a candidate's funding. And this is for The Level Playing Field, where the rules were devised by Democrats who were supposed to be the Progressive party, the Liberal party, the more multicultural party compared to donald trump—which of course isn't saying much.

In a two-party system, the bar for engaging Latinos in general has been set very low: you simply have to not attack Us. Most of the discussion of these 2020 debates focused on donald trump's anti-immigrant rhetoric, which, as in the case of the Slaughter in El Paso, proved that stereotypes can kill Us. This spilled over to threatening democracy during the January 6, 2021 Insurrection—such a loud and obvious narrative that it made the Democrats the "good guys" by default without them having to do much. In the case of Latinos, it was enough to simply not call Mexicans rapists and not directly attack and vilify immigrants.

However, yes, the trump administration was covertly and openly hostile to the varying segments of the Latino population, beginning with Mexicans—when he attacked immigrants from Mexico and called them rapists; then moving on to Mexican Americans, when he attacked Judge Gonzalo Curiel and said he was incapable of presiding over the lawsuit regarding trump university because he was Mexican—when in fact Judge Curiel was born in Indiana; to abandoning Puerto Rico, when it needed help after a hurricane disaster; to attacking more immigrants with travel bans; and so on.

And We all watched as the Democratic Party devised its own rules which kept Julian Castro, the lone Latino candidate, off the debate stage.

In a subsequent debate, the rules of the game on The Level Playing Field kept both African American presidential candidate Cory Booker and Latino candidate Juliián Castro off the stage. This meant that the star players—the only players competing on The Level Playing Field—were white.

Which is to say, the players on this Level Playing Field looked a lot like the players on The Level Playing Field of the Ninth Circuit Court of Appeals.

The rules are rigged under Our noses, because english is brutally honest about its oppression. We are just too traumatized, busy, scared, lusty for Our own mythical turn, or too numb to notice. The very reasons that keep Us from competing on The Level Playing Field keep Us from changing, challenging, or usurping The Level Playing Field altogether. Worse, We have been trained to speak english, and act right, and defer to white folks the same way on both Level Playing Fields: The Ninth Circuit Court of Appeals and the 2020 Democratic Presidential Primary debate.

Both myths are rackets.

I want to shed light on what America thought was a minor moment—which was not—in order to prove that a Chicano lawyer would not be granted the same latitude as Chemerinsky.

Back on the debate stage, a heated debate ensues. Julián Castro grimaces, smirks, shakes his head, just as Chemerinsky did in the Ninth Circuit Court of Appeals. He means the same thing. He is shaking his head for all of Us, telling the old, white power structure, *Come on. Get with it. You are so wrong.*

He is not talking to an elder anglo reagan appointee. He is talking to Joe Biden, elder anglo Obama appointee. We did not know he would become president at the time. He had tried before and failed.

Then, Julian Castro, Ivy League graduate, Obama administration cabinet appointee, lawyer, former mayor of San Antonio, Texas, went too far. He schooled Biden.

At the time, I cheered. Yet as I retype the comment from the transcript, it really is pretty friggin' mundane: "Are you forgetting what you said two minutes ago?" Castro asked, "Are you forgetting already what you said just two minutes ago? I mean, I can't believe that you said two minutes ago that they had to buy in, and now you're saying they don't have to buy in. You're forgetting that."

white America gasped. There were boos in the audience, which of course consisted of white folks.

Old America had a heart attack over this. Mainstream news and pundits revealed themselves. They were shocked. How dare Castro do that!

You would have thought Castro had mugged Biden.

Perhaps white America did fear that Castro was "stealing" Biden's chance at the white house. Old school mainstream newspapers and anyone with an old mindset dug into Castro.

In other words, when Castro made it onto the stage, America scolded him for raising his voice to an older white guy.

Castro's campaign plummeted. It was not just that moment. But that moment revealed the racket of The Level Playing Field.

This also revealed that the maxim "All publicity is good publicity" only works for white guys who already have power. Those under their spell, under their domain will stand up for them, control media for them, unleash other bullhorns, dog whistles, and attack dogs to subdue, kill, or drown the wrong narrative.

We don't have that luxury. For Chicanos, for Mexican Americans, for Latinos, Hispanics, Latinx, the adage does not hold true. Not all publicity is good publicity when you get no publicity, when you do not have access to the publicity machine, when, as in Castro's case, and as in all of Our cases, you are not in the American imagination, the media's imagination, voters' imaginations, when you are not worthy of addressing presidential topics, but only a talking head for immigration issues, when the fact that you might or might not speak Spanish is a major issue for you.

This goes back to demonstrating how smart the Chicano civil rights lawyer Richard Martinez was not to handle the case himself. Martinez, Esquire could not compete on The Level Playing Field equally because the price of admission is too high and success is based on generational wealth and power. This oppression is branded into Our DNA.

Of course, folks who want to uphold the façade of The Level Playing Field will read through Chemerinsky's resume. Again, I think he is brilliant. I think he is a hero. I think he handled the case brilliantly. And it is clear only he could have won.

Richard Martinez is humble and brilliant for not just the obvious reasons. He is brilliant because he knows what profound racism looks like. That is why he can take on the far right-wing republican racists of Arizona. Arizona's laws were blatantly racist, but as a lawyer Martinez also deeply understood the myth of The Level Playing Field. He understood that he could have never said to that old white Judge, "Look it up," just as Julian Castro was not allowed to school Biden on stage.

Even if they spoke english.

Unidos

*"AZ 2281 Prohibits Courses that treat students as a group and not individuals
. . ."*

The United States Court of Appeals for the Ninth Circuit dropped
the closing gavel.

We broke into mist as the next cloud rolled in to form against the
next case of alleged oppression.

I was on an intellectual adrenaline high.

We were all starving for justice and tacos. So We reconvened at a
Mexican Restaurant. (C-SPAN did not cover that.)

There is more to say about the game on The Level Playing Field.
However, this Book is about the CCC that got Us there, got Us
through it, got Us here, and is moving Us towards the next Tip of
The Pyramid. I know that. I am a CA. So I know that it is difficult
to navigate back and forth from Tip of The Pyramid to The Base,
because We always have to eat.

I have heard the wealthy romanticize the myth of "The Starving
Artist." Starving is not romantic. Starvation is a real threat hanging
over Our Community. Starving kills CCC. Even right now it's killing.

I learned this during my first job. When I was a kid, my job was to
learn english as quickly as possible, and I figured out, also as well as
possible so I could translate the outside world into Spanish for my
mother and father. Sounds pretty straightforward. But, of course,
it was, is, not.

I learned to quickly cross borders, to navigate South Side Chicago
english, english with Polish, Italian, Mexican, Puerto Rican accents,

and Spanglish and Spanish with all kinds of other accents, from Michoacán, CDMX, Guadalajara—all on the fly as I got things done like helping my father buy a fridge, my mother get a refund for returned clothes, neighbors pay bills. In school if I did poorly, I failed. At home, if I did poorly, We got poorer.

I learned in school that there is the legal "I" and the ego "I," but school never taught me about the community "I" that actually helped me survive school and then school school. The Court Case at the Ninth was vital. The legal "I" knows that. That "I" shapes the law and policy that usher forth and destroy or edify Our CCC in every corner of the US, because We are everywhere and the nation needs Us. I could read the moment. We were going to win. I was already envisioning Our next Tip of The Pyramid once We reached this one.

But first, We had to eat, which was also a chance to feed the Community "I." Our mission was Mexican food in the Mission District.

Our Community forms.

Some of Us become lawyers, educators. Other of Us become artists—including writers, painters, musicians, media.

Some of Us form groups, collectives.

Some of Us, more and more of Us, now fight Our way to the paper, the parchment—degrees.

Once paper is involved, We are approaching the pale pale of the mythical Level Playing Field. College degrees and now advanced degrees are the bleacher level tickets to The Level Playing Field. This does not mean you count or are counted, yet. This does not even mean you get to actually compete on The Level Playing Field. If you have to ask, you do not have the generational wealth or power to compete on The Level Playing Field. And, by the way, the goalposts on the field are being moved again as We speak.

Earning your college degree allows you to prosper but not rule.

Still, some of Us earn advanced degrees, form professional guilds. Some of Us form nonprofits.

A line in the Internal Revenue Service regulations engenders 501(c)(3) nonprofit organizations. This is how the IRS quantifies

CCC. The law, as is the case with rules for The Level Playing Field, does not directly say that but that is what it is saying. That is the user agreement.

english, if you know how to read it, is forthright with its oppression. These 501(c)(3) rules are not for prophets. They are for folks with discretionary money, time, energy, and resources for legal, accounting, and public relations advisors.

I founded NP in 1998. In 1999, I documented the CCC of La Raza in Houston, Texas by forming the 501(c)(3) nonprofit organization Nuestra Palabra: Latino Writers Having Their Say.

Of course, "getting documented" is the term used to refer to Our Gente's immigration status. I use the term here because it is the same racket. I was born in the US, so I was born a US citizen, but that does not automatically mean my Art, History, and Culture are documented. No, that CCC remains in the shadows. Just because I am born on this side of the line bordering the US does not mean I am treated like an American. I have to unearth my Art, History, and Culture.

In graduate school, MFA candidates imagine. We imagine the struggle to exist on paper. In the ivory tower, We mean poems, short stories, novels. In Houston Barrios, We mean immigration papers, nonprofit papers, and dollar bills.

In this nation We are free on paper. So, We best get documented when We can. We best work the paper. We best author Our authority.

Paper is the basis for the pale pale of the mythical Level Playing Field. The case at the Ninth is incredibly important to Our History. But We must remember and act on the fact that neither the court annals nor C-SPAN tell the entire story, or Our Story.

Only Art can save Us.

Lawyers cage language by day. Poets free the words at night.

Chicano civil rights lawyer Richard Martinez used his legal capital to create the legal dream team that would fight Arizona's racist law banning Mexican American Studies from the Arizona courts to the Federal Courts in California. That had to be his focus. If he fumbles anywhere along that line, Arizona's ban of Our History and Culture stands. And spreads.

We as activists and artists have no direct role in the proceedings in the Ninth and on C-SPAN. However, as Librotraficantes Our goal was to make sure that the racist ban was not copied in other states. We also needed to make sure that the rest of the nation knew about this attack on Our Culture, and We had to support the CCC of Tucson, which developed this brilliant curriculum and stood up to this head on oppression.

It was because We were involved with the Gente of Tucson that I learned to identify the tactics the far right was employing to desta-bilize Our Community. I realized that Only Art can save Us because that act of Art, an artful line, an artful bus of contraband prose and pros, Accelerated Our argument and touched hearts and opened minds.

Librotraficante's approach also snuffed out the stereotype that helped form the basis of Arizona's law, since the stereotype that Mexican Americans are violent also engenders the stereotype that We are not intellectual, that We do not like to read and write. This plays a role in and is also spread by all the negative roles that por-tray Latinos in film, TV, media.

The falseness of these ideas gets harder to argue if there are near-zero portrayals of Latinos, let alone positive portrayals to counteract the false narrative.

The House On Mango Street pierces through all of that.

Here is where CCC comes in. *The House on Mango Street* is beloved. First published in 1984, the book was and is still a bestseller. The last time I checked there are about six million copies sold. (If you never heard about it, ask yourself.) Sandra Cisneros, the author, was the first Chicana to earn an MFA in poetry from the Iowa Writers Workshops. She had two books on the prohibited Mexican Ameri-can Studies curriculum.

Also, I knew the writer. She was my friend. We are in a Chicano Renaissance when a young Chicano writer can read a great book by a Latina and then meet and befriend that very same CA.

Nuestra Palabra: Latino Writers Having Their Say hosted Sandra several times, including at Our massive Latino Book and Family Festival, which during the peak of bookstores and the mainstream book industry in the early 2000s, drew over thirty thousand people to the George R. Brown Convention Center. We also interviewed Sandra on Our radio show and promoted her on Our social media, which was just taking off at the time. At all of Our events, We combined established voices from the mainstream racket with voices from Our Community. Our Terms on Our Terms.

This is just a quick inventory of the power of Our approach. The. Power. Of. CCC. These tactics work. Our Community is powerful. And Our power is growing. Mi Casa on Mango Street es su Casa on Mango Street.

Mi Renaissance es su Renaissance.

If Our opponents were to address specific texts taught in Mexican American Literature and Ethnic Studies courses, they would be forced to recognize that the supposed charges against these curricula—such as Chicano teachers inciting students to overthrow the US government—are totally false. None of the over eighty banned books is about that. As long as Arizona right-wingers attacked a general curriculum, their attack played on stereotypes.

I must point out that these tactics demonstrate why Our Crew mounts campaigns that leave in the dust anything Madison Avenue or mainstream PR or advertising agencies slap together regarding Our Community. The Librotraficantes hit back.

I have unpacked just one line from the discriminatory law to shed light on who We really are, and aren't. Now let's look at just one more line from that legislation, another prong of Arizona's law banning Mexican American Studies that I believe is even more sinister than the criminalizing provision.

It is little studied at the time of this writing. It also received very little attention during the actual ban or during any of the court cases. During Our campaign of Cultural Acceleration, the Librotraficantes did not have the time, or place, or audience to address it. A decade later, for this Book, I must.

Arizona's law also prohibited courses that treated students as "a group and not individuals."

Of course, as I read the law for the first time every line of it stunned me. Each was the result of deeply based stereotypes, myths, generalizations about Our Gente. The legal english of the law sentenced Us to live those stereotypes forever—without ever directly mentioning Us, while clearly directly targeting Us. And it was done so often, absorbed so much by corporate english that reporters assigned to the story often did not understand the problem. But as time passes, this provision still strikes me as particularly pernicious.

Treating students as individuals only and not thinking of them as part of Our Community flies against Our embrace of extended families. Chicano scholars have documented Our Gente's practice of defining Ourselves in the context of Our families and extended families. If you Cultivate CCC, you know how large a role this plays in Our personalities and Community. I suppose if that law were still in place, this Book itself would be furthering a prohibited idea of Community. That's why I am a pro in contraband prose.

Of course, this provision of the ban, and the individualism that informs it, ignores the fact that political parties are groups. For anyone in a political GROUP to tell Our Gente We should not form groups of Our liking is hypocritical. It also feeds into the mentality that leads to the racket of The Level Playing Field. In a now infamous 2012 campaign speech, Democratic President Barack Obama once said that if you have a successful business, you did not build it by yourself. Our Gente gets that. The far right, on the other hand, berated him for that. They defy that those in power crank out laws to keep themselves in power and to keep the rest of Us scrambling, preferably alone. They defy that the rulers create rules to maintain their rule.

Here is what We must remember. When We appear as a dot on The Level Playing Field, We are headed toward The Tip of a Pyramid. But if We allow The System to break Us off from Our base of CCC, We become rubble.

We cannot compete on The Level Playing Field because We do not have generational wealth and power. We can only compete on The Level Playing Field with Our generational wealth of CCC.

That's why Arizona right-wingers straight up attacked that power and banned Us from thinking Ourselves into a group.

Texas right-wingers are sneakier.

As stated, I first saw this "individuals only" line in the Arizona law banning Our History and Culture. When We returned to Texas, I saw that line again in the 2012 Texas republican party platform. There was also an additional line that read: "We oppose the current teaching of multicultural literature."

The Librotraficantes attacked this right away.

We spoke out against it on Our radio show *Nuestra Palabra: Latino Writers Having Their Say*, which broadcasts at one hundred thousand watts, during prime time, in the fourth-largest city in America with a population that was 45 percent Latino, on 90.1 FM KPFT. This was in 2012, at the height of this classic media platform.

I wrote an op-ed in the *Houston Chronicle*. We posted on Our social media platforms and the websites for Our groups that I built and updated. We spoke out about it at all of the Community events, charlas, lectures, keynotes We were invited to, attended, crashed, before being invited to speak. And I organized some of Our own.

We learned how the Texas far right rolled.

They did not attack back.

There is a trade-off: Arizona's direct attacks on Us also fueled notoriety of Our Community. You are as mighty as the rivals you struggle with. The Texas right-wing tactic was to ignore Us so as not to give Us fuel, the same tactic employed over generations.

They were not dealing with Our grandparents or parents, however. They were dealing with Librotraficantes.

We had direct access to Our Gente, Our media, Our intelligentsia, wisdom. So as they resisted directly attacking, We continued, gathering victory after victory, reaching the next Tip of The Pyramid in Texas and then building on those as foundations, creating and refining Our own networks. We were powerful because We had achieved self-determination. We knew Our History, We knew Our Culture, which edified Our Voice and kept it tuned to Our Community.

The next version of the 2012 republican platform did not contain any anti-collective language.

This proved that Texas right-wingers did look to Arizona right-wingers.

This proved that Texas was watching Arizona regarding the ban on Ethnic Studies.

This proved Librotraficantes are CAs.

This proved the power of CCC.

Still, We kept the heat on Texas right-wingers, who never adopted a ban on Mexican American Studies, though it was clear they were considering it.

The Librotraficantes talked them out of it.

Our Gente across the Southwest, across the nation, and all of Our allies, instead could keep the pressure on fighting the ban in Arizona.

Now, about those tacos...

We assembled Our CCC at a Mexican restaurant in the Mission District. This was the legacy Chicano neighborhood in San Francisco, succumbing to gentrification. We did not call it CCC at the time. We called it comida. We were hungry, tired, hopped up on adrenaline, trying to make sense of The Cultural Acceleration We were part of, the History We'd just witnessed.

I felt good. I was optimistic. However, I am prone to optimism, so I wanted to commiserate with Our crew to see what they thought.

There were folks from California, of course Arizona, of course TEJAS, and Nueva York. We were eating with Sean Arce, Curtis Acosta, José Gonzáles the original MAS *profes*. César A. Cruz Teolol from California joined Us to break bread, er . . . tortillas. Cuban American journalist Roque Planas flew in from New York City to cover the oral arguments. He helped put the struggle on the national radar from the early days in Tucson. I was joined by Librotraficantes High Tech Aztec and Lilo.

There were way more of Our Gente in the courtroom and now spreading all over the city.

That morning, Aztec Danzantes from El Paso welcomed the Sun. There, in the concrete swirl of Old Downtown, in front of the Greek columns of the US Ninth Circuit Court of Appeals, with gentrification trying to cement itself around Our Gente, Our gentification re-defined the center of the universe.

Over five hundred years before this trial, the spanish conquistadores razed the pyramids of the Mexica. They burned all the Books, all the Art of the Mexica for the same reasons as Arizona's far-right-wingers: to dehumanize, demoralize, destabilize, colonize.

Conspiracy theories claim that only aliens could have built The Pyramids, because the complexity and precision of The Pyramids defies the abilities of Us Indigenous. No. The colonizers burned the Books of the Mexica, including those that explained how to build Pyramids. Others inspired architects, philosophers, intellectuals. All of that was destroyed.

Our Gente has been even more brutally gentrified before now—land taken away, people lynched, Histories violently erased, whitewashed, sent into hiding. Generations of Us were trained to be illiterate, illiterate of english, Spanish, Nautl. That became doctrine, subsumed, until the nation forgot its atrocities, and forgot it had ever needed to fight hard to keep Us in Our place. Now, they just starve Us. If We do not uphold The Level Playing Field today, get documented with the right credentials, We will not work. But if We do, We are allowed to prosper—but not rule.

Yet We assembled in Califaztlan, occupied Mexico, and Our Gente recapitulated, over years, the very movements, sounds, and grace taken away from Us, returned in full form.

That is what terrifies those who hate Us.

We have been attacked, ignored, oppressed. Our Art, History, and Culture, destroyed—yet, here We are, thriving, on Our Terms, happy, and growing underground, under your very noses, void of hate.

There, in Our suits in 2012, in line to watch Our champions on the court, these memories swirled with the divinity of the futures I imagined.

And afterwards, again, the starving.

It was an authentic Mexican restaurant We found Ourselves at. Raza-owned and operated. Tables made of wooden beams painted blue in rows. The windows wide open to the street.

Gorditas, carne asada—not over-priced.

Hot warm, tradition, surrounded by Our Gente. Familias eating there, and you know you are home. I tell los clientes from the barrio why We are there, who the visitors are, what is at stake, how We may have won.

They are Our CCC.

There was so much to witness.

I needed to rest, to get my heart back in order, to talk to the intelligentsia.

Of course, We also need capital. But let's get one thing clear.

Capitalists create pyramid schemes to steal your capital.

CAs draw schematics on Pyramids to *create* more Culture.

Since We live in a capitalist system, American Airlines will not accept CCC as payment for flights. However, We did use CCC to help pay for the flights of Maya Arce and her family to attend the oral arguments.

We, I, the Librotraficantes fundraised to get Maya and her family to San Francisco to the court case. As you can now see, their presence was not required. But how could she and her family, how could We, have missed it?

There is much more to say about the events not chronicled that day. There is much to say about each of Our champions' role. But I am filling in more than was possible during the Cultural Acceleration.

And I want other CAs to realize their power, and to invest it in Cultivating CCC. Of course, Our Community grows and keeps growing without these words. With this Book I hope to build on Our past successful campaigns to inspire Our generation to unite to Cultivate CCC. More CAs need to reveal themselves, foster links to Community, and unite. The time is now because of Our sheer numbers, Our talent, Our technology. The nation needs Us.

We can also inspire so many others by showing them how valuable Our knowledge, networks, time, and energy are.

I was present with my crew as the media We created did its work. The Librotraficantes grew out of the Art and Media We were expert at for almost two decades in 2012, even more so now. We transmit the History and Culture of Our Community. We helped spread the word to the media, *Flashpoints*, Radio Bilingue. I called Univision to make sure they were there. I pointed them to the *profes* who spoke Spanish. Roque Plana broke the news to America via the *Huffington Post*, as he had been doing from the early days. He interviewed me, Sean Arce, Curtis Acosta, Maya Arce, Korina Lopez. Bryan Parras shot video, grabbed sound, posted on social medial. Liana Lopez called more media, took shots, posted live as the court continued. We all hit Our social media: text, pics, video, interviews.

I gave interviews in english, Spanish, and Spanglish, posted, and blogged for the *Huffington Post*, on my blog(s), on Our websites. I wrote op-eds. And. We. Are. The. Media. Bryan and Liana recorded audio and video that We would air on Our radio show in Houston, week after week after week, leading up, during, and after.

And I would reiterate it live on TV, including the weekly political talk show I appeared on, Fox 26 Houston's *What's Your Point?*

And We made History. Recordings of the Nuestra Palabra Radio Show are preserved through the University of Houston Digital Archives. Our hard copies are preserved in the Municipal Hispanic Archives at the Houston Public Library.

Today I will walk into college classroom, high school classrooms and teach the youth this History and Our Ways. We organize readings, panels, Community charlas. And. Then. Some.

This is Our valuable CCC that We invest in the Community to make more Culture.

Of course, to do this, We have to raise capital as well. These are valuable services that We do not charge Our Community for. We engage in a fair exchange of CCC. I charge everyone else. And We also get support from Our Gente, in-kind or financial.

I will point out that Nuestra Palabra did not receive grants at the time because the process was (perhaps it still is) unfair to Our Community. Those "blind applications" are just as unfair to Our Gente as The Level Playing Field. Many give funds based on the amount of money an organization raised the year before under discriminatory practices, policies, and realities, which leads to a constant cycle of underfunding. Those funders then blame Our Gente. No. Basing grants on a group's previous year's operating budget is like imposing an artistic poll tax.

Chicanos, and Mejicanos, are terrible about talking about money. Artists are too. I had to learn to be forthright about it when I first founded NP. I had zero funding, and I had no discretionary funds. During Our first readings, to Our packed houses of hundreds, I would pass around a basket and ask folks to pitch in what they could. Others would buy me drinks or food, since We were in the party hall of Chapultepec Restaurant, and it was a party, and they were open twenty-four hours. At the end of the evening, I would have a stack of wrinkled singles, fives, some twenties, and it never failed, some fifties and a hundred.

We gotta eat. That would go towards flyers, books, and, sometimes, I used it for groceries. Like I said, a vato has got to eat. The people's generosity fueled Our literary movement, and sustained Our CCC which then grew to include artists donating their writing, their visual art, their performances, the street marketing, their advertising skills, photocopies of Our flyers at work, and so much more.

Seventeen years later, We have grown from Chapultepec Restaurant to space—which got Us to San Francisco.

This time around, I did not pass the hat. Here is how CCC works in the era of High Tech Aztecs—an era when you can't yet pay for this Book with Bitcoin, yet near the end of the era when massive book signings and *mitotes* will be built around the launch of this Book. People were visiting the website I built for Librotraficante.

One day, all of a sudden, We were getting lots of donations. They were clicking Our donate button and money was being deposited into Our accounts, donations ranging from $5 to $10, and then all of a sudden someone would donate $500.

Mind you, before this, We were not getting donations all the time. So I had to track down this influx of love. Going over Our analytics for Our social media, email blasts, and website (I own over one hundred domain names; the Librotraficante website was the fourth one I built, and I built dozens after that) analytics and other trails, I tracked down the boon to an article in *The Guardian* from England.

It featured a picture of Isabel Allende, the brilliant Chilean writer whose work formed part of the outlawed curriculum. In those days, publications would not only include the avatars for social media, they would also show how many times a piece had been shared via Facebook, Twitter, and LinkedIn. By the time I tracked it down, this piece had been shared over one hundred thousand times.

It was a badass piece, too, published May 18, 2012 and titled "Anti-intellectualism is taking over the US" by Patricia Williams, whose work forms part of the contraband prose in *Critical Race Theory: An Introduction*.

Ironically, even as I write this, the right is busy vilifying and attacking Critical Race Theory, directly this time, not as part of the Ethnic Studies Curriculum.

Clearly the struggle is not over—just now I paused in the writing of this page to work on a press release for a press conference I am helping to organize tomorrow morning. I have worked with Latina Texas State Representative Christina Morales to submit a bill that would make Mexican American Studies and African American Studies, and subsequent Ethnic Studies, count toward high school graduation requirement in Texas.

This is the CCC those who hate Us fear.

And that hate and fear morphs.

In fact I've interrupted the finishing of this Book several times because the far right is repurposing the very attack that I'm writing about. I'll talk more about this at end of the Book to explain how the work continues. But I will say here that those campaigns can be defeated only by profound grassroots organizing—which this Book is all about. And these attacks are cyclical, as is clear by the fact that ten years after the Librotraficante Caravan, enemies of the imagination and knowledge are still summoning retro-discrimination.

They hate to see Our youth reading and writing, lest they become adults who do the same. In the past, I can imagine how this would grind, demoralize, intimidate Our people. Today, I am blessed to be part of the generation that can fight back, survive, and thrive. I have not only been part of protests, but I have also been able to see Our campaigns work and create policy change. We are powerful.

Back to Williams' *Guardian* piece: The number of shares kept skyrocketing, like a scoreboard for Cultural Acceleration. And We were winning. It trended on Reddit, and folks were hurtling it further. Eventually it hit over two hundred thousand shares just on FB. Those clicks and shares translated to folks donating through Our website. Through Our bank account, under the name of Our umbrella nonprofit, I donated the funds for the Tucson *profes*, and to help fly Maya and some of her family members to watch Our champions fight on The Level Playing Field.

And, yes, I paid for lunch that day in the Mission, as We sat with each other, united, as We bolstered each other's optimism. I suspected We would win. The Tucson *profes* were wary. They had been disappointed before.

The cards are stacked against Us. The court rules. Those rules shape The Level Playing Field. And the rulers create rules to maintain their rule on the mythical Level Playing Field.

I knew Our cause was fair and just. We were right. We were on the right side of history. And not even We realized just how fucking mighty We were, but I had a pretty good fucking idea.

I shall ruin the ending and give you the splendid news: the Ninth sent the case back to the Arizona Supreme Court, demanding that the evidence of Latino student achievement and higher graduation rates as a result of the Ethnic Studies curriculum be included. The case would get overturned in AZ.

There is more to discuss about the court case. Some other time, I will write about the lawyer for Arizona stuttering, hemming, hawing.

I will write about the older white reagan-appointee judge wondering if Chemerinky was personally attacking his friend Judge Tashima, who presided over the Arizona Supreme Court.

I will write about Arizona arguing that student achievement is irrelevant—guess We have been doing it wrong all these years.

That thought is scary. What if society truly believes that student achievement is irrelevant?

One thing the trump administration taught Us is that anything We thought was unimaginable had just never been tried yet. After all, there is no law that says student achievement is fundamental. A state's secretary of education evidently could further the very opposite premise as a policy.

They left me with one nagging, terrifying thought.

Arizona had a long time to devise a few key answers. They had time to figure out how a course could be designed about a group of people, without discussing that group of people, and not attracting just those people, and why this would even be desirable—as they were asked about in court and must have known they would be asked about.

So: Are We safe from that parallel universe where Arizona figures that answer out, defends it in court, and Ethnic Studies is banned in several states?

Did Arizona simply need a better lawyer or an extra lawyer to spend more time imagining evil?

Or is discrimination so illogical that it cannot be coherently, logically defended?

In a room full of students, I pause on this question. I pause dramatically, and then say good night.

Here on the page together, I let you know Librotraficantes are on the case making sure We are not sentenced by a single, simple sentence ever again.

CULTURAL ACCELERATION ESSAYS

These essays were precursors to this Book. They were published during Librotraficante's Cultural Acceleration towards The Tip of The Pyramid: overturning Arizona's ban on Mexican American Studies. Each played a role in a campaign.

Each fueled Our movement towards The Tip of The Pyramid.

As a writer, I did not wait for publishers or outlets to realize they needed this work, though of course I happily submitted when asked. But I was not acting to advance my career, if that word can even be used nowadays, or status as a writer. Instead, I was creating Art in tandem with the needs, issues, and views of My Community as We morphed into the forms necessary.

As CAs, We were unearthing the fact that Our Crew is the media. We are not taught this in school or college, and I sure as hell was not taught this in graduate school. In fact, the UH CWP tried to unlearn me of this.

Instead, I grew as a writer in sync with CCC.

Nuestra Palabra: Latino Writers Having Their Say was always making news. Sometimes it lined up with mainstream news, sometimes not. Sometimes mainstream news caught up.

On the Librotraficante Caravan, I did about seventy-five interviews in english, Spanish, and Spanglish for outlets from the barrio to TeleSur, from ABQ to England. From Tucson to Canada. corporate media wants one person to talk. These interviews, this coverage was set up, coordinated, and helped by the Librotraficante co-founders: Laura Razo, Liana Lopez, Lupe Mendez, and Bryan Parras, with social media support and sweat equity from the thirty caravanistas on the bus with Us, and then all the Community members who added their granitos de arena.

We also created outlets.

These are further proof of how powerful We are. We do not need the mainstream publishing racket. They need Us.

CAs are also translators. corporate education thinks of time in terms of semesters. corporate media thinks of time in terms of fiscal years. The Tip of The Pyramid encompasses lifetimes, generations.

Or, sometimes, with the right cause, guided the right way, in step with the Community, We Accelerate, and the seemingly impossible is delivered—in Our Time.

This Book is not simply about how We are attacked. This Book is about and part of The Movement We have propelled.

Grammar serves writers. These Cultural Acceleration essays are printed here as they appeared online, in hard copy publications, and as read for broadcast. As a result, they do not follow some of the rules for capitalization or acronyms the rest of the Book employs.

Texas GOP Platform Would Discourage Multiculturalism

Originally published in the Houston Chronicle *July 11, 2012.*

Are you the type of Republican who will spank our young the way our elders were hit for speaking Spanish in school long ago?

The Texas GOP 2012 platform makes it sound like that. It advocates, "Corporal punishment is effective and legal in Texas." The GOP agenda goes on to describe what it considers intellectual transgressions: "We believe the current teaching of a multicultural curriculum is divisive."

That line concerns me even more. The Librotraficante (or book trafficker) Movement was founded to defy Arizona legislators' prohibition of Mexican-American studies. Last March, we organized a six-city caravan from Houston to Tucson to smuggle the banned books back to Arizona. Along the way, 1,000 books were donated from around the country, we opened four underground libraries and unleashed the Latino literary renaissance. We had just returned from Tucson, where we opened our fifth underground library, when we learned to our surprise that this type of prohibition could happen in our own backyard.

So are you the type of Republican who would prohibit the teaching of the story of Texas military legend, who served during the Vietnam War, Roy Benavidez from the classroom? His memoir will fall under the rubric of multiculturalism. He's an American hero. His life story is not divisive.

The language of the Texas GOP platform sounds similar to the language that Arizona Republican legislators used to justify Arizona House Bill 2281 (AZHB 2281) which prohibits "courses that promote the overthrow of the government." This was the legal trigger used to prohibit Mexican-American studies in the Tucson Unified School District. The Librotraficante Movement was founded to fight against the banning of our history in Arizona, and we'll be damned if we put up with it in our own backyard. Arizona is well known as the origin of the anti-immigrant movement, and it is now the center of the anti-intellectual movement.

You might think that this would never happen in Texas; however, the Texas GOP platform goes on to say, "We favor strengthening our common American identity and loyalty instead of political correctness that nurtures alienation among racial and ethnic groups."

This sounds like the Arizona-speak that led to AZHB 2281, which says, "The Legislature finds and declares that Public School Pupils should be taught to treat and value each other as individuals and not be taught to resent or hate other races or classes of people." Our books don't cause resentment. These laws cause resentment.

Will you ban Mexican-American studies? Will you spank my son if he reads the speeches of Dr. Martin Luther King Jr.? Will you ban the writings of Maxine Hong Kingston? These works are powerful examples of multicultural literature.

Are you the type of Republican who will sabotage the American dream for all of our young and ruin their chances for being admitted to elite schools because you "... oppose the teaching of Higher Order Thinking Skills (HOTS) (values clarification), critical thinking skills and similar programs..."

Arizona's anti-intellectual movement must not spread the way its anti-immigrant movement has spread.

On Sept. 21, during Hispanic Heritage Month, the Librotraficante Movement is organizing "50 for Freedom of Speech," which will feature a teach-in in every state of the Union. This will also include freedom of speech report cards on political officials. So before you get to discipline our children, we'll be grading you.

So what type of Republican are you? You're not an Arizona Republican, are you?

The House on Mango Street Goes to Trial: #MayaVsAZ

Originally published on The Huffington Post Blog *December 31, 2014.*

Mayra Arce even resembles Esperanza, the protagonist in *The House on Mango Street* by Sandra Cisneros. That was one of the 80-plus books that were part of the Tucson Unified School District's K-12 Mexican-American studies curriculum before the program was dismantled under Arizona House Bill 2281.

But Maya isn't the main character of a book. She's the main plaintiff in the lawsuit against the state of Arizona.

On January 12, 2015, Maya heads to the Ninth Circuit Court of Appeals in San Francisco to overturn the law used to prohibit Mexican-American studies in Tucson.

This is a major case of truth being stranger than fiction. And it will take several semesters of Mexican-American studies courses to fully appreciate, comprehend, and document all the nuances, cultural subtexts, historical facts, and fiction against our fiction. We are a blessed generation that can fill that San Francisco courtroom to witness a young Chicana making history and fighting for every American's freedom of speech.

I first met Maya Arce at the conclusion of our 2012 Librotraficante Caravan to smuggle the books banned in Arizona back into Tucson, organized by me and alums of Nuestra Palabra: Latino Writers Having Their Say: Liana Lopez ("Librotraficante Lilo"), Laura Acosota ("Librotraficante La Laura"), Lupe Mendez ("Librotraficante Lips Mendez"), and Bryan Parras ("Librotraficante HighTechAztec"). Thirty others joined us on our six-city caravan, which started in Houston and led to opening four underground libraries along the way, and thousands of Americans donating over $20,000 in banned books to the cause.

My fellow Librotraficantes and I convened with Maya, Korina Lopez, also one of the plaintiffs, and Nick Dominguez, who was also on the case but lost his standing when he graduated from high school, at the John Valenzuela Youth Center, site of the Tucson Librotraficante Underground Library. It was thrilling to hand the donated books to Maya and her fellow students and the original teachers of the Mexican-American studies program. They were like love letters from supporters from around the country, who we hope will join them once again as we close in on the happy ending to this landmark court case.

We interviewed Maya and one of her lawyers, Richard Martinez, just before Christmas, on the *Nuestra Palabra* radio show, which airs on 90.1 FM KPFT, Houston. (I co-host the weekly program with Librotraficante Lilo and Librotraficante HighTechAztec.) Maya told our listeners:

> I'm doing this for future generations to come [so they] can learn about their history and the history of people in their community, to better understand the contributions Mexican Americans have made to the United States and better understand how Mexican Americans play a part of society.

Her father is Sean Arce, co-founder of the Mexican-American studies program. I asked him via email how he felt about his family being delivered into this monumental civil-rights struggle. He replied:

> While this case, on a day-to-day basis, has been a tremendous stress on our familia, we know that many who have come before us have struggled so we can be in the position to carry this lucha forward. My conversations with both of my children, Mayita and Emiliano, often center on this struggle and its importance. They have been inspired by this struggle,

and it has led to the further development of their critical consciousness that they practice daily in school and in their social circles. We do this in the spirit of social justice, and, more importantly, we do this in the spirit of asserting the humanity of El Pueblo Chicana/o.

Richard Martinez, the legal eagle organizing the lawyers for the case, told our listeners:

> I think the likelihood of this ending up in front of the Supreme Court is extremely slim because it's a statute that deals with Arizona but no other states. So the likelihood that they would place national importance on it and the Supreme Court take it up is very small.

He continued,

> On the other hand we'll find out a week before our hearing who our panel is. If we get the right panel, there's a very good chance we'll get one of the things we are asking for: either send this back for trial under our equal-protection argument or invalidate the statute on our vagueness argument.

He added that the case had been prepared for as if it *were* going to the Supreme Court. The lawyer conducting the arguments is Erwin Chemerinsky, who is the dean of the University of California Irvine School of Law and a leading constitutional scholar who has argued cases before the Ninth District Court of Appeals as well as the U.S. Supreme Court. (More information about the case is available at the Seattle School of Law website.)

Six amicus briefs supporting the students' appeal were filed, from a stellar group of individuals and organizations, which the Seattle School of Law website listed as:

(1) Authors of Books Banned from TUSD; (2) National Education Association and Arizona Education Association; (3) Freedom to Read Foundation (FTRF), American Library Association, American Booksellers Foundation for Free Expression, Asian/Pacific American Librarians Association, Black Caucus of the American Library Association, Comic Book Legal Defense Fund, National Association for Ethnic Studies, National Coalition against Censorship, National Council of Teachers of english, and REFORMA; (4) Chief Justice Earl Warren Institute on Law and Social Policy and the Anti-Defamation League; (5) 48 Public School Teachers; and (6) LatCrit, Inc.

I asked Barbara Jones, Executive Director of the American Library Association's Freedom to Read Foundation, why the FTRF submitted an amicus brief. She wrote:

> Growing up during McCarthyism in the 1950s, I view this as a blatant attempt to stifle diversity of expression. . . . We are proud to take part in this lawsuit. We believe that the best way to promote harmony among people is to challenge each of us with characters, ideas, and themes that may make us uncomfortable at first. It is through reading and discussion that we attain a more peaceful world, that we bridge gaps between police and community, that we bridge gaps between recent and more distant immigrants. (Remember, we are all immigrants except for the indigenous Americans.)

The 1930s Called, Arizona; They Want Their Racism Back

Here are more ironies. The main far-right Republicans who engendered, passed, and enforced this law are now either out of power or on their way out.

John Huppenthal, former Arizona Superintendent of Education, who is named in the lawsuit, lost a Republican primary for his post to another Republican who did not even bring up anti-Mexican-American-studies rhetoric, which Huppenthal had used to ride into office. That race included a press conference that featured Huppenthal crying after he was busted for posting racist comments online under fake names, even using state-owned computers in some cases. Thom Horne, another enemy of Mexican-American studies, also lost in his primary. Even Arizona Gov. Jan Brewer is leaving office. She signed into law not only H.B. 2281 but S.B. 1070, famously known as the "Show Me Your Papers" law.

Of course, even with this Republican "dream team" out of office, it is vital to remove this law from the books.

The actual wording of the law does not limit its scope to Mexican-American studies. It could do all kinds of damage to other courses if it is allowed to remain. It prohibits courses that "PROMOTE THE OVERTHROW OF THE UNITED STATES GOVERNMENT," but it also prohibits courses that:

2. PROMOTE RESENTMENT TOWARD A RACE OR CLASS OF PEOPLE.

3. ARE DESIGNED PRIMARILY FOR PUPILS OF A PARTICULAR ETHNIC GROUP.

4. ADVOCATE ETHNIC SOLIDARITY INSTEAD OF THE TREATMENT OF PUPILS AS INDIVIDUALS.

Overturning this law will also probably save further teaching of *Romeo and Juliet*, which made me, as a teen, resentful against the Capulets. This could also save the teaching of the Civil War, seeing as the rebel South not only advocated the overthrow of the U.S. government but actively attempted to achieve it.

I asked Maya why she thought it vital to allow the teaching of Mexican-American history and culture. She said, "I feel like students my age and who come after me, like my brother, won't be able to get to learn about all of this, and it is important."

Sean Arce wrote to me:

> One lesson that we have learned is that a dominant culture
> that demands assimilation as a condition of entry and places
> little premium on diversity (that which brings strength and
> richness to this society) will constantly seek means to deprive
> colonized/marginalized children of the training and tools we
> need to carry out the processes of asserting our rights. H.B.
> 2281 (now A.R.S. 115-112) is the example of this deprivation,
> a law passed that makes it illegal to study our history, litera-
> ture, and cultura in schools.

It is clear to me that on Jan. 12, 2015, in San Francisco, we will see
if America is still America. We will find out if freedom of speech
and intellectual freedom are still alive and well in America. We will
find out if there is still a balance of power in America. And we will
find out if a young Chicana can take on Arizona oppression and
win.

Welcome to the Chican@ literary renaissance.

What is Community Cultural Capital?

First published November 27, 2018 on TonyDiaz.net. Broadcast on the radio show Nuestra Palabra: Latino Writers Having Their Say, *90.1 FM, KPFT, Houston.*

1. Your grandma's recipe for tamales.

2. 300 volunteers.

3. Your college degree.

I began this essay with three examples of Cultural Capital because you already understand what it is, but I want to really delve into the concept to accelerate it.

And because I am a Cultural Accelerator, I'm going to discuss the topic as I put it into practice so that more of us will get into the habit of quantifying it and investing it back into our community. That's what I am focusing on—our Community Cultural Capital.

I'm going to begin with a basic definition from a dictionary from the internet to not merely enrage 98% of professors and english teachers but to also start with a very relatable reference point for you to use with your cousins, the person who cuts your hair, or in a tweet.

Then, I'm going to take it to the next level by providing a definition from Chicana visionary, the late, great Gloria Anzaldua, who, like so many other Chicanas and Chicanos, has been writing about this for years but is overlooked by the mainstream.

Finally, I'm going to end with a definition by French sociologist, the late, and also great, Pierre Bourdieu, since he possessed a PhD and might make mainstream academics feel more at home, and I really enjoy his writing.

These are going to be short essays that I'll publish once a week, every Tuesday at two, as they add up to a book.

The reason I want to dedicate myself to dissecting Cultural Capital is because, as I explained in my essay from last week, policy change is The Tip of The Pyramid, and our community's cultural capital is the base.

Mexican Americans have **directly experienced the power of cultural capital through two potent examples.**

1. In 2017, the Chicana/Chicano community overturned the banning of Mexican American Studies in Arizona.

2. In 2018, Chicanas and Chicanos advocated and succeeded in getting Mexican American Studies endorsed statewide by the Texas State Board of Education.

I want to break down what transpired, not just for posterity but also as a guide for our community to understand its power in order to quantify, cultivate, and accelerate it.

The Oxford University online reference defines Cultural Capital as:

> the symbols, ideas, tastes, and preferences that can be strategically used as resources in social action.

Your grandmother's recipe for tamales is a perfect example. It has manifested into delicious food your entire life and, in the process, shaped your tastes, sense of family, and sense of culture.

And I want to thank you for turning that Cultural Capital into capital as a fundraiser for the Librotraficantes by selling tamales and donating the funds to our 2012 caravan to smuggle banned books back into Arizona. Of course, protect that recipe so that hyper capitalists don't appropriate it, gentrify the community, open a restaurant and sell $10 tacos based on her recipe without giving her a cut of the profits.

The *Merriam-Webster Dictionary*'s definition for "Capital" builds on this:

> accumulated goods devoted to the production of other goods

We will be addressing quantifying and investing Cultural Capital into the community. This involves risks, but this can also lead to additional Cultural Capital to build on for larger goals, even eventually policy change.

That is why some folks fear this.

I am positive that Arizona wanted to sabotage our Community's Cultural Capital by banning Mexican Studies in 2012. At a surface level, most folks can understand this, but it is vital to delve even deeper.

"La facultad is the capacity to see in surface phenomena the meaning of deeper realities, to see the deep structure below the surface." Gloria Anzaldua writes about this in her potent text *Borderlands/ La Frontera: The New Mestiza*. Her book was one of the books on the prohibited Mexican American Studies curriculum at the Tucson Unified School District.

"Seeing deep structures below the surface" is a potent way to unleash an individual's ability to quantify Cultural Capital, which makes it easier to invest that power and to protect that power.

For example, my Master of Fine Arts (MFA) in Creative Writing helped me examine more profoundly the aesthetics below the surface of writing fiction. An MFA also plays into the role of Educational Capital that Bourdieu writes about.

The website Social Theory Rewired talks about him like this:

> Bourdieu's concept of cultural capital refers to the collection of symbolic elements such as skills, tastes, posture, clothing, mannerisms, material belongings, credentials, etc. that one acquires through being part of a particular social class.

That is based on their analysis of his thrilling book *Distinction: A Social Critique of the Judgement of Taste*, which leans toward the academic but sets up his powerful manual, the badass how-to manual, *The Field of Cultural Production*.

He bases some of his findings on research conducted with working-class folks and immigrant Moroccans to France. When I first read those passages, I swore he was talking about Chicanos.

That is a working definition of Cultural Capital. I will expand on this, but I also want to get the ball rolling.

Did this work?

Email me examples of Cultural Capital at Tony@Librotraficante. com. I'll talk about it in upcoming essays and on the radio show I co-host, *Nuestra Palabra: Latino Writers Having Their Say*, which airs live Tuesdays 6p–7p cst on 90.1 FM KPFT, Houston, Texas, with a Livestream at www.KPFT.org. Check out podcasts of our past shows at www.NuestraPalabra.org.

If, as you read that, you said, "that radio show is another example of Cultural Capital," then we are on the same page!!! I bet we are. I know we are.

Again, I will address more nuances about the definition of Cultural Capital, but I also want to get moving onto more aspects, but we have time. This is going to be a long book that we will live together.

So, as we part, here are three more examples of Cultural Capital. Send me yours:

1. Sandra Cisneros's and Dagoberto Gilb's cell phone numbers.

2. My Master of Fine Arts Degree in Creative Writing.

3. A list of 100 Chicanas who spend $100 MINIMUM when they visit a bookstore.

What is Community Cultural Capital? Part II

Written July 2020 for a grant proposal which we did not receive. We are right. They are wrong.

Broadcast on the radio show Nuestra Palabra: Latino Writers Having Their Say, *90.1 FM, KPFT, Houston.*

Community Cultural Capital consists of assets that we, in this case, Mexican Americans, Chicanas, Latinx have at our disposal to use (spend, invest) as we see fit. This includes our stories, our time, energy, the art—including literature—we may create, our sheer bodies, and our network of family members, friends, neighbors. This also consists of our family history, the history of our community, the history of our culture as conveyed via recipes, folklore, Cuentos, poems, short stories, and the additional works they inspire.

The metaphors of owning, buying, and investing cultural capital, teach our community that these assets are valuable. Often, our community does not imagine our writing, our stories, our family to be valuable in a capitalistic system. Articulating the framework of "Community Cultural Capital" or "Cultural Capital" engenders new metaphors and analogies that drive home the point.

Of course, the two passages before this, and this one, suffer from academic privilege. It would take too long to explain this to a room full of 300 community members, and we would bore the hell out of them. However, art is a cultural accelerant and a testament to our community's intelligence. This we know because we love literature and art. However, the framework of Cultural Capital allows us to expand this privileged view to others.

A Chicana at a Nuestra Palabra reading on the North Side of Houston, who shares her story about her family, and brings the audience to their feet with applause, is a powerful example of Community Cultural Capital. If after she reads, I were to go up to the audience and explain how that is a testament to how powerful we are, the power of our words, and the value of our experience—we accelerate the process of our community realizing the assets we possess but overlook. That would also inspire others in the room to value their stories, value literature, and value poets. And the investment of our time and energy to plan, manage, and conduct that reading would result in the creation of more culture—at some point. We would most likely be in the red as far as capital goes, but we would reap a bounty of Community Cultural Capital.

Our community has been brainwashed into believing that our stories are only valuable when a capitalist enterprise such as a New York mainstream publisher has copyrighted our stories and sold them through corporate bookstores. A more basic example is the fact that we might not consider our household, our family, our friends, and neighbors a "network." However, a bank would spend tens of thousands of dollars to organize an event in one of our communities to get our names, emails, and addresses to later market bank accounts, CDs, and loans to those folks. Moreover, my list of 100 Chicanas who will drop $100 bucks during one visit to a bookstore is invaluable. I know better than to give that away.

I use "Cultural Acceleration" more extensively in describing a plan for achieving a specific goal. In that case, I also use the metaphor of the pyramid. The desired policy change is The Tip of The Pyramid. Community Cultural Capital is the base. One example of this policy change would be pushing the Texas State Board of Education to endorse Mexican American Studies statewide. We invested our Community Cultural Capital to thwart the bills of lobbyists to erase Ethnic Studies in Texas, and we achieved a goal typically realized by corporations, politicians, lobbyists. Only a decade before this, the Texas State Board of Education famously villainized Mexican American Studies. With our tactics, the Community accelerated the process. We did in 6 years what had not been accomplished in decades.

Poetry Doesn't Make Money

First published December 11, 2018 on TonyDiaz.net & December 12, 2018 on LatinoRebels.com. Broadcast on the radio show Nuestra Palabra: Latino Writers Having Their Say, *90.1 FM, KPFT, Houston.*

Poetry doesn't make money.

That sentence is intended to sentence our senses to cents. Yet, we hear it all the time.

I aim to write about Cultural Capital to defy sentences like this.

Because here is the truth: poetry does not create direct capital, but poetry creates a gold mine of Cultural Capital. And our community thrives on it.

We will not be kept from it, but our community needs to profoundly understand the power of Cultural Capital, and they must know that others actively attempt to make us relinquish our voice.

At the most basic level, teachers, parents, and even editors tell potential poets and writers that poetry doesn't make money as if they are repeating a universal truth.

Most folks might consider this a harmless statement. The harmful part is that it's a stereotype that has gained traction and is repeated more often than poems are probably read.

Too Poor For Poetry

"Poetry Does Not Make Money" becomes a brilliant advertising campaign. The result is that our community is sentenced to a reality where poetry does not matter because, evidently, we don't have enough money to enjoy it.

At the very least repeating, "Poetry Does Not Make Money" might persuade a young person not to read poetry, a college student to reject his or her dream of choosing to major in Literature or Humanities, or an editor not to publish a collection of poems. Folks then assume that our community does not care about poetry or literature. All humans have the desire to relate their voices, their visions, their stories. All people want to. "Poetry Does Not Make Money" sentences the community to silence. Writer Dagoberto Gilb says it is more accurate to call this "invisibility."

2 of Dagoberto Gilb's books were in the Mexican American Studies curriculum outlawed in Arizona. This is from the introduction to *Mexican American Literature: A Portable Anthology*:

> ". . . historians and scholars are inclined to attribute that unawareness to an "invisibility" of the community. But the implication of this becomes that it must be something of a quaint, natural character inside MexAm people, and not the effect of poverty or consequence of a lack of political power. I'd suggest that it's more of visual degeneration in the center of the dominant culture's eyes."

Mind-Altering Prose

It is what Gloria Anzaldua calls facultad that transforms us and inspires us to pierce through this manufactured "invisibility." Endowed with facultad we are on the road to becoming Cultural Accelerators.

Anzaldua's book *Borderlands/La Frontera: The New Mestiza* was also one of the books on the prohibited MAS curriculum at the Tucson Unified School District. In it she writes, "La facultad is the capacity to see in surface phenomena the meaning of deeper realities, to see the deep structure below the surface."

Mind-altering poetry and prose reveal to us what is missing. And then we write about what we see in our minds. And we dispel that myth that poetry does not pay because we are proof that poetry creates Cultural Capital. If we invest that Cultural Capital into our community, we are poised to accelerate it for the good of not just our community but for humanity.

I have seen this happen before my very eyes.

In 1998, I founded Nuestra Palabra: Latino Writers Having Their Say in the party hall of Chapultepec Restaurant in Houston's Montrose neighborhood.

At the time, people did not quite say to me, "Poetry Does Not Make Money." Instead, they used a lot of synonyms and euphemisms.

The worst thing I would hear, even from other Latinos, was that our community just was not interested in literature.

Let that sink in. Our own community deeply believed we did not possess the basic humanity to want to tell our story. That is profound damage. I would simply tell them they were welcome not to attend, but this train was moving, and I kept looking for other Cultural Accelerators who were ready to unleash Aztec muses.

From the outside world, I would hear that there were not enough Hispanic writers in Houston to sustain a series.

I had just become the first Chicano to earn a Master of Fine Arts in Creative Writing from the University of Houston. I moved here specifically for that. This was shocking to me. I always wondered why Houston had to import Mexican Americans from Chicago when, being occupied Mexico, it had plenty of its own. Examining Cultural Capital peels the structural issues that explain this.

MFA students are taught to flee to New York to starve as soon as they graduate and try to get an obscure novel published by a small New York press. I looked into that and ascertained that NYC already had enough writers, actors, and hitmen. Instead, I decided to invest my Educational Capital into Houston's Cultural Capital.

In graduate school, you're not supposed to leave the ivory tower unless it's for a reading of your novel in progress. I adhered to other habits.

My instinct has always been to stay connected to my community. At first, I thought that meant only my family. However, I realized as early as high school that if I was going to navigate the halls of education, I was going to need my community's support.

For that reason, I continued to make history during graduate school. I was the first to teach Creative Writing courses at places like the Chicano Family Center and Talento Bilingue de Houston. I also helped organize press conferences for Central Americans seeking and being denied, political asylum.

For that reason, I knew that there was not just a need to share our voices but a deep pool of talent.

Sitting in those workshops, I was thrilled to hear people who resembled us tell their stories on their terms for the first time. Everyone should experience an edifying moment like that. It is thrilling to be part of. I wanted to give more people a stage for that. And Houston wanted to be that stage.

So, when folks told me there were not enough Latino writers in Houston to sustain a reading series, I would tell them they were wrong because I knew that if we ran out of writers, I could create more.

And I would convene with the founding members of Nuestra Palabra such as Russell Contreras, Alvaro Saar Rios, and Carolina Monsivais, and others like them who shared their time, energy, and genius with our cause and who have gone on to publish nation-wide and earn advanced degrees and inspire the next generation of writers, and on, and on, and on.

When I think of the 2.6 million Latinx students in Texas public schools right now, I envision 2.6 million poets and writers.

But don't be scared. Even when they are all freed into their Cultural Capital, the number of poets and writers will probably stay the same percentage-wise, but they will have an army of readers who have become doctors, lawyers, professors, accountants, politicians, board members, and so on, and so on, and so on.

If you don't believe me, you simply need to refer to the research by Chicanas and Chicanos submitted as evidence in court to overturn Arizona's un-American ban of Mexican American Studies. If you need more proof . . .

Sociologists take too long to explain the dagger at our throat.

Writers render the moment.

The poets make us sharply feel the import.

Librotraficantes hit back.

I bring all three to this battle for Cultural Capital and have 10 more waiting in my car.

PART II: UNEARTHING NUESTRA PALABRA: LATINO WRITERS HAVING THEIR SAY

Librotraficante Under Ground Libraries exist under your nose.

A Librotraficante Under Ground Library is a Book Oasis in a Book desert.

Librotraficante Under Ground Libraries don't take the place of the Public Library. Think of them as starter libraries.

Librotraficante Under Ground Libraries are not new. They rise from the Mexica Libraries razed by the spanish imperial land pirates.

Ultimately, Librotraficantes always defeat the spanish pirates.

Librotraficante Under Ground Libraries are Our Terms on Our Terms.

I'll be chillin' right here at the intersection of these borders, waiting for the Cultural Border Patrol, with this baseball bat in hand. Oh, wait—it's a pen.

Defining Cultivating Community Cultural Capital

This phrase is a tuning fork. CAs will automatically catch on. They have been doing this. They will recognize. It will dawn on them that the phrase and the approach puts into words a tactic We have had to adopt to survive. And now We can name it, and use it, and plan with it, and realize We are not crazy, and communicate with others if not to act, then to simply identify who else is a CA.

We are looking to work with those who We do not need to define CCC too much. Closer to the Base of The Pyramid, I don't need to explain. So We can get to work instead, and build bridges with the work We have been doing, perhaps alone, perhaps with low pay, perhaps no pay, perhaps on the periphery, on the side—not just a side hustle, but on the down-low as We do Our work for the mainstream system.

Because We spend all day in the world of the mainstream, where certain words and terms are not defined or explained. They are considered facts, they are considered law. They simply are. On the mythical Level Playing Field of corporate education, in the MFA academy of the kings english, if an MFA in poetry candidate used French in their poem, We were expected to know the reference or look it up. If I used Spanish or Spanglish in a short story, my classmates lost their minds and would waste the entire workshop attempting to intellectually deport my code from el camino real.

And if We dare ask about them, We are considered foolish. We are ridiculed. We are pegged further as outsiders. This then creeps towards hallucinations of Our incompetence, of Us as affirmative action kids given chances We did not deserve. Or being ignored.

There are terms that are baked into the experience of the shrapnel latchkey kids of the rulers.

We have to figure it out, and We are not given a clue.

This is similar to the corporate english of the mythical Level Playing Field of the courts.

The lawyer representing seventeen-year old Chicana Maya Arce against Arizona, presented solid evidence that Arizona officials were targeting Raza because the then Arizona secretary of education said, "I'm going after La Raza." But even on the liberal Ninth Circuit Court of Appeals, only the elderly white republican-appointed judge could ask, "Does saying you are going after La Raza mean you intend to go after the Mexican American Community?"

When I show one of my classes or a Community group the C-SPAN footage of that moment from the court case, We, La Raza, have to laugh or cry, knowing a judge does not know the most basic thing about Us: Our name.

If you don't who We are, if you don't even know what to call Us, how can you judge Us?

This is the most basic question from the Judge. He sounds foolish to Us because We are here. We know the right-wing republican Arizona official meant Us, was targeting Us, was going after Us. We know it plainly. You don't have to explain it.

But because he is the ruler and appointed by the past rulers, in his case ronald reagan, he was appointed by the rulers to maintain the rules that maintain their rule. And We have to explain the obvious to him.

And We have to ask, just as We have to ask every day, every time Our oppressors, the power brokers, use code to talk about Us, to hide success from Us, to make life harder on Us, to overlook Us as they carve up the world for themselves and then they carve out the crumbs, too, We have to ask, do We exist?

"What is La Raza?" in the mouth of the white reagan-appointed judge is Our existential question on a rigged playing field where We are teased. We are not asked.

Questions and answers work differently for Us.

We know that. CAs know that. Librotraficantes hit back.

We are not being asked. The white ruler is wondering out loud if this childish word bears his attention, if it should be struck from the court.

He is not asking Us.

He is speaking out loud to no one. To him, We are no one.

That is what We go through every day.

Of course, one stage of Our work is to Cultivate CCC. Of course, those acts, these assets, those things I cherish have no value at work, in the office, at the university, on the news, but I know they exist.

I know they don't matter because I don't matter. Unless I do.

And I can see that there are layers to Our work.

I see that everything We have done to merely survive will now help Us thrive.

However, to make you think like a Librotraficante, and to dramatize that you have Librotraficante in you, I want to take you back to those moments which you will encounter probably today, but when you do, you will encounter them differently.

Every day, We see and hear words, phrases, or practices that the mainstream, your boss, your coworkers, know, or at least know enough to get by, or at least know enough to not ask. That is Our college experience. Those are the parameters of the workplace still.

Today, We have flipped the script. And I remind you, We have been trained for this. As a kid, I had to learn to translate on the job. I would transform the english, with Polish accents, with Italian accents, into Spanish for my parents on the South Side of Chicago.

I was a kid bartering with adults. And I had only two choices: Break down from shame, humility, laziness, or just from being a kid—or grab the words, hold them still, and choke 'em until they either coughed up all of their secrets, or at least did what I wanted them to do.

We have to learn what the oppressor means, so We can excel there. We must learn their facts, and then also their myths, and then

We must also learn what they ignore about Us and what they want to see in Us, which might not make sense. We must translate their expectations of Us and learn how to respond.

We are also torn.

Do We lean into the work? That is one obvious place where We extract the capital We need to survive via paychecks. And We have been trained to fight for minimum wage as a marker so that if We make any bit more, We feel as if We are blessed, and We can ignore the clear fact that We are allowed to prosper but not rule. And the more that sinks in, the more depressing it is, and the more We have to decide to ignore it or acknowledge it . . . but, to who? Report it to who? Who do We tell about it? What do We do about it?

In order to survive, you must separate the work you do at work, within your family, at school, and your other worlds. This applies to just about everyone; however, for Mexican Americans in particular and Latinos in general, We are also reduced to invisibility even though We can see each other, traces of each other, evidence of each other, everywhere—especially anywhere in Texas, especially anywhere in Houston, Texas.

So, do We get more involved in the Community? That is not clear either. Where? How? Why? How can that help? Where is the Community? Aren't I the Community?

Do I get involved with activists? Will that affect my work? If I get involved too much, will that hurt how I put food on the table? Will that hurt my family, me? Will it make a difference?

What does it mean that I asked myself this last year? The year before? Five years ago, when I graduated from college?

Now, We can break it down.

Activists like the Librotraficantes Accelerate CCC. We need help from other CAs who spend years Cultivating CCC. There are many folks to thank; for example, the Mexican American Bar Association of Houston (MABAH) is the first organization that made a large donation, enough to pay for the bus for the 2012 Librotraficante Caravan. They donated $1,000. That was a stamp of credibility. Other organizations soon followed.

More importantly, MABAH's membership consists of many lawyers who are also CAs. They donated their legal minds, advice, and clout. During the caravan, We had lawyers on speed dial in every state We passed through, just in case. We also consulted with lawyers regarding the law banning Mexican American Studies, regarding how courts worked, regarding what Our words may or may not mean or imply. It made Us bolder to have access to a deep bench of lawyers in case racist-ass right-wingers wanted to drag Us into court.

Both Cultural Acceleration and Cultivating CCC take a lot of work, concentration, smarts, and genius.

However, Acceleration is thrilling. It is fucking awesome. On. The. Way. Up.

But what goes up, must come down.

What remains afterward, after the hype and anticipation and excitement, is true CCC.

We must Cultivate that base of CCC throughout the campaign, before, after, and into the future. This is harder work, especially as We are not taught this in school. We cannot go anywhere for Our license.

And worse, it hasn't even been clear that what We are doing and believe We are doing is possible.

Until now.

Yes, We *can* delineate the work of Activism, as it builds on Cultivating CCC.

One handy example of such delineation is this Book. I am here to break down the role of Nuestra Palabra: Latino Writers Having Their Say in creating, planning, conducting the Librotraficantes. However, I should add that this also sheds light on the efforts required to Quantify CCC, especially for others.

In this book I must Quantify CCC for CAs. It is harder to Quantify CCC for the rulers, because they are illiterate about Us. We have to define the basics. To go back to the older, white, reagan-appointed judge on the Ninth Circuit Court of Appeals, he had to have La Raza explained to him.

In any attempt to Quantify CCC to such an audience, I'm sure We would similarly have to explain Our Terms, especially Our identity terms, on their terms. And then We would have to teach them how to see how We use or don't use those Terms on Our Terms, as filtered through their terms.

The mainstream gives lip service to wanting to know this information, but they do not. For them to truly begin to understand, they would need to realize they are illiterate about Us.

They would have to want to learn to read Us.

And they would have to ask Us to teach them.

And then We could begin.

We are not there yet, but We will get there, not just for humanitarian and intellectual reasons—for them to get over their racism and racist practices which will hurt them psychologically, morally, and on a humanitarian level—but this will also hurt their businesses, their government and democracy.

Quickly, here in Houston, the city loves to call itself diverse, but visitors will see through it as only a slogan if they can visit and easily find the Texas Mexican Food but not the Mexican American Art. Texas is famous for Tex-Mex, the corporate version of Our abuelita's food. And tourist after tourist, and even long-time residents, actively search for the great Texas Mexican cooking abundant in Houston. If it is that hard for them to find the food they covet, it is even harder for them to unearth Our History which they never think about or are taught.

Worse, Houston's population is over 45 percent Latino, yet the city has never had a Latino mayor. Currently, there is only one Latino city council man out of fifteen.

This is an American Apartheid.

It hurts business. It hurts tourism. It looks bad. It is not a profound Democracy. It is proof that the status quo is built on structural discrimination, and you all know it.

Before all these issues were too large to deal with. They are daunting. This Book breaks them down to break them down.

You must first humanize Us.

If they don't know what to call Us, how can they quantify Us? Cultivating CCC demands humanizing Us.

This demands using Our Terms on Our Terms. We are not only well-versed in Our History, Culture, Art, We are part of it. We are from the city and state in question. We know how Our Community Works. We have receipts.

Building on the assets, Art, Culture, and History of Our CCC involves identifying it—again, Quantifying Our assets as CAs.

We respect CCC. We study it. We edify it. We spread it. We volunteer for it. We engage it every day of every year. Again, this is hard work. It may go unnoticed, ignored, or overlooked by design.

It may get co-opted by Our own. Some folks may have Spanish surnames, or blood relatives, but might still be illiterate about Us. However, We win over the long term.

When Our CCC is co-opted, a good test is to see if there is long-term gain or love. For example, when white-founded and controlled arts nonprofits use their infrastructure to engage Latinos, but they do not do so on Our Terms—no long-term gain, no love. They pursue Us as dots to fulfill their grant requirements. Those same grants might be specifically meant to develop Latino Art or Culture that they are illiterate about, without Our Community hearing about it or being eligible to apply. Our Artists, Our Community gets a few pennies from the dollars the white org gets to pretend to develop Our Art and Culture. Worse, they strive to become the agency that gets funded to Cultivate Our CCC. These nonprofits want to profit from Us as dots to check off points on their diversity plan or to maintain their progressive credentials. They are colonizing Our CCC.

Some folks who are non-Latinx want to help but are not sure how.

A semester of extra credit for attending Nuestra Palabra: Showcases is valuable to Us and you. However, that was one semester. We were here before, during, and after.

We need you back.

Live among Us. Live with Us. Hang with Us. Know Us by name. Come to Our house. Come to Our events, often. Come hang out. Come hours before to set up. Stay hours later to clean up and then to celebrate.

Come on days the spotlight is not on.

Write a check. Give unrestricted funds. Don't get mad when you don't get a thank you note, your name on a brick, or the red carpet treatment, because We don't have a Development Department. And to be frank, your donation did not change Our struggle for funding year in and year out. It would take millions of dollars over the course of several years to stem the neglect of decades and generations.

So yes, thank you, but it was not all that. We still have to put out fires. You did pay for an extinguisher. We used it up, last week.

We are too tired, too burned out to write you a nice note on vellum. And We have a long list of folks We should thank but won't be able to.

Read Our Terms on Our Terms. Learn them.

Learn Spanish. But also know that is the colonizer's language. We are nostalgic for it, but We are also wary of it. And no—I don't feel like chatting with you in Spanish just because you feel like it. I am not your free tutor. I do appreciate your love of it. But you need to adopt Our Terms on Our Terms.

Read Our stories, Our writers.

Don't steal Our stories.

Don't co-opt Our stories.

The mainstream publishing industry is illiterate about Us and, in the worst cases, simply wants to clip the tip of a Pyramid and co-opt Our stories, Our Terms on their terms. They want to profit from it. They also want to say they are open to Our stories.

They are not. They are colonizing, co-opting, stealing. The mainstream publishing world revealed these dirty tactics in 2020 with the publication of the terrible novel *American Dirt*. This Book was not intended to Quantify CCC, so I will not delve further into it. I will, however, focus more on Our Art and Culture.

We will develop specific practices for Fair Exchanges of CCC, and you should follow them. Otherwise, you are co-opting, colonizing, even stealing.

Write. Create. Artists, writers, performers from Our Community who are CAs are Cultivating CCC.

Write, read, promote, archive Our History and Culture over several years. This may also require, at times, defending Our History and Culture. However, you must also not exploit, colonize, co-opt, disparage, or hurt Our Community.

I will explain what this means.

I founded Nuestra Palabra: Latino Writers Having Their Say in 1998.

The Librotraficante Caravan was launched in 2012.

Ten years later I am writing this book.

Twenty-five years after Our first celebration of Nuestra Palabra: Latino Writers Having Their Say, We will celebrate chapters across the nation.

The Cultural Acceleration of The Librotraficantes revealed a lot about Our Power, Our History, and Culture. It also clearly burned into Our imaginations the path Art can blaze to edify Our Gente, especially when it was clear there were forces that fear, resent, and will attack Our intellectual edification.

Oppressors, rulers, and institutions that benefit from the status quo and The Level Playing Field mowed and stamped by decades and generations of structural discrimination will thwart, defy, undermine and passively—if not outright—attack Our Community Cultural Capital.

This is enough of a definition for CAs. This should be enough to inspire action.

The models as they exist do not serve Us. Artists create new models. Together We are part of the intelligentsia shaping the terrain, devising, creating.

Author the Authority

You think you speak english? Let me translate your language for you.

You don't speak english until you've had it rip through your life, bounce back through your head, and then you held it still, for a split second, to force it to cough up its secrets. Then spit it.

english is brutally honest. english is brutally honest about its oppression. But We have all been brutalized for so long, We fear the truth, and so hide it in Our minds.

Allow me to mine your mind as they've mined mine.

Let's go back to 1998 english.

That's 1998 english in Texas—Houston, Texas.

Some Texans think they're friggin' english 'cause they're rich— well, Texas rich, oil money. Some money does go back a few generations. Some is the result of a recent crime, some is in the ticking time bomb of a Ponzi scheme called Enron—but they're feeling good about themselves.

Mind you, I'm not judging them. I'm not judging people. I'm judging the kings english as its crimes are inherited by its bastard son corporate english and persecuting the Texas english of 1998.

To prove that: even I—the first Chicano on earth to pass the scrutiny of all the tests, rackets, rules, policies, requirements of the University of Houston's MFA, all the submission tricks—do not yet fully speak texas english. In any month of 1998, my 1995 chicago english was still wearing off. When I first moved to Houston, Texas, Mexicans would love to hear me say things in Chicagoan. Some of these sounds clattered around words like "car," "roof," "route." In 1998, there were still a few times I slipped up and called a wrecker a tow truck or a washateria a laundromat.

But my on-the-job training as a translator for my parents on the South Side of Chicago impressed on me the reality that no single word ever sounded the same, meant the same thing, or was worth the same in english. english kept moving, never getting captured for its crimes. This, too, was the early formative training for my Librotraficante tendencies. I grew up watching and listening to words melt, sometimes slowly, mostly quickly, and you had to move at just the right speed to make them count.

I do love Houston.

Of course, in Chicago, Houston does not exist. It's a place your relatives sneak off to, God knows why. They tell you it's 'cause of work, but you know there are so many hustles in Chi. But, it's nun ya business. Houston is generalizations you hear about someplace near San Antonio, a city you hear more about 'cause it's like little Mexico, or something. But really, you don't hear about it much or think about it.

In Chicago I was also a goofball. Most twenty-something guys, esp. from Chicago, esp. from the South Side of Chicago, esp. with a college degree, a Buick, no student debt, no kids, no wife, and two grand in the bank, are goofs. So my own definitions of "men," "women," "family," and "work" were all immature.

Worse, I had reached the North of El Norte, the border of The American Dream, and realized once again, me and mine were on the wrong side of yet a whole new set of borders. The South Side of Chicago was a racket like the entire country was, starting with that American Dream. On the other hand, I can appreciate a good hustle. And at the end of the day, it got my folks the fuck out of picking crops in Texas—which saved me from profoundly learning *that* definition of hard work. It also got my folks out of Mexico, which was in a civil war, and got my ass into a school seat to learn about bigger and bigger cons that, evidently, I could easily understand and earn high grades for participating in during an era when teachers and schools were looking for troubled youths to edify. That was me, a troubled, edifiable youth. Even though I didn't feel troubled. Having dodged becoming a migrant worker, living in the shacks the ranchers put up to keep their workers on the land during their season, and instead getting to go to school on the regular, I felt like a fucking prince. We even had a car.

Better yet, my folks were just nicer than folks were back in the day.

At first, I thought it was just my sisters talking smack about how spoiled I was and how I was treated better than they were and given more stuff. The more I found out about Our family's history in Texas, the more I realized it wasn't just about favorites—in Texas, my folks were poor. Really poor. They were simply busting their ass all day, every day, with hard work. Even as I write those two words, I still don't profoundly know the meanings of those words for my parents.

My father's heartbeat was shaped by having to drag cotton out of Texas fields when he was a teen. His back was hacked by slowly strangling the life out of crops. His bones must still bear the brunt of the sun that passed through his skin as it beat down on him, trying to stop him from pillaging the earth's fruits and veggies. His organs are dried up by now, but when he was alive, a teen, alone, loose on this world that wanted to kill him by working him to death, slowly, in a grind, baited with this friggin' mythical American Dream racket—yeah, I woulda drunk a lot, too. That definition of "hard work" robs your body, your mind, and you try to forget it, and you save the cents that come from it to survive and maybe, one day, thrive.

So yeah, by the time my mother and father raised me in the shittiest, two-story brick house in Bridgeport, as one of the first Mexican families in that neighborhood, I guess I made Us Mexican American. My mother no longer had to work—outside of the home—when We had a fixed address, so I could attend a school, and my father had a hard-ass job that paid way more than migrant work, on the regular, and he was the member of a union, so they had time and a half, benefits. … Yeah, my folks were just nicer parents to me than when they were struggling to barely survive. Like I used to tell my sister, she shouldn't blame herself. It's how I destined it.

And whereas my sister learned shame because her parents didn't speak english and she had to translate as well as pick crops without going to school, I grew up on the South Side of Chicago, surrounded by rackets, so I learned early on to recognize the ones that shape the most.

Yes, at first it sucks to translate, especially if you aren't good at it. But that's why I was sent to school: to learn english quickly and well, so I could translate for my parents.

That's not what they said, but as a South Side Chicago Translator, a nascent Librotraficante, you learn to read between the lines, and then one day, you realize you can add your own lines, and if you get really good, you can erase lines, mash up lines, create dotted lines.

There was power in language.

Josie and I were the only Mexicans in the class at the catholic school at the time. I loved that We could speak Spanish together, talk about the teacher—in front of her—and she would never know.

While other kids had to sit down and shut the fuck up, when my parents came to school, I was a player. I sat there with the adults talking, taking one set of words, adding, or taking off a bit and passing them to the other. Then one day, I was asked to translate for Josie's parents. I knew then that I was on to something.

This made me better at english.

Some of that was my own skills, some of that was studying all fucking day in school, but some of it was the power I saw.

And it was easy.

All I had to do was repeat exactly what the teacher told Us, and I would get good grades.

And even some of the white kids were worse at it.

I would even beat them at their own language.

In second grade, We would break into tiered reading groups, based on Our literacy skills. Each group had names that were supposed to mask who was a slow kid, a medium kid, and a smart kid. Even though it was supposed to be egalitarian, We all knew what was up. I was mistakenly put in the slow group because . . . well, because I'm Mexican, and yeah, once the first white kid opened his mouth, I knew this was the slow group. But I also knew I could read my way out of it if this guy would just hurry up. When he was finished reading, I jumped in and read next.

One paragraph later, I was helicoptered to the fast group, covertly titled "The Flying Eagles."

Even in that group, those white kids were not that great at reading.

The teacher had a contest where the student in their particular group who read the best out loud would get a gold star. I started winning it and kept winning it.

Long story short, it was not long before Mrs. Monniham did not stop me, instead making me read an entire page. I guess she thought it would tire me out, but nah, I practiced like that. I just stopped at the end because . . . well, no one read *two* pages. When I looked up, she was staring at me funny, that way people look at you when they think ya stole something or said something smart-ass, but they just aren't sure. I was sure I had not, because I stuck to the words. I did not add to the words, but I did pause just a bit between sentences.

And she said, "Antonio did a great job, again. So he is not going to be part of the reading contest anymore." And that was the best gold star ever.

From then on, when I saw the punk who got the star for the day, I thought to myself, *Nice job winning second place*, but I knew better than to say it out loud. I figured the teacher would get mad, yell at me, and probably tell my dad, and if she told the story, he would get pissed off and hit me with the belt.

So, nah. I didn't want to ruin the victory. It was enough to drag their star into the ground with me.

That's where the nice story should end. But, nah.

I knew the power of language when I created my own racket.

Because my mother did not speak english, I would write my absentee notes. I remember the first ones I had to write. My mother would say, *He didn't go to school because he said he was not feeling well. That's all I have to say.*

But there was no way on earth I would convey that message to the institution.

I rewrote it: *My son missed school because he had amebic dysentery.* I had used a thesaurus to look up other words for diarrhea.

It worked.

I would have written "stomachache," but I thought that was the oddest spelling on earth. Later I would have to use it, just to vary the notes, as well as "sick in the stomach."

They worked.

At some point, I would also begin to sign the notes for my mom.

By the time I was in eighth grade, I would take days off when I needed to study, wanted to read more, or needed a rest. I liked the *Dune* series, and *The Lord of The Rings*, and the shit they were giving Us in school was as boring as fuck. When We learned religious stuff, which was always pretty standard, I would write myself another day off.

I learned to author the authority.

There's an expression Mejicanos use: Arregla tus papeles. This refers to somene who is undocumented, perhaps from Mexico, going to the US Immigration Department, whatever it might be called at the time, and filing out the proper PAPERwork to adjust their immigration status and comply with the US immigration laws. Someone who is illiterate about my Community would translate that literally as "Get your papers fixed." This terrible translation illustrates the difference between oppression in the kings english vs. oppression in the kings spanish.

This is the wrong way to translate the phrase into corporate english. In corporate english, papers are not fixed. Copy machines are fixed. Paperwork is completed. Papers are filed. However, in the hands of a poet who melts borders between words, the translation is perfect, because the kings english on the South Side of Chicago knew baseball games or boxing matches might be fixed, as in the winner was pre-determined, rigged, set up. I grew up in a household that knew the immigration system was just as fixed.

So, who has the right words? Who decides the meaning? When is the meaning set? I grew up discovering one step at a time that it was not my parents, it was not the teachers, it was not the principal, it was not my neighbors, it wasn't the mayor. Sure, my teachers graded Us on grammar this, spelling that, but even they were in charge one test at a time, and when they got annoyed with Us they sent Us to the dictionary. Who wrote the dictionary? Who built the skyscrapers downtown? Who owned the schools? Some one, some people were in charge, and they sure as hell weren't living in Bridgeport, on the South Side, anywhere near me.

On the other hand, words got things done. Words that led to action were defined by the acts. I enjoyed learning and studying the theories. But I also liked getting shit done. Between those two lines, the AztecMuse took form. I didn't have those words for it at the time, but it was clear someone needed to fix the words to fix the papers to fix the world, or at least my block.

Translating the kings english on the South Side of Chicago forged the imagination that helped me duck the Cultural Border Patrol keeping Raza out of the University of Houston Creative Writing Program.

I loved poetry, I loved fiction, I loved reading, I loved writing. The 10 percent of the program that was about that was brilliant. The other 90 percent was the oddest racket I had ever ran into.

I was trying to catch up on generations of a racket that no one was willing to explain. The acolytes and priests all spoke of writing universally, even though they all sure as hell were against writing any part of the world that was not the imagined "universal" in their mind that would keep their writing at the center of the fictional, or poetic, Universe not too many other people seemed to visit.

The english of the ivory tower was the kings english of the 1800s, not the english of Texas 1998. Thus, it was my 1980s Chicago english—the kind I'd learned and authored and re-authored in school—that the UH Creative Writing Program tried to stuff into the forms, types, intellectual fonts of yore. At the UH CWP I got to read some cool books, but I could also tell that the program consisted of New Yorkers continually lamenting that they were not currently in New York, were instead banned to Houston swamps for some reason, at least for part of the year—to make enough to live in NYC the other part of the year, evidently, paying for their wine with their whine. These writers would tell Us to write in the templates of the past: past NY, past US, past France, past UK. They rarely left the ivory tower, even though they berated that this tower was not as high, as modern, as shiny as the NY ivory tower.

On the fiction side of the program, I did learn a lot from cool white writers. Daniel Stern became a mentor of mine. James Robison was a fun as hell instructor and a great writer. They were cool sentries in the last ivory tower in the hinterlands of the White Whale of Literature. But I could see other instructors were too crushed by NYC to enjoy the racket they were part of.

We were never to ask about getting published. We were never to ask about making a living as a writer. Yet, Texans' tax money went to a program that imported and paid writers from New York, who were published in New York, to teach one class, live in Houston a few months, and then get the hell out of Swamp City—which they always complained about.

In the ivory tower of Houston, lording over the swamps and trees, the myth of the American Dream was replaced by the New York Dream: Once you earned your MFA (by the way, no one fails their thesis defense, no one, so if *you* are getting your MFA: hurry the fuck up, finish, and put the paper to work), you are supposed to leave for NYC to get published—well, drink a bunch and hang with writers, same as in Houston, but not with writers who are in Houston.

And not surrounded by Mexicans.

I had already been to the North of El Norte, as in the end of El Norte, so I knew that New York had too many dancers, writers, and hitmen—they did not need or want any more. Also, elite NY is not only illiterate about Mexicans; elite NY treats Texans like Texans treat Mexicans.

My MFA, despite the indoctrination of the ivory tower, transformed me into a Mighty Fine Aztec. I realized why they had to import Mexicans from Chicago to the UH CWP even though they were in the middle, well, on the southeast side, of Occupied Mexico: Texans are illiterate about Mexicans and, of course, as a logical conclusion, illiterate about Latinos. Two topics I was expert at. I didn't need to be given a gold star to know I had struck a gold mine.

The Texans were in need of translating services, and I was a child prodigy of translations. I learned early in life that adults did not know what they were saying, on top of the fact they sometimes did not say what they meant, on top of the fact that they often did not profoundly understand themselves, what they could do, what they should do.

I also did not give a fuck about a job, especially not in the ivory tower.

My goals were to earn a black belt, earn a master's degree, publish a book, reject masters. That was my Chicano Dream.

And then I did it.

Now I just needed to unleash my Librotraficante, and I needed to mine all the CCC surrounding me in Houston. I didn't have the words for it at the time, but I was authoring the authority to forge them.

"Forge" for the working class means melting iron and beating its ass on an anvil. "Forge" for rich fucks means faking it, ripping Us off.

Those same skills were necessary for me to navigate Houston as I worked to open Nuestra Palabra: Latino Writers Having Their Say.

Texans were honest when they said they did not believe there were any Latino writers in Houston. They could not imagine enough Chicana writers to fuel a reading series. They could not imagine the movement I was announcing. My english defied their english.

They were confessing that they were illiterate about Latinos, but they were used to intellectually bullying Us. They were used to "owning Us" figuratively, because their forefathers literally owned Us.

They were used to putting their blinders on others, sharing them, making Us wear them, and if We wanted to work with them, work for them—which was mostly the case—or get graded by them—

which they always thought was their right—then it was best to conform to their forms, to submit.

Of course, I was an expert in Us.

I spoke many languages. I spoke 1980s Chicago. I mastered the kings 1800s english per my master's degree. I spoke 1998 mexican spanish.

And most importantly, I now spoke 1998 texas english.

I learned it from the dingy ivory tower of the MFA program, the run-down campus around it. I learned it by crossing the concrete moat of streets and highways surrounding it, to get to the Salvadorans and Guatemalans speaking their versions of Spanish on the southwest side as I translated their narratives into governmental english for their applications for Temporary Protected Status; I learned Mexican from all the Raza EVERYWHERE, at the tae kwon do school, at Fiesta Mart, at the Pulga, the cantinas, the restaurants, the bingo halls. I learned it from the drawl of the white folks at the comedy club I performed at, the small-town newspaper I covered city hall meetings for, the bars and clubs I strolled into to watch boxing matches. And some of it would work its way into the classrooms where I was a teaching assistant for Composition I courses—with zero training or experience, but with the credential of my bachelor's degree and acceptance into the UH Creative Writing Program. That translated into "You can teach this class."

So, when white Texans admitted to me that they could not imagine Latino writers in Houston, I knew they were confessing they were illiterate about Latinos. I did not bother to argue with them and explain that I was an expert on Us. That was too hard. Looking back, I think even then I knew it would take too long to Quantify Our CCC for them. And it would slow me down from Accelerating CCC by planning, organizing, and conducting the Science Fiction they said did not exist, and doing so by making the TV news, radio, and print.

The white reading series never made TV news. We did.

I learned about Our power and the power of Our Art, Language, Metaphor. And I see now why the powers that be try to con Our youth into believing reading and writing don't matter, even though they have dedicated generations to keeping Us from it, from making literature illegal to segregating Our schools, to burning Our Books, to banning Our Art, History, and Culture.

If it is not powerful, if it does not matter, why are they so scared of it, working so hard to snuff it out?

They were trying to make me illiterate about my power, too. They were trying to make me fit into the template, where in order to create Latino writers, "we" must import Mexicans from Chicago. The program pulls candidates away from their base of CCC. We submit. We move to a new terrain. We are supposed to focus on learning only the useful knowledge of the perspective and aesthetics of the Writing Program. If We can't read the landscape, We dedicate Our time to the ivory tower.

This is the same tactic corporate universities use to pay lip service to Community Engagement even as they undermine it—along with CCC. The rulers create rules that rule out applicants from particular Communities. Meanwhile, the folks they hire from far away who meet the rigged criteria will be worked so hard they won't have time for or interest in learning to read the CCC of the area, the home of the other students in the program.

But when I got here, I created my own racket, like when I started writing my own absentee notes.

In Houston, I crossed cultural border after border to become the first here and then the first there.

I got my writing license, aka an MFA from the UH CWP. MFA stands for más frijoles and arroz.

I gave classes. I knighted other writers. I authored Our authority.

If We counted on NY to forge Our writers, We are fucked and stupid.

And on Wednesday, April 22, 1998 in Houston, Texas, I launched Nuestra Palabra: Latino Writers Having Their Say and changed the world, mutherfuckers.

Texans insisted We did not exist. We insisted. Houston's CCC formed a powerful platform for the expression of Our Gente's Art,

History, and Culture. We needed it. We demanded it. We created it. We sustain it.

NP would become The Tip of The Pyramid that would lead to the creation of many other works, which helped Us organize to defy the looming direct attack on Our People.

I say this after Arizona banned Our Culture—the worst form of psychological warfare.

This was state-sanctioned violence engendered against Our CCC. We had to act to overturn that.

And then We won.

But still, Our oppression is ignored and erased, and discussion of that fact is banned.

I am writing this ten years after the Cultural Acceleration that forged the Librotraficante movement. In the hands of the mythical Level Playing Field of the media, Our movement was an interesting component of a marketing campaign, perhaps, or a cool term, maybe, or what may or may not have been the dismantling of courses. corporate media could not comprehend the CCC at the base of this Tip of The Pyramid. Mainstream media feared, or could not fathom, the true situation, would not call the oppression We were responding to what it was.

So Librotraficantes made it news: We Broadcast Our Terms on Our Terms and revealed the power of CCC, especially through Literature, and the fact that only Art can save Us; revealed how many are threatened by Our intellect and the fact that there was an ongoing, overt effort to sabotage Our intellectual advancement and destroy Our CCC.

Even as We succeed in defying, in authoring Our own authority, We must understand how to Cultivate CCC leading up to and leading through those key moments. We can't expect the mainstream to Quantify Our CCC, or, even more importantly, as this Book accomplishes, to explain the inner workings, tactics, reasons, and strategies for Cultivating CCC. The Librotraficantes did not appear out of thin air. We were formed by fourteen years of work through NP, which was built on the CCC of generations.

We must mark Our victories. We must acknowledge that, with Librotraficantes, We reached The Tip of The Pyramid and will again. We must look at the risks, the costs, the beauty of it.

We must study the tactics.

We must archive it.

We must Quantify Our CCC for CAs, on Our Terms.

We must measure Our capacity. Study it.

And most importantly, We must build on it. This is vital because the goalposts on The Level Playing Field of the courts, where Our Community was successful, and The Level Playing Field of Academics keep moving.

Things keep moving.

We are used to moving, working, grinding. We must move and grow and study. As such, I write this now to articulate the power of The Pyramid and to showcase the power of CCC.

I am also building on it.

This Book fills in the blanks and shatters the stereotypes and generalizations that obscure the movement.

This Book outlines the next generation of the movement. Together We must find the frequency for the next Tip of The Pyramid. However, I won't speculate on individual ones at this moment, as they must arise from the moments in which they are meant to exist.

At this stage, there is the work of Our larger movement to liberate Our Librotraficantes, to edify CCC so that We can Cultivate CCC. CAs must reveal themselves. We must unite.

Each force shapes Our move up The Pyramid. Our Community chooses a Tip of The Pyramid that We embrace, that the Community vets in Our Way, and that Art Communicates in Our language, imagery, values, system. For decades, these forces and movements were coded in novels, poems, essays, short stories—especially those on the banned MAS Curriculum.

That is the theory. Let me get specific:

We go back to 1836 with the war with Mexico.

We go back five hundred years to the spanish pirates' invasion.

We go back to the Olmecs before then and those before them who coded Art, Culture, History, Wisdom, Knowledge into The Pyramids We constructed.

the kings english imposes arbitrary lines on Us for political power, for profit, or to try to carve up time to maintain its supremacy.

Instead, We CAs, We Librotraficantes, defy time. Art is a time machine.

El Camino Real

It's called a master's program.

We as Americans tolerate it because We suspect it means We are on the road to becoming masters, even if it is only of english.

But We are wrong.

Metaphors are forced confessions. And english is brutally honest.

The master's program belongs to the master.

We must submit before We are admitted. We fill out the forms. We actually jump into the forms they create to make sure We will conform. We submit to corporate english which is the bastard son of the kings english.

the spanish kings killed to monopolize reality. In spanish, "real" translates literally into "royalty." "El camino real" means "the royal road" at the same time as it means "the real road" at the same time as it means "trail." It means the road to money. The spanish kings paid you in reals. With each payment you took, imagined, conveyed, you enforced the fake real world where the king, monarchs, forged reality.

If today We have augmented reality glasses, Our sovereign states are built on contracted reality blinders. Back then, the user agreement you signed to download the blinders on Our head was accepting, buying into the real of the king.

They forged reality so that all roads led to them. They made life much harder off the beaten path. And if this reality was hard to maintain in teeming and contentious Europe, imagine the challenge of taming the imaginations of strange peoples across the ocean in the new world that you had to forge into this fine old world—with kings at the center of the universe.

There was a royal need for institutions to institutionalize the reality of the royalty. As Americans, We like to believe that We are immune. We are surrounded by the kings english, the taint of monarchs.

As a translator, you pick it up, but you have to figure out how to put it down.

You could translate el camino real into "the royal road." corporate english would like to contract that to "infrastructure," dusty roads that are tourist attractions in the southwest USA. That is a synonym for the kings highway. To Americans, that sounds antiquated—we did, after all, kick the british kings ass to become independent. True, the colonies rebelled and deposed that monarch, but We kept so much more. We rid Ourselves of the KING'S highway, but We kept highway, and the model, a central source paying to forge the easiest path. We maintained the practice of imposing highways over lands once indigenous turned barrios, overlooking erased neighborhoods, mapping that which touches el camino real and obscuring all that is other. We even kept the metaphor and employed it to erect the information superhighway.

We dreamed it would be egalitarian. Yet, even now, in Houston, Texas, the fourth-largest city of America, the COVID-19 shutdown has revealed how Our communities, Our barrios, Our casas are shaped out of prosperity, health, vaccines, and stable Wi-Fi access.

How did corporate media, publishing, education, politicos, et al. learn to shape Our cities, neighborhoods, houses, bodies, Our imaginations? There was a need to tame the mongrel spanish of the barbarians of the new world after it was imposed upon them. kings needed to forge a reality that keeps them at the center: royal language, real art, true religion, caste systems, real people, and gold.

MFA programs are the bastard children of the royal academy of spanish.

I must be careful how I say this because I want to make something clear for my Community: I do believe in Education. That is why I work to transform it. I am proud and glad I earned an advanced degree. I would love for as many people as possible to earn doctorates. I love cultivating a life where all of Us Read, Write, and Create.

However, I am able to write these words because I maintained a connection with my CCC during my submission to the master's program.

Even as I type that sentence it sounds like a sentence from a handbook, or a "how-to" manual or a self-help guide from some corporate publishing house—so, let me shatter that similarity.

Older Mexican American parents traditionally don't let their children fly the coop.

I altered that. A bit. I moved my parents with me to Houston to attend the master's program.

Again, I must defy the types, myths, and images that occupy imaginations. Picture a "father," picture a "mother." That is not what my mom and dad looked like.

My parents were older.

I was raised by my biological grandmother and grandfather since the day I was born.

I promoted them to my real parents in eighth grade when I legally adopted them. That was when I chose my real name—Tony Diaz. I remember imagining being baptized one name and then baptizing myself with another, my true name. (My mom was very Catholic by the time I was growing up, so I knew better than to say that blasphemy out loud.)

That act began changing the path of el camino real for me.

My father was retired. My mom was in poor health. I still translated for them, except now my battles were with the social security un-administration, doctors, nurses, pharmacies.

My sister and her husband lived in Houston. They had moved from Chicago years before, in one of the waves of all those White Sox and Cubs Fan you see at Astros games.

Activism is one level of Community Organizing that inspires myths.

Yes, instead of going to only readings, parties, or bars, in graduate school I would also go to protests and marches and organize press conferences. None of that counts towards yer thesis. I dated an an-glo poet who could not understand why I was VOLUNTEERING to give free citizenship classes at a Church. She tried to talk me out of it. I didn't listen.

I worked with the Central American Resource Center (CRECEN) on the southwest side of Houston. Teodoro Aguiluz, the director, would organize marches in front of ICE facilities, demanding that Central Americans receive political asylum for the secret, not-so-secret civil wars the US instigated in their home countries—similar to US interventions across the same path of continents the spanish monarchs razed.

I was bilingual, so I would help translate the narratives of Salva-dorans and Guatemalans on their applications for political asylum. The US denied this request because it could not admit there was any civil war that the US played a role in. Instead, it granted them TPS—temporary protected status.

I would squeeze the plight of Guatemalans and Salvadoran into the forms acceptable to corporate media to cast/e broadly the words in the kings english that would inform and capture the hearts of good Houstonians. Those speeches did not count toward my thesis; corporate education never counts Community Work.

And of course, my classmates would lose their minds if I used Spanish or Spanglish in a short story and all of a sudden begin asking me about who was my intended audience. Under all other circumstances, intended audience was "too commercial" to address in this program meant to produce professional writers. On the other hand, the universal form racket *did* lead to readers gushing over french or greek in a piece. So the right foreign languages were "universal"—whereas the wrong one, mine, was absurd to use in a made up work.

I would go on to document stories of refugees staying at Casa Juan Diego.

I defied the gravitas of the camino real to unearth more of my CCC. To dig deeper is more work.

When I moved to Houston to become the first Chicano to graduate from the University of Houston Creative Writing Program, *me treje mis chivas*. There is no best translation for this.

So, I'll endeavor this:

And it is hard. Language is intended to form Us, conform Us.

So I will first say this in american english this way: I lived with my parents.

What a loser. That plays for laughs on TV. That is not the bohemian artist life of MFAs.

After my mom passed away, my wife and I added an addition to Our house, which was its own mini-house, so that my father could live there. He was by then using a wheelchair, and We wanted to make it easier for Us to help him with groceries, doctors visits, nursing visits. My wife was expecting Our youngest son, too.

My father did get to meet Our newborn, and he adored him as much as he adored my oldest son, Antonio, named after him, and me. Yes, as my wife pointed out, that was a bit patriarchal of me. She indulged me but refused to also name Our second-born Antonio. I named him Pablo, after Pablo Neruda.

I don't want to be too glib or academic about how all of Us lead Our lives. Also, I am not a robot. I can't detect all oppression in every act. I also don't think of the origin of every act. However, I am a writer, a reader. I love to read, sit, learn. And as a writer, I do love to hear how deep words can get.

As I type this, I am touched by a memory of how my mom made me feel like the center of the universe, so much so that I was stunned to find out later that I was not the center of anyone else's.

When Antonio was born, We lived about twenty minutes away from my parents. My mom was bedridden. My father could still move around on his own, slowly using a walker, but I did have to take his car keys away because he could no longer drive.

Carolina and I would buy Our weekly groceries, now adjusted for the baby, and also buy my parents' groceries, stop to pick them up fajitas for dinner, and then stop to drop off the food, set it in their fridge, count out their pills, hug, chat, then drive to Our home and do baby stuff.

One day in particular I remember pulling up the driveway in a white Nissan Altima that could barely fit all the groceries, and then the baby seat in back, and then the stroller. Grocery lists were the only prose I wrote on days like that. Nuestra Palabra loomed as the monthly showcase of other peoples' writing while I wrote to-do lists, not books. I was unglamorously exhausted from sleep deprivation that new parents undergo, numb from scrutinizing grocery store shelves for items, comparing prices and portions, and it was hot. Houston is a hot, wet octopus, humidity accosting me with eight arms as soon as I stepped out of the car to unbuckle Antonio from the baby seat. I carried him up the driveway and was ecstatic that the fence opened, the rusty nail I'd twisted to fasten the handle together holding up for one more day. My folks had the front door open, and I could see through the screen door to my mom's bed set in the living room. I told them time and time again that We could afford to pay for the AC and that I preferred they lock the door so they would not get robbed.

I walked a few steps onto the lawn, my son cradled in my arms, and I could hear my mom saying in her loudest voice possible, raspily, "Ahí viene el Rey. Ahí viene el Rey."

I smiled. She continued as I approached the *unlocked* screen door, and I could see she was holding a picture of my son and kissing it, repeating "Ahí viene el Rey" until I could get my son close enough to lay him on her chest, and she could put down his picture, wrap her arms around him, kiss him, and say, "Aqui esta el Rey."

I could just imagine what she was like with me when I was a baby. All that adoration even before I began forming words.

She repeated that incantation, created that ritual. Eventually, I stopped wanting to be the center of the universe. It was enough to have been the center of hers, for a bit, and even now.

Heart. That melts all. Inspires. Only Art Can Save Us. Shattering borders, limitations. Expanding.

When she died, she asked me to take care of my father. We did.

Even though my father passed away many years ago, I still live with my parents.

I am typing this from the house We just bought that follows what is currently called a "Next Gen" model, meaning it contains a private suite within the layout of the house. This time the occupant is my wife's mom, an elderly Chilean woman. Our sons are now young men. Antonio is a senior in college, Pablo is a senior in high school. During the COVID-19 shutdown, We were all here in the Diaz Family Compound. I loved it.

No, We are not the sandwich generation that has to take care of the generation that came before Us and the generation just after: We are the burrito generation, because We are wrapped by those other generations and consumed—yet, We get bigger and bigger. From Us, more is created.

It is a hard path at times. Still, all these stones forge the base of my CCC.

Here is one more layer.

Folks hear me mention that I am Chicano or that I'm advocating for Mexican American Studies, which was banned—so, because corporate media has trained them this way and they don't read enough books by Us, they might assume that I champion only Chicanos. That is wrong, as wrong as the myth that Latino Artivists only champion Latinos.

To prove that is a myth, I remind you that my sons are Chicano-Chileans.

I fell in love because of CCC.

I met Carolina through my great friend Cliff Hudder, who I met at the UH CWP. Cliff Hudder is one of the best short fiction writers I know. There was a young Chilean woman named Carmen who lived in his apartment complex, which We nicknamed Melrose Place because it resembled the TV show that was a huge hit at the time. Both featured sexy, fascinating young folks in weekly dramas with pop references, humor, and booze. Carmen told Cliff that she was having a dinner party for her friends visiting from Chile who used to host parties in Chile with a bunch of writers. So she wanted to do the same, but We were the only writers she knew. She said I should come, but she told me not to hit on her friend. I was definitely going.

The chicken was lousy, but the moment I saw Carolina I was smitten by Cupid's crossbow. She was gorgeous, spoke Spanish, and, like all Chileans, loved wine, poetry, and politics. She had protested Pinochet. She was friggin' brilliant. She had just finished law school and was visiting her mom who lived in Houston, and she planned to return to be some bougie lawyer. I wanted to hang out with her as much as possible before she went back.

That might be the Melrose Place version of events.

Here is how CCC love works.

I had a dilemma. My mom was scheduled for a doctor's visit the same day We had organized a protest in front of one of Houston's immigration facilities with CRECEN.

I was torn. I told Carolina about this.

She. Offered. To. Take. My. Mom. To. The. Doctor.

Carolina picked up my mom in her car. Of course, Caro not only speaks Spanish, she is a trained lawyer. So she chatted all the way to the doctor's with my mom and then grilled the doctors and nurses. My mom had famously disliked anyone I dated. She came back home in love with Carolina.

Of course, Caro planned to leave the States. She had a career to attend to.

I began writing her a love letter a day. I would make them arrive by all different means, snail mail, messenger, flowers. I would hand them to her, leave them in her mailbox. We would see each other just about every day before she was scheduled to leave; regardless of whether I saw her or not, another love letter would arrive.

Three months later, I proposed. Six months later, We were married.

That damn Poetry Crossover class I had to take in the MFA Program had finally paid off.

She jokes that I stalked her; I joke that she married me for her papers.

CCC changes. We change. Words change. Language adapts or constricts. We create or conform. In reality, there are many, many ways. #Plur

Here is the reality I imposed on my universe: I lived CCC as I steeped myself into the ivory tower, deep into the kings english bent on propagating its reality.

I turned earning my MFA into The Tip of The Pyramid I would reach.

The institution saw me as a dot.

Thirteen years into their existence, sitting in Occupied Mexico, with a rising Hispanic population reported on the news to their trustees, revealed by all the Spanish surnames enrolled in undergraduate courses, the University of Houston Creative Writing Program needed Us.

Of course, it did not know what to call Us, it could not see Us under its very nose, and it had to create rules to maintain its rules.

I literally submitted the forms they created to see if I could conform to their forms. They saw me as a dot on their graph for diversity. They did not know I was The Tip of a Pyramid. They tried to chip me off my base.

But I brought my base with me.

This is a struggle. It is hard. But all of Our paths are hard. We are defying an invisible caste system that, on a good day, ignores Us and, on the worst days, obliterate Us.

Of course, it's just school. But school is rarely just. And MFA programs are not programmed for justice. They are programmed to do the kings work. However, Our Community has learned to thrive, for generations, off the grid, off the charts, under ground, under the kings very nose.

Forget the cliché of "pick your battles."

I am putting into words how We chart the war.

The University of Houston contracted the legal "I" who submitted to their forms to become documented as a writer.

The ego "I" forged a voice.

The Community "I" is the foundation before, during, and after.

I didn't have the words for this then.
I have extracted the words from Tejas.
They are this Book.
And now, We accelerate.

I Began My Revolution By Summoning The Poets

Librotraficante Maxims:

1. Learn the system.

2. Don't trust the system.

3. We are the system.

There is another vital facet of this Renaissance.

We CAs are blessed to have powerful heroes who We can meet in person, who can become Our mentors, and then become Our friends, and then familia.

What is the unifying term for Our Community? That's simple: Familia.

No Nuestra Palabra, no Librotraficantes.

No Raza writers, no Books to teach or ban.

Nuestra Palabra: Latino Writers Having Their Say created tenth-degree black belts in CCC. I founded the group in April 1998. In January 2012 We began organizing to answer Arizona republican officials attacking Our History, Culture, and Community.

When the five co-founders of the Librotraficante Caravan sat around a table, each member had over ten years of experience in Community Organizing—the real deal, not Hispandering, not re-sume packing, not one-shot deals. Those five founders were Libor-traficante Liana Lopez, aka Librotraficante Lilo; Laura Acosta, aka Librotraficante La Laura; Bryan Parras, aka Librotraficante High

Tech Aztec; Lupe Mendez, aka Librotraficante Lips Mendez; and me, Tony Diaz, El Librotraficante. Each one of Us had at least ten years experience with Nuestra Palabra and brought particular skills, experience, connections. They all had skills, they were all empowered through CCC, and each one of Us was connected to Our Community, which made Us each CAs. Each one of Us shaped NP and would shape the Librotraficante Movement. This is what happens when CAs unite.

Of the crew, only two of Us were writers. I wrote prose, and Lupe is a poet. In fact, this Book comes out the year he is named Poet Laureate of Texas—the damn entire state! He was great at working a poem, a crowd, an army of volunteers, including the almost four hundred folks who helped run Our massive Book fairs.

Liana was originally into Science and even worked in Accounting. She showed up to one of Our volunteer meetings one day and then just started getting shit done. She was soon Our stage manager who helped Our live showcases run smoothly. But she ran a tight ship. She once told a well-known publisher that he had to get off the stage because his time was up. The other writers working stage crew that night were scared to say anything because they wanted to get published by him some day. I'm sure if Neruda woulda come back from the dead for one of Our showcase, Liana woulda told him he had only one minute left—when it was time. She later brought that sensibility to the radio show and helped Us become badass. Lilo, along with Bryan, captured many of the most potent photos during the Librotraficante Caravan, images that then became part of Our social media, websites, flyers. Liana received grants for her photo work, including her series on the relics of revolution in Panama.

Laura grew up in Baytown and then earned her degree at St. Thomas University in Houston, so she brought in volunteers, donors, and audience members from Baytown. She was also an expert in education administration. She helped Us organize Our first workshops for administrators and was always showing Us how to reach out to working-class as well as upper-management Latinos.

Bryan loves film and broadcast. He is a hardcore activist, especially for environmental issues. He had been on caravans before, so he brought that experience to the Librotraficantes. For NP, he ran the board for the radio show and chose the soundtrack for Our revolution. He always pushed Our movement to the next level of technology, making sure We were moving fast but keeping the Community with Us.

We were not interested in simply becoming nonprophets of nonprofits. When We gathered around the table to plan, of course there was great food, beer, and wine, but We also brought over fifty years of experience delivering great feats by, for, and about Our Gente. We each invested at least ten years in the group, and some of Us up to fourteen years.

The ban of Mexican American Studies pushed Us to break the boundaries We had become accustomed to. Arizona banned Our History and Culture. We decided to make more.

Every year as part of my praxis, I devise what some folks might call new year's resolutions. Some I share with folks, some I keep to myself, some I follow for years. As a matter of fact, you are reading one of my goals for this year—this Book. Praxis is the praxis. All. The. Time.

One of my goals for 2012 was to create more videos. Librotraficante High Tech Aztec had been giving me a hard time. He loves film, video, audio, thus his moniker, and I could see how the mainstream book industry was in flux, if not quite a free fall yet, and the world of video was booming. This paired well with one of my other goals: building websites.

Orlando Lara built one of the first versions of the Nuestra Palabra website as an undergraduate student at Stanford interning for Us. Subsequent versions were created by writer Cliff Hudder and Community member Alberto Diaz. They put in time and energy to get Our movement online, but it also would take a lot of time and energy to update the sites, so I wanted to attempt to learn to do it myself.

The year before, I had made it my goal to engage in social media, diving into Facebook, LinkedIn, and Twitter, among other platforms. So all of these activities tied nicely into one another, and none of them were anything I would ever learn in my MFA program. Instead I'd have to learn this in my Community MFA Program, which would make me Mas Frijoles y Arroz.

I'll tell you about the fourth video I shot that year.

I figured, *I write novels, this short, quick stuff should be easy. Maybe I make this thing ten minutes, twelve minutes? I talk on the radio for an hour—piece of cake.*

I shot a five-minute video about what We were planning. It sucked. It was hard to watch. I bored myself, and I love me. I tried to shoot another video about a different topic. Maybe I was too close to this one, I figured, and maybe four minutes would be enough.

I have erased the contents from my phone and my memory. It was that bad.

I was, however, undaunted. The week before We shot the final video to launch The Librotraficante Caravan, I started dreaming up different scenarios. I pictured renting a U-Haul, getting folks to act as if they were loading books in the truck. We did, after all, actually move books. We moved them to readings, to Community centers. We even set up readings and book signings in spots where no one had before, from parks to church basements to parking lots. But We were running out of time, energy, and resources. The longer We took to move, the fewer other actors We could involve, until there was time for only one actor: me.

I decided to aim to create a video that was just one minute long. I worked on a script based on the coolest lines from what We had been saying on Our radio show. I fired all the rest.

So, I memorized the script, practiced it on my phone, and was ready, just waiting for Bryan Parras, Librotraficante High Tech Aztec, to show up at my crib to shoot it. We had a big enough budget to shoot live on location. That meant We had $0, so We would film in front of my house, with my garage door open and my black Nissan Xterra with black-tinted windows, hatch open, displaying the boxes of books We trafficked across the city on a regular basis. It was a pop-up book display featuring the racks and shelves I'd bought from a Borders bookstore liquidation sale, which We used at book signings We organized and magazine launch parties for *Aztec Muse* magazine. Promoting *Aztec Muse* in different Texas cities revealed to me how different each city was. That awareness would serve Us as We planned the Librotraficante Caravan.

Here is the text of the video, as presented on YouTube and as published in Dr. Cliff Hudder's dissertation, "The Capital of Elsewhere":

In the video, wearing aviator glasses and a brown leather jacket, Diaz stands near the open cargo area of an SUV filled with books. As he mentions "new words in the lexicon," these appear superimposed in front of his image:

"My name's Tony. You might have heard that Arizona had the audacity to ban Latino studies. Well I'm here to introduce a few new words into the lexicon of Arizona, courtesy of the Protestors Handbook, written right here in Houston, Texas.

"First phrase: 'Libro-Traficante.' Me and my fellow Librotraficantes will be smuggling contraband books back into Arizona this Spring Break, March 2012. If you want to get involved, visit the website, Librotraficante.com.

"Second phrase: 'Wet-Book.' These are books that We smuggle illegally across the border to be used in underground classes where We will conduct Latino Literary Studies. It's a lethal dose of Dagoberto Gilb coming at you Arizona. [Holds up Gilb's story collection, *Woodcuts of Women*.]

"Third phrase: 'Dime-Book.' These are paperbacks that used to be worth only ten dollars, but are now invaluable thanks to your fascist laws, Arizona.

"*House on Mango Street* [holds up the book]. Twenty-first anniversary edition by Sandra Cisneros. I hear she's leaving San Antonio. Maybe We can convince her to come live . . . in Arizona. Contraband people!

"Arizona, We're throwing the book at you. 'V' for victory, *vatos* [a rooster crows in the background]." (*Wet Books: Smuggling Banned Literature Back into Arizona.*)

After filming, Bryan and I met with Liana Lopez, Librotraficante Lilo, at Agora Café in Montrose, the chill, artsy, gay neighborhood in Houston that has since been gentrified. We drank beer, wine, and ate as We plotted and schemed this Librotraficante Caravan. That means it was a Tuesday. We did this before every edition of Our radio show, *Nuestra Palabra: Latino Writers Having Their Say.*

I co-hosted the show with Liana, who was also the producer. Bryan ran the board and was Our music curator, choosing the soundtrack for a revolution. And any week, We may have had an army of new interns, a guest with their crew, two guests with their crews, and then run into folks We know from the barrio, 'cause between Us all—we knew a shitload of people. If We had live guests, We would meet and shoot the shit before the show, which meant a few beers with a cool poet, or several. The studio was packed, the interviews were dope, and the musical breaks were parties.

It is fun as hell being a Librotraficante.

We would all ride that adrenaline high from the broadcast to *really* chill after show. We would roll into Avante Garden Café, owned by an Argentine woman, maybe twenty or thirty deep on some days. Of course, it was not just Latinos. We interviewed and worked with all cool, down, artistic, and Community-minded Houstonians across the rainbow. We are pluralistic.

This was one way We had such a deep base of CCC. We chilled with the people. And Tuesdays were the intelligentsia, activist, artistic think tank pop-up parties.

This was one part of Our real-life love for that which corporations try to copy as "community engagement."

But they can't hang like Us.

And this love was part of the reason why back in the day, when We organized the Latino Book and Family Festival, We had almost four volunteers helping Us to organize the massive event that drew over thirty thousand people at its peak.

I say this to remind CAs that this is the basis for Our Movements: Community. corporations and politicians want to reach thirty thousand people in one swoop. They want to dig into all their pockets at once. They want to generalize Us. Our movement humanizes Us at every level.

As We ate hummus and drank Duvel at Agora Café, Lilo began organizing the radio show lineup for that evening. The radio show lineup would include calls to writers Dagoberto Gilb and Sandra Cisneros, both now contraband authors whose works formed part of the outlawed curriculum. Lilo sounded great on the air, was laser focused on the details, and came prepared.

As a team, We had a work rhythm that was what I'd once dreamed school, then maybe college, then maybe graduate school, might be like—but they never were. I'd also hoped that flow would come from a great job, but that never happens either. The higher paying the job, the more likely you are to die stressed in some office, which is just a fancier version of a cubicle.

Turns out I'd find the flow in a different context altogether: No one could pay the Librotraficantes to do what We did. We invested Our CCC to make more CCC, and We simply kept unearthing more and more and more.

We hung out at the very least once a week to put on a badass, intellectual show. We texted each other all week long at odd hours of the day with show ideas, cool posts, new writers, new films, cool readings, openings, concerts, and parties.

Because folks wanted to be on the air, We found out about great shows, performances, and readings way ahead of time, and 'cause We also organized readings, workshops, parties, and protests, We just kept meeting cool folks throughout the entire city.

The entire crew had a context, too.

While We were fighting for more of Our youth to be exposed to their Cultura, not only did We read Dago and Sandra's work, We got free copies, We got copies to give away, We hung out with them when they got into town, We hung out with them when We visited San Antonio or Austin. We didn't have to Google or get bios from their publicists—we had Our own personal stories about them.

Between all this socializing and how confident she was on the show, it took me a while to realize that Liana is shy. She helped Us run the NP showcase, she flowed on air, she defined space by taking shots—but she was straight up mortified when We did a talk together at a local bookstore. I had never seen her so nervous. She told me it was because she had never spoken in public as just herself. At first I had no idea what exactly that meant. But I then understood that her on-air confidence grew from her preparation—the show rundown, the research, Our talking through ideas and approaches—whereas a lot of the time, Bryan, Lupe, and I were just talking smack.

Lilo, like the rest of Our crew, is an artist of the beautiful. Yet so many from Our Community are not given license to say they are writers, artists, poets. The rest of the world says you need this degree, that degree, this publication there, that title here, in order To. Be. A. Writer.

We Librotraficantes author the authority.

We print out writer's licenses like green cards and pass them out at one hundred thousand watts, or one Mexican at a time, even if you are not Mexican.

We are flagrant about Our crimes: Dagoberto Gilb would say on air that he felt like he was getting an Emmy by being banned by Arizona. He appreciated the honor.

Sandra Cisneros invited Us to stay at her famous Purple House and volunteered to organize a fundraiser for Us at the Guadalupe Cultural Arts Center in San Antonio, which We decided would be the first stop on the 2012 Librotraficante Caravan to smuggle the banned books back into Tucson.

corporate hacks try to bite Our style. When We interview corporate zombies, they try to compare, they make the mistake of calling Our crew a "staff." Nah, We'll hit ya with a bolt of lightning from Our staff, contraband prose at one hundred thousand watts.

The Agora Café where We'd plan the show is only about one mile from the radio station and about another mile from Chapultepec Restaurant. It was in the Party Hall of Chapultepec Restaurant that I'd organized the first Community reading for Nuestra Palabra: Latino Writers Having Their Say fourteen years earlier, in 1998. All of these spots are in the aforementioned Montrose neighborhood of Houston.

In January of 2012, pre-gentrification, Montrose was still the artsy part of town, with a long history for the LGBT Community. It was the site of the largest Gay Pride Parades in the nation. And, like all Houston neighborhoods, it was full of Latinos, including a lot of Our Gente who predated the Latinx movement, who were living it via familia, friends, neighbors, co-workers, bosses. The graphs and surveys of the city always want to reduce Communities to dots. But the poets united communities that were living in the closet and living undocumented, off the grid, but forming powerful components of Houston's CCC.

In spite of this, Montrose was by no means considered a Latino neighborhood back then. As I organized the first event for NP, Houstonians were shocked I was organizing it in Montrose. They thought I should hold it in one of the two Houston City Council Districts that were considered Latino. Those were City Council Districts H and I, which contained the Legacy Mexican American neighborhoods of Magnolia, the East End, and Denver Harbor.

Of course, I knew those areas and had organized events in them. But I also knew that Montrose was Latino.

Montrose was about readings, cafés, visual art, open mikes, slam poetry, bars, clubs, free thinkers—and among all those cool, artsy, and queer folks were Mi Gente.

But Houstonians were married to their tags and insisting that I follow them:

Montrose was "a Gay (white by default) neighborhood with Art."

City Council Districts I and H were "the Latino (straight by default) neighborhoods without Art."

Wrong.

Mexicans are everywhere in Houston. Houston forgets Texas is occupied Mexico. Texas has a genius for erasing Us and then wondering why its citizens are illiterate about Latinos.

Then again, folks who cling to the generalizations often think Latinos, especially Mexicans and Mexican Americans, don't read, write, enjoy poetry, prose, teatro.

In this day and age, corporate media constricts discrimination to a manageable data point on their charts by discouraging the direct utterance of the worst stereotypes and slurs of the past.

But these implicit assumptions are just as ugly.

So why would anyone propagate them? They are generations in the making. They are baked into the DNA of the kings english. It is not just white folks who are programmed this way. Latinos are programmed, too.

NP's naysayers could not see me as the expert on this despite the fact that I am the first Chicano to earn a Master of Fine Arts from the University of Houston Creative Writing Program, despite the fact that I had already had a novel published—and despite the fact that I was not asking them.

I was not asking them for advice, yet, they offered it. I was not asking them for money, though I could have used it.

I was certainly not asking them for permission.

I was gonna organize in the Montrose, and all around the city, because I had empirical evidence that a shitload of Houstonian Mexicans, Mexican Americans, Salvadorans, Guatemalans, and a few Chilenos and Argentines were dying to amplify their voice.

As writers We examine words as their own Tips of Pyramids, unearthing layer after layer of their meaning as the definitions change with time, culture, insights, and Art.

Yet some Houstonians still don't know how to read Us.

I do. And I can throw back at them the very dots from the graph they tried to string Us up with. Based on the census, Every. Houston. City. Council. District. Is. Latino.

It is now a cliché to say that "Houston is 44 percent Latino." What should really be focused on is the way Our population is distributed. According to the 2020 Census, the lowest percentage of Latinos live in Houston City Council G, with 20 percent of that population counted as Latinx. This is the census that was sabotaged by donald trump's efforts to dissuade Our entire Community from filling it out—so these numbers are certainly an *undercount*. That means that in the district with the lowest amount of Latinos, AT LEAST one in five residents is still Latino.

District C is next lowest, at 25 percent Latinx. And the numbers rise district by district after that, culminating in the only two districts typically associated with Latinos, Districts H and I—and granted, both are over 75 percent Latino.

But just like corporate media nationally tries to reduce Our Community to one Hispanic dot on their graphs, Houston's imagination reduces Us to two Communities based on tactics from the past, the way past.

For generations Artists, Activists, and Educators have been offering humanitarian reasons on why this limiting perception must change, reasons I'm going to translate into business, corporate, and marketing english.

Houston, along with other places, likes to say that it is a "Diverse City." This is a marketing ploy for a Blue City in what has become the reddest state of the Union. Here is the harsh reality: This is just a slogan if visitors to the city can easily find the Texas Mexican food, but they can't find any Mexican American Art—if they even think to look for it.

The kings english is forged from stereotypes, generalizations, myths. It is the bastard sibling of the kings spanish. Both burned caste systems into the DNA, history, and skin of generations in order to maintain their spot as the center of a universe that then created universities and subjects who created the subjects who would subject the rest of Us to the only subjects that sustained that uni-universe. The kings english is now broadcast broadly by corporate media, politicians, education.

This is not a Lit class. This is lit prose. Got the theory? Here comes the action.

When I arrived to become a writer, Houstonians had no idea that they had one of the leading Creative Writing Programs in the nation. When they heard I was from Chicago, they would be shocked and ask if Chicago didn't have a better one.

I would say, *Writers from all over the country are killing each other to get into your Creative Writing Program, paid for with your taxes*—for not only was UH's program high caliber, it was fully funded.

I, too, bought into the branding.

The main goal was to go where I could write my ass off. Right after I finished my bachelor's degree, I had invested a year in a bullshit, wannabe corporate job. It sucked. I didn't like them, and they didn't like me. So I believed in school, but I also believed in getting it over with ASAP while enjoying each moment. Three years seemed like a friggin' long-ass time, but I would burn through it, write my ass off, get an MFA, wrap that up as soon as possible, and write my novel.

And then do what? Whatever the fuck I wanted, wherever the fuck I wanted.

At first I told myself that as soon as I got the MFA, I would head back to Chicago. Or I would go shake up the big boys—NYC or LA.

I would wind up staying.

Texas was the land of wildcatters, speculators, braziers who take chances. What did I fall in love with? All that power, teeming.

I can see how immigrants write home that the streets are lined with gold. It isn't the gold of the spanish pirates. That has all been swept up, and there is a long line of kings and queens killing for it.

But there was so much plenty that extras spilled over at Our feet.

Most wore blinders the boss placed over their heads to harness the gold, the oil, for the bosses.

I was used to Chicago rackets, qualitatively different from Houston rackets. I came because Houston had enough profits from oil to invest in Creative Writing, to become a city that could buy enough class to pay writers to write.

I also had yet to learn that all these rackets were created by communities tilling, mining, working all the spaces in between the legal or nationalized rackets laws, policies, rules created by the rulers to maintain their rules.

And, like my parents, I would cross borders to re-set, re-boot, re-start. But when I did it, I had my papers: citizenship, degree, cash. And once I crossed city lines—and neighborhoods, south side, north side, and then state lines, and then the Mason-Dixon line—I would find out in Texas how a different state of the union bred an altered state of mind. And when you walked into not just Texas, but Houston, fourth-largest city in America, the lines were blurred, buried, and even invisible.

Every city has its laws, then rackets, and then the blinders the state imposes on The People.

My blinders were forged in Chicago, which made it harder for me to see Chicago Mexicans. I was blinded to Our full power in the place that I first called home.

We sign away Our vision all day long through user agreements We don't, can't, or have just stopped reading. Politically, We are starved into it, especially when We think We are bourgiouse, or upper middle class, or have made it—maybe even mostly then. The corporate world traps Us inside one business card for a title, to a post in a cubicle that is so constricted that a corner office with a peephole sounds like progress. To the outside world it seems like We are MOVING UP, trapping Us in a metaphor that clearly states We are on a track, a lane, a friggin' ladder.

Metaphors are forced confessions. english is brutally honest; We are too brutalized to fight back. We sign more and more user agreements for Our blinders every day.

When I first got to Houston, I was blind to the Texas blinders.

But it was Houston that lured me, paid me, and knighted me.

Houstonians' blinders prevented them from seeing the Mexicans among them as artists. But I could see them.

Growing up, the borders in Chicago were like invisible fences for dogs. I couldn't see them, but I sensed them. And I watched others to see when they got burned crossing them, revealing them, letting you know how close you could get and then figuring out ways around them.

But I was not taught from a young age in Houston where the Mexicans could or could not go. I did not know which neighborhoods were Ours and which were not. Instead, I saw what I saw—which was the Raza. I could see all the Raza in Houston. All I could see was the power running through Our people. So much, so many.

Meanwhile, I also had a license to write.

I had a license to author the authority. I was working on an MFA—as in Muther Fucking Artist—so ya had to get out of my way. I resembled a Texas Mexican, especially if someone can't tell Us all apart. My last name was similar, my thick, course Aztec hair was similar, I spoke Spanish. But I also acted like a Chicago Mexican, ready to argue, fight, or party; spitting english like I didn't grow up in a state that used to lynch Mexicans, immune to the timeworn tactics used to erase colonized Mexico.

In Texas, the invisible borders had become gentleman's agreements, and I was no gentleman. Worse, I had a big mouth, I worked hard like a Mexican, I liked to shoot the shit with everyone, and I liked to make friends; I was well-read, thus, interesting and charming, in Spanish, english, and Spanglish. I was a citizen. I spoke good english—great, even. And I was pursuing a Master's Degree in a town shaped by the old masters, so I could see through the ghost of the masters plans.

Our Gente could not see this. They were convinced We were not writers or thinkers or artists, bullshit that Houston bought at a cheap price.

Instead folks worked and got a big-ass house, a big-ass truck, more vacation time, even money for a cruise now and then. Not bad. white Texans had figured out that a lil prosperity like this was a better way of keeping Mexicans in line than lynching them.

But of course, they did lynch Gente. I researched that. They traumatized generations by stringing up some. But at the rate they were going, they would've run out of Mexicans.

Besides, you couldn't kill the wrong person. You couldn't kill the talented Mexican who follows the rules and overtly tries really hard. That one you gave stuff to. Otherwise, it would be too clearly unfair and unjust, and it would shatter the peace.

Because if you bothered to count the bodies, there were more and more and more.

And more and more.

And some had not just your confidence; some had the future of whole Texan ranches in their hands. Some knew the business so well, inside and out, that they would be the ultimate competitor. So they couldn't be allowed to break off on their own. You needed to make *that* look too risky, and you needed to make *this*—subjugation, secondary status—look too comfy.

And worse, some of them had the keys to your house, and some the keys to your heart.

What kind of treason would that be if they openly rebelled against your secret oppression that everybody knew about?

Then and still, We, La Gente, are allowed to prosper but not rule. Here are quick facts for proof.

As I write this, Houston, at 45 percent Latino population, has never had a Latino mayor. In fact, only one out of sixteen City Council members is Latino. The majority of students in the seventeen public school districts that overlap Houston are Latino, yet the majority of school board members and superintendents are not.

I won't go on; you can Google more oppression.

On the flip side, here is what texans in power want Us to act like:

This texas senator ted cruz has a spanish surname that games the identity label racket. His father was born in Cuba. ted cruz the kid was born in Canada. He famously renounced his Canadian citizenship when he ran for US pres. He lost. He alludes to his father's experiences, but I have never heard ted cruz say he is proud to be Latino.

Worse, he does not champion the only topic corporate media sees fit for Our Community to discuss: immigration rights. He condemned the Obama-era policy of DACA—Deferred Action for Childhood Arrivals, which helped youth who were brought to the US from other nations when they were children—thus through no choice of their own—who grew up in this nation, attended school, stayed out of trouble. Under DACA these youth could then legally work and legally obtain licenses, two years at a time.

If you know anything about Houston, you need a car to simply survive. The public transportation system is not on par with Chicago or New York. Everything is twenty minutes away by car. The houses, businesses, everything was built for cars and constant air conditioning.

As for work permits, there is a massive underground economy of undocumented labor operating right under all of Our noses. As I'm typing this, I hear hammers and saws building all around me, Our Raza working in that ninety degree heat and humidity. If you eat at any restaurant, Our Raza brings the food—that Our Gente picked. As essential workers, We bus the tables and work the kitchen. Visit any park in any affluent neighborhood during lunch, and you will see all the nannies who resemble Us tending to the children of the same right-wingers who vilify Us on corporate news.

Republicans may try to say that I am hating on Our Cuban brothers and sisters by critiquing cruz. That is not the case at all. I don't do that. ted cruz, on the other hand, did not stand up for the Cuban American Community when President Obama ended the Cuban Adjustment Act, which helped many Cubans adjust their immigration status when they arrived in the US and touched land in Florida, putting them on the path to citizenship. Cruz did not address this even when trump was president. The program stayed gone.

In other words, ted cruz and his family benefitted from a rigged and broken immigration system and then refuse to help Our Community still suffering under that same broken system.

Maybe that is what right-wing Texans would like Us to act like.

Well, fellow Houstonians, that ain't me. Given that it took you thirteen years to admit a Mexican to your University of Houston Creative Writing Program MFA program, odds were it would be a wild one.

Texas Mexicans, artist Tejanos—how the hell could I ignore them? I loved them right away because I love myself.

Nuestra Palabra: Latino Writers Having Their Say is Community Cultural Capital

The base of Our CCC in Houston, Texas, is deep and profound. Some easily believe it goes back to 1836 when Texas broke away from Mexico.

Others go back to 1592, when the spanish imperial colonizers first came into official contact with the Mexica.

Keep this sentence in mind to sentence your imagination to a longer view: If We think of the deep roots of indigenous Meso American timelines, the Olmecs were as far back to the Mexica as the Aztecs are to Us. Who were the Olmecs of the Olmecs?

I see how they worked. I feel how they created. I sense how they shaped. Our Art, Culture, and History coded into The Tip of The Pyramid.

When I founded Nuestra Palabra: Latino Writers Having Their Say, I was told it was in the wrong building in the wrong neighborhood for the wrong people who did not exist.

Raza came out of the woodwork. Well, let's smash that cliché: Raza came *off* the woodwork, because Raza had been working all day long, studying, teaching, waiting tables, at their nonprofits, at the bank, at the post office, at the airport, at the construction site. They put down those tools and picked up their writing tools.

There were over two hundred people there that night.

I am so glad Houston did not convince Us We did not exist.

Alvaro Saar Rios made his stage debut that night. He also made the front page of the *Houston Chronicle* Metro section. He read his short story "Finding Peter Z," which I would wind up publishing in an issue of *The Pennsylvania Review*. He would get published in the newspaper *The Tejano Times*. He would form part of Our NP MFA Initiative, earning an MFA in Theater from Northwestern University. He is now a professor. His plays have been commissioned all over the US and include the Spanish version of "Rapunzel" for the Houston Grand Opera. Even as I write this, Arizona State University is advertising the full production of his play *Luchadora*, which will be presented virtually, because I am also typing this during the COVID-19 shutdown.

(By the way, back in 1998, when NP's first showcase took place, if an institution was "virtually producing" your play, it meant they were *almost* going to do it—but they did not. Today, it means they gave it a full production that folks from all around the nation could attend online, and ya got paid.)

Nuestra Palabra provides a living, feeling, thriving example of the investment of CCC. This is a dramatization. This is me, and Our leaders, demonstrating the Cultivation of CCC before your very eyes.

We are not taught this in school. You shall be: This Book is the school.

There was not a clear audience for these lessons before. There is now. And many of Us operated with the sense of these words before We could, should, wanted to, needed to, or had time to articulate.

Now is the time. This train is moving. You can stand to the left or to the far right, but do not get in the way.

I distinguish between this prose and the prose for Quantifying CCC. The Books in my Quantifying Community Cultural Capital Series will break down more of the people, the organizations, the History, and the Culture that built up to NP. Here, I'm providing the poignant parts. I am writing at the speed to Cultivate CCC. These words and images are tuning forks to guide CAs in their work and entice others to open their minds just a bit more, to pave the way for that series.

That means there are some terms, values, insights that I simply won't explain because We who are in the field, and from families who have worked the fields, profoundly understand those terms, visions, values. I engage in some of those concepts during lectures, town halls, classes, panels, meetings, on the radio, in person, with audiences of mixed familiarity with Cultural Acceleration work.

We as Writers, Artists, Thinkers find the frequency for forming the right terms at the right moment for Our audience. This might sound like the basics of a speech course, rhetoric, debate—it is not. Those subjects were created by the subjects who create the subjects to subject Us to the kings english, where the ghost of a monarch is at the center.

We must define Our Terms on Our Terms.

I think Our Writers are at an advantage if they understand the game and its full implications. And We as a Community should not be fooled into believing that this approach of prioritizing superficial concerns, like clickbait topics such as "Latino vs. Latinx," helps Our intellectual edification, satisfies authentic Community engagement, or paves the way for authentic change. These approaches are examples of Hispandering. All Cultures can relate to the idea of pandering politicians who are running for election, which is when they just might visit Our neighborhoods, maybe shout out a street, a leader, maybe take a bite of a tamale, perhaps, in Our case, mutter something in spanish—only to never be seen again until the next election.

The mainstream just wants to make Us easier to Google.

My aversion to this also epitomizes my manner, which is in the tradition of my father, my mother, and Mexican American families: I don't tell you everything. I don't explain it all. It may seem as if I explain a lot. Those are the basics, the parameters, the ground rules. But there is more. I can't even teach it all to you. So I'll test you. I'll see if you pay attention. I'll see if you care. I'll see if you offer to help. I'll see how much teaching you require when you ask.

Do you watch? Do you learn? Do you dive in and start helping?

Do you read the situation, listen to the goals I have mentioned, and then help towards those goals?

Do you help and criticize? Do you help to help yourself? Do you help a little bit and take more credit than you deserve? Do you need constant affirmation that you helped? Do you take? Do you grandstand?

Are you out to promote yourself instead of the group?

If you require more teaching than you can actually help me with, I will withdraw. And if I withdraw for just a bit, and you leave, that was a wise choice. Because I am here for the long haul. Are you?

We raised Nuestra Palabra where Our History, Culture, and Art had been razed.

This proves Only Art Can Save Us.

Sure, I am going to dance for you. I will thrill you with how badass We were, are, and shall be—but I also want to indict mutherfuckers, at least bring them before the people's court, try them even if they are let off the hook by all the technicalities their ancestors have benefitted from.

There is an entire class of people in Houston, Texas, and every major urban area, telling Us We do not exist. In Texas, they're the most polite oppressors, and they tell you this over a fine lunch, and they tell you this in the nicest schools. At some point, it seems plain rude for you to insist you exist.

Also, let's suppose I was not good at my job, the job I created, the job invented with the authority I authored.

Even if that day I was in the party hall of Chapultepec Restaurant alone, with empty chairs behind me, Carlos Calbillo and Raul Rodriguez training their cameras to a stage with just the writers I had assembled, the ten of Us and none of the other secret writers who would come for a chance to read for the first time in front of Their Gente who did not exist like they did not exist, with the poems in the hand, their stories in english, Spanish, and Spanglish that did not exist—even if it was just Us, just Us ten and Our friends, Us twenty, then the lowest number We could have had was twenty of Us not existing.

And if Carlos Calbillo recorded the writers playing to Us, still just as nervous, not quite as high without the large audience; if the recording of their voices would ring more in that empty room, no mass of people for the sound to bounce off, none of their applause, their raucous joy at Our existence—even if it was just Us, it would still have been a badass victory of assembling those of Us who dared to cross the border of nonexistence, who defied the Cultural Border Patrol. We would have won.

Even then.

Instead, I am very good at my job.

We packed the house and have never looked back.

So many voices.

In reality, We were resisting, not simply existing. We were breaking the rule that We did not exist, coming out of nonexistence to flaunt Our existence.

That day, each voice was the Tip of a Pyramid. They each survived in a city that insisted, argued, worked to convince Us We did not exist, in a system that rewarded Us with minimum wage, even if We thought We were professionals scoring just above it, but still below maximum wage, and worked to starve Us out of existence, Our words blurred, ignored, erased. We defied.

Under the way We are imagined, erased, oppressed, told We do not exist, it can be at the very least frustrating and in the worse case maddening—no: in the worst case, silencing. We are also frozen by fear and indecision because We know We have a History, important stories to tell, a legacy of Culture.

There is no one to tell Us how to process, translate, or understand.

However, Librotraficantes are born for this. We are trained for this as children during Our first jobs: translating the language of adults from the outside world, from the polyglottal streets of the South Side of Chicago into the Spanish of Our living rooms and kitchens for Our mothers and fathers. That too can be frustrating. However, those of Us who can dive in and those of Us who can learn to thrive in that, and even enjoy, and perhaps take it for granted, are already on the road to Librotraficantes.

Our broad shoulders must raise Our even broader imagination to consider Our profound History, getting closer and closer to the

155

base of The Pyramid, while also standing alone at The Tip of The Pyramid, then doing both at the same time. Then three things, then four things, then five.

Then infinity.

CULTURAL ACCELERATION ESSAYS

Importing Mexicans From Chicago

First published January 22, 2019 on TonyDiaz.net. Broadcast on the radio show Nuestra Palabra: Latino Writers Having Their Say, *90.1 FM, KPFT, Houston.*

I am the first Chicano to earn a Master of Fine Arts in Creative Writing from the University of Houston Creative Writing Program. I came from Chicago to study writing in Houston. When I first arrived, I had to keep explaining this to Houstonians, especially Latinos. They found it hard to believe that Chicago didn't have such programs first.

Folks were shocked to find out that Houston had one of the leading Creative Writing Programs in the nation. "People are killing each other to come here," I would tell them, "And it's in your own backyard."

Some folks remembered they had a cousin or relative who attended the University of Houston. Maybe he was in it, too, they would think out loud.

Some would say that Rice was a better school. Maybe I could still get into Rice.

I had to point out to them that I didn't want to enroll at Rice University because they didn't have a Master of Fine Arts Creative Writing Program. Others would say they swore they took a creative writing class there. I explained that was undergraduate.

My first summer in Houston, I invested time telling Houstonians about their city and their program.

Once I began the University of Houston Creative Writing Program, I understood why the community had so many questions.

I was the only Mexican in the program.

This blew my mind. No, that phrase is too light, too much of a cliché. I was shocked, stunned, surprised, sickened, dismayed.

I grew up on the South Side of Chicago. There are a lot of Mexican Americans and Puerto Ricans in the city, a lot of Latinos.

But we never had a Mexican American mayor like San Antonio did. Of course, that's San Antonio, not Houston. However, at least Houston was a 2.5 hour drive away from a Chicano mayor of a major city. Chicago still has yet to elect a Latino mayor.

Chicago didn't have a Center for Mexican American Studies like the University of Houston did.

And I didn't really pay attention to this before I graduated from college, got my well-paying-but-crappy first job out of college.

So, in all fairness to those first folks who I talked to in Houston, Tejas when I arrived, I would have asked me those same questions, too, if I had met me when I was a senior in college or just about to graduate from my undergraduate program.

I would have confounded me too if I had met the me who was ready to quit a regular paying job to become this crazy thing called a writer and was willing to leave the center of his universe—Chicago— to return to the state where his parents had to pick crops to survive.

And I did have to leave to do this. For all its brash talk, Chicago didn't have any Master of Fine Arts in Creative Writing programs in the city at the time. Now there are several.

And Houston was willing to give me a fellowship and also give me a job as a teaching assistant to a, I imagined, beautiful poet professor, for whom I would help conduct research on great writers and bring her poetry tomes that I had to extract at great lengths, which we would both read and discuss over wine.

Yeah, we didn't have any of that in Chicago.

But Tejas is also in my blood.

My father was a teenager when he was loose in the fields of Texas, without parents, going farm to farm to pick to make his pan de cada dia. He didn't speak english. He had not gone to school. And soon he would also have the responsibility of children to raise.

On the other hand, I spoke the language. I was the first male in my family to graduate high school and the first of my family to go to college. I didn't have any kids. And I had a car.

I decided I wasn't going to put up with my bullshit, sick-dream job, and I quit.

I was going to Texas to become a writer.

I was turning the world upside down.

My parents had picked their way North out of Texas.

I was writing us back South.

Of course, in Mexico, the American Dream was always in el Norte.

My Mexican American Dream was South.

But I had to turn the world upside to down to understand why in the world the University of Houston Creative Writing Program had to import Mexicans from Chicago while they were surrounded by a sea of raza.

That gap between the Ivory Tower and the Cultural Capital of our people is what I'm about to expose. And that day of reckoning is here, and I am happy to deliver it.

My parents paid their dues. I'm here to collect.

Allowed to Prosper But Not Rule, Part I

Originally published June 11, 2019 on TonyDiaz.net. Broadcast on the radio show Nuestra Palabra: Latino Writers Having Their Say, *90.1 FM, KPFT, Houston.*

Mainstream sociologists take too long to explain the knife at our throats.

Activists break the arm holding the knife and fight back.

It will take an activist to explain how we can thrive individually even as collectively we remain disenfranchised. And that activist must become a writer to convey that.

Texas has powerful examples of our wealth. It is a prime setting to demonstrate how we are allowed to prosper but not rule.

In fact, the only reason that we are at the table is because there are now so many of us. Most studies or analysis picked up by corporate media consist of different versions of telling folks that there are now a lot of us. Feel free to google "Latino population," "Hispanic population." If you are fascinated by that, add the name of your city and town after it for more hits.

The next most popular way to think of us is in terms of money. So, most reports about us, especially from every Hispanic Chamber of Commerce in every state, is to give examples of how much money we spend. Again, if you must, google "Latino buying power" or "Hispanic Buying Power." I'm sure even as I write this, somewhere in some city someone on a board believes they have devised the very original idea of quantifying how much wealth we don't save.

This seems reasonable to people.

There are a lot of us. We are prospering. Why don't we rule?

We Don't Rule:

In Texas, with its whopping Latino population, only 3 Latinos have served as mayor in its 4 largest cities. Two of these cities have never had a Latino mayor.

Houston's population of 2.3 million is 44.5% Hispanic. 0 Latino mayors.

San Antonio's population of 1.5 million is 64% Hispanic. They have had 2 Latino mayors.

Dallas' population of 1.2 million is 42% Hispanic. 0 Latino mayors.

Austin's population of 900,000 is 34.5% Hispanic. 1 Latino mayor.

Worse: At a presentation at the 2019 NACCS Tejas Foco Conference in Houston, a scholar quantified that out of the hundreds of Dallas city council members in the history of the city the number of Latino city council members barely made it to double digits.

Houston is no better. While we are almost half of the city's population, only 1 Latino sits on the city's 16-member city council.

Of course, addressing the structural reasons behind this is not popular. Some scholars in small journals dissect the reasons why this is the case. Some sociologists write about this for their dissertations or own research. These are not typically conveyed to everyday folks affected by these issues.

But this needs to be discussed.

We have all the intelligence to succeed. Yet we can't lead?

This clearly is an example of the structural forces that shape our minds.

If we individually thrive, we are not seen as a threat. We are seen as an example. We are rewarded for not ruling.

Here are three quick ways this is stamped into our imaginations and heart. There are many more.

When Arizona banned Mexican American studies, one component of the law prohibited students from being treated as a group. They must be thought of only as individuals. Of course, this is not how we define ourselves. We define ourselves in relation to our families and communities. This is conducive to building voting blocs, yet we do not.

Even the 2012 Texas Republican platform alluded to, without directly referencing, the Arizona law banning our history and culture. It, too, said that students should be treated as individuals and not as a group. Again, it is clearly demonstrated how our community's natural tendency to build groups, which should result in major political engagement, is thwarted in many ways—including a direct attempt to "teach" that tendency out of us.

This also demonstrates the importance of Mexican American Studies. Of course, this seems obvious to me, but it is clear that this is not obvious to folks—especially from those outside of our community. So, I allude to a European sociologist to help translate.

Antonio Gramsci wrote about this connection in his prison writings when he addresses "Philosophy, Common Sense, Language and Folklore." He wrote this while jailed by Mussolini's fascist regime. He says of a sustainable and authentic philosophy: "This means working to produce elites of intellectuals of a new type which arise directly out of the masses . . ."

Again, something that is obvious to us, but is not to the mainstream world, so we must remind each other of this and teach this to others:

> In school the teacher . . . must be aware of the contrast between the type of culture and society which he represents, and the type of culture and society represented by his pupils, and conscious of his obligation to accelerate and regulate the child's formation in conformity with the former and in conflict with the latter.

We must fight for this in our schools. The fact that Mexican American Studies was banned in Arizona proves that there is an overt attempt to thwart our intellectual progress. Additionally, the status quo advanced by the far-right Republicans also attempts to undermine the values and gifts of our community.

You need only to look to Texas Senator Ted Cruz to see the working example of what far right Republicans would like to see us act like. They want to divorce individuals from our community and reward them if they act and think like Ted Cruz.

He does have a Spanish surname. However, he was born in Canada. He is definitely not Chicano or Latinx, although folks who support him might not really know the nuances between each term.

He might be Hispanic. His father is Cuban. However, I have never heard Ted Cruz say he is proud to be Hispanic or Cuban American.

That is a basic rule for Chicanos, for example. You can be born Mexican American, but you have to choose to be Chicano. Self-determination is essential to our identity.

Additionally, Cruz does not advocate for issues that directly influence our community, such as fighting for Ethnic Studies or fighting for Dreamers—who are at the mercy of a broken immigration system that he was able to manipulate for power. Again, he was born in Canada and even renounced his Canadian citizenship when he ran for president, and lost.

Through the policies they enforce and the candidates they support, Republicans reveal how they would prefer all Latinx, Chicanos, Latinas to act and behave.

This was not addressed even during the very close 2018 Senatorial race when incumbent Cruz was challenged by Democratic candidate Beto O'Rourke. This race was very close. Ted Cruz won by just 2%, or about 200,000 votes.

Ironically, mainstream media outlets nonchalantly alluded to Ted Cruz's "structural advantage" in Texas. It is stunning for them to bring up structural oppression so matter of factly.

Again, none of the complex issues regarding identity were addressed at length by the corporate media or political parties.

But the message is clear: Latinos are allowed to prosper but not rule.

Gramsci addresses this contradiction: "The theoretical consciousness of the man in the street can indeed be historically in opposition to his activity."

Logically we are talented enough to make money and do well. That should mean we can rule. Yet we do not rule. Gramsci says this "produces a condition of moral and political passivity." We are rewarded for not ruling. We then do not shape candidates, we then don't shape voting blocs, we then don't shape voters, we then don't shape intellectuals. We then don't rule.

Likewise, Pierre Bourdieu writes that those who don't vote even when they are eligible to vote are rejecting the system by abstaining.

Gramsci tells us that political parties are responsible for taking our community members and "turning them into qualified political intellectuals, leaders, and organizers of all the activities and functions inherent in the organic development of an integral society, both civil and political."

Republicans want to divorce us from our community. Only then will they take us in. This threat chases a large part of our community into the arms of the Democrats—who do not then need to profoundly address these issues.

Chicano poet Lalo Delgado dramatizes the cost of this in his poem "stupid america":

> stupid America, remember that chicanito
> flunking math and english
> he is the picasso
> of your western states
> but he will die
> with one thousand masterpieces
> hanging only from his mind.

—Abelardo "Lalo" Delgado, "Stupid America" 1969

Allowed to Prosper But Not Rule, Part II

Originally published on www.TonyDiaz.net on October 22, 2019 and on LatinoRebels.com on November 1, 2019. Broadcast on the radio show Nuestra Palabra: Latino Writers Having Their Say, *90.1 FM, KPFT, Houston.*

Every family should thrive enough to create a poet.

Every family should thrive enough to cultivate an elected official.

Each of these vocations requires a lot of hard work, talent, and public scrutiny. Each is admirable.

Yet, in our community, we don't often talk about the costs of cultivating either one. The real question is, are we ready to pay that price?

Let me get really practical really quick.

Early voting began in Harris County yesterday, so right now especially, I hear people wonder why more Latinos don't run for elected office.

This is the same as asking why more Chicanos do not become poets. In 1998, I founded Nuestra Palabra: Latino Writers Having Their Say because I and others were asking the same questions. Looking back, I can tell you that the answers are very similar.

Here is the good news. If you are a Latino with a master's degree and bilingual, you are in demand. However, you do have to make a choice.

There are two avenues of true success for our generation. One road to profound success is strictly American and has to do with strictly capital, money. Most people understand that, and the American Dream is really perhaps the myth that all of us can get there. The other road is to prosper via Cultural Capital, which means not simply money, but also intellectual capital, educational capital, perhaps thriving by creating art or literature.

I've written about different definitions of Cultural Capital in the past, and I will write more about these two facets in future essays, but for now, these two roads represent the choice that our generation must make.

Here is the bad news. At this time, you can't do both. You must now decide if you choose to prosper or rule. Here is one quick example: I run into so many accomplished professionals who tell me about the book they want to write—most, if not all, will never write it.

We are successful at this time because we are allowed to prosper. We are not allowed to rule. Those who rule have generational wealth, so they can do both.

To put it another way, some of the structural barriers that in the past prevented us from middle to upper-middle class incomes have been removed or addressed. Again, just this sentence can be, and is, the basis for an entire book, but for the purposes of this essay, I'll summarize this fact this way: due to civil rights victories and access to education, Mexican Americans and Latinos now have access to upwardly mobile jobs.

In Texas alone, Mexicans used to be lynched, there were "No Mexicans Allowed" signs at restaurants, we were denied access to higher education, and so on and so on and so on. As I write this in 2019, these barriers have been addressed enough for some of us to gain access to positions that pay well.

This, again, I must stress, is powerful. I should also stress that there were also allies from other races and ethnicities that got us here.

However, I would also point out that this has afforded a segment of us to prosper but not rule.

Yes, a bilingual Latina with a master's degree is in demand. Early into her professional career she will get hired at a corporation that pays well in Houston or Dallas. However, this will probably mean she is in the Community Affairs Department, or she may be working on Latino outreach.

That is great.

But at most corporations in Houston, Dallas, or Austin, the highest-paid administrators are not Latino. Those positions at the top pay salaries and benefits that lead to generational wealth.

The Latina who is entry level, even mid-level, is prospering, but she is not ruling the corporation. Few of us do.

More importantly, in order to accumulate wealth, she may fall into the myth of the workaholic. In other words, she may believe that by working 60–80 hours a week, she can move up to the upper echelon ranks or may accumulate enough wealth to manage that capital to pursue generational wealth. That does not work.

Again, do not mistake this assessment as dismissive or judgmental. I am removing any emotion from this analysis.

Here is the reason that quantifying our cultural capital is important.

If that Latina chooses to pursue the path of accumulating continued capital, she would clearly not want to run for elected office or become a poet.

School board members in Texas are not paid, but they give, "work" enough volunteer hours as a full-time job. Texas state representatives make $7,200 a year. Houston City Council members make $60,000. These are internship level and entry level salaries for Latinos with advanced degrees.

These volunteer positions require a lot of time and energy, and running for the posts costs money, time, and energy. Also, to do the job well requires different skill sets that are the very skills that allow the Latina in question to make a lot more money in the corporate world.

If a person is pursuing generational wealth, why would they put that at risk for a full-time job that does not pay, is exhausting, and requires submitting yourself to public scrutiny? Why would that person become an elected official or a poet?

Of course, there are other reasons besides money to run for office. However, without generational wealth, it is a bigger risk for members of our communities.

This is the same for writers and poets. Ironically, we need more poets and elected officials than ever to break through the new structural barriers that allow us to prosper but not rule. Our elders were fine until they realized how unfairly they were being treated. Once they realized they had to act, an entire generation fought for more rights that we are still benefitting from.

However, unless we set the course to invest in more Cultural Capital, we have hit another ceramic ceiling.

Mind-Altering Prose:
"Somos Librotraficantes"

Originally published on www.TonyDiaz.net on December 18, 2018 and on LatinoRebels.com on December 19, 2018. Broadcast on the radio show Nuestra Palabra: Latino Writers Having Their Say, *90.1 FM, KPFT, Houston.*

Protect the Cultural Capital. Live on the dividends.
Banking on your interest as my hashtag trends.
How do I make my coin?
I coined a phrase "Somos Librotraficantes."

I grew up on the south side of Chicago. With my broad shoulders and broader imagination, I could'a dedicated my life to busting skulls or opening minds. Lucky for you, I want to do time behind books.

It's ironic because my folks told me that going to school would keep me out of trouble. Little did they know that those small doses of mind-altering prose were simply starter books. I would grow up to get into harder and harder stuff.

Worse, I became a kingpin of contraband prose.

I am just evil in nature. I suppose my parents could see this in me all along. They tried to save me. They sent me to a catholic school. But not even the nuns, or the brothers, or the priests could change my evil ways—no matter how much they hit me.

So, no, reading Nathaniel Hawthorne's "Young Goodman Brown" did not turn me into a young good brown man. Instead I would turn *All Quiet on the Western Front* into "All Chillin' on the West Side."

I turned *Macbeth* into "Emcee Beth."

I couldn't stop myself no matter how much I was punished. There was no boundary to my imagination. I was always capable of the unimaginable.

I respected no limits.

I had to get out of Chicago for my own good.

Back when I was a kid, and a punk would ask me why I was reading a book on the corner, I would reply, "It's this or beat your ass."

I will beat ya with the book.

I came to Houston to check out their literary cartels and to get my papers—an MFA, which stands for Mighty Fine Aztec.

I'm the first Chicano to get an MFA there.

Of course, it made no sense to me that I would be the first Chicano to become a Mighty Fine Aztec in Tejaztlán. The sense that makes is non-sense. Texas is occupied Mexico.

Being from Chicago I can smell a racket a mile away. I wanted in on the action, so I started a gang.

In 1998 I started our outfit—NP.

Our alias for the outside world was Nuestra Palabra: Latino Writers Having Their Say.

We were running the streets from day one. We had a crew of two hundred capturing imaginations, stealing hearts, and breaking literary rules right and left.

By 2002, we were out of control, going from monthly mitotes to larger and larger and larger joints.

We put on mega events, drawing thirty thousand people at the George R. Brown Convention Center, attracting celebrity authors like George Lopez and Jorge Ramos in limousines at our disposal.

All the Big Dogs saw was money flying around. They saw capital being made in sales.

That was no big deal. You can sell anything. What I saw was our Cultural Capital building and building and building.

All the other players could fight for their cuts of the capital. I knew we were monopolizing the real power, we were cultivating our Community's Cultural Capital right under everyone's noses.

And the outside world barely understood it. That meant we could just keep cranking out more and more Mighty Fine Aztecs, on our terms, our way, who would become Cultural Accelerators.

But that wasn't enough. I needed more, and more, and more.

There, under the street lights, in the alley of the Convention Center, running our hands over the literary gold we were trucking across state lines, that our people were consuming in massive doses on the streets of Houston, I knew what we looked like.

And instead of being ashamed, it made me more flagrant.

And someone one asked me, if police roll up on us and ask us what we're doing here so late, what do we say?

This time I said, "We tell 'em 'Somos Librotraficantes.'"

And we became bigger and bigger, and more and more flagrant.

We took over the airwaves, broadcasting NP at one hundred thousand watts on 90.1 FM.

We took over social media while it was just coming of age.

We were on TV and conventional media.

Our addiction to Cultural Capital knew no bounds.

Of course, there were people watching who wanted to put us in check, but they couldn't. Not just yet.

We did not know there were Mighty Fine Aztecs in Tucson, Arizona who were running Cultural Capital factories of their own on different fronts and at different scales, and they were about to be attacked.

Our destinies would soon be more directly linked.

I've told you before about Arizona's Ban of Mexican American Studies. So, you know how we launched the 2012 Librotraficante Caravan to smuggle the books banned in Tucson back into Arizona.

But now you need to see the larger picture. The far-right Arizona Republicans who attacked our Cultural Capital were flagrant too. They accused our Community's Cultural Capital of promoting the overthrowing of the government.

I know language rackets. They wanted Americans to think we would try to change the world violently because at that time it was hard to imagine us as intellectuals.

What was really happening was that some Republican politicians were scared of young Chicanas and Chicanos cracking the spines of books instead of each others' spines. The far right knows how to control gang members but not Cultural Accelerators.

This ain't a mystery novel. So, I'll ruin the ending.

Mexican Americans have directly experienced the power of cultural capital through two potent examples:

• In 2017, the Chicana/Chicano community overturned the banning of Mexican American Studies in Arizona

• In 2018, Chicanas and Chicanos advocated and succeeded in getting Mexican American Studies endorsed statewide by the Texas State Board of Education.

So now, I'm on to a bigger racket.

There's a new game in town.

I'm gonna be dropping weekly doses of Cultural Capital for our edification.

Spreading mind-altering prose to the entire nation.

Been to Arizona, guess now I'm a litigator.
Gonna run for office, guess I'll be a legislator.
How do I make my coin?
I coined a phrase "Somos Librotraficantes."

PART III: CULTURAL ACCELERATION: THE LIBROTRAFICANTES

I type these words five hundred years after the spanish imperial pirates razed to the ground Mexica Libraries, burning their texts and persecuting all who touched any that remained.

This Book is first published on the ten-year anniversary of the 2012 Librotraficante Caravan which smuggled back into Tucson the Books about Our History and Culture banned by Arizona far right republican legislators.

That happened fourteen years after I founded Nuestra Palabra: Latino Writers Having Their Say in 1998. Even though Houstonian after Houstonian told me We did not exist, that Our Community was not interested in reading and writing, We united to organize the largest Book fairs in Texas among many other feats that would Cultivate the Community Cultural Capital that would form the foundation for the Librotraficantes.

La Gente

This Book is for La Gente.

Thank you to the youth, the elders, the writers, poets, the moms, the dads, the cool aunts and uncles who spread the word about Nuestra Palabra the old-fashioned way, one person at a time.

This movement has grown from your work. You paid attention. You donated your time, energy, genius, stories, emotions, fuerza, dollars, cents, blood, sweat, and tears, lit candles, bought books, started home libraries. You defended Us. You promoted Us. You gave Us cariño. You gave Us advice.

We paid you compliments.

Forgive me for not listing you all, yet. Again, this book is just shy of Cultural Acceleration and a few miles before Quantifying CCC which will include the Nuestra Palabra Census of which you are a part and which you made possible.

I pay you back, We pay you back with consistency, pride, staying true to Our Values, edifying others, and Cultivating CCC for decades—and, when necessary, defending Our CCC tooth and nail.

And winning.

There is so much History, talent, joy, and support in Our Community that it will take Books and Books to name everyone, and as We do so more, and more and more CAs will join Us.

Some of The Gente who have helped Us are not even obviously from Our Community, or writers, or do not expect their voices to be raised or edified. They help because they want to Cultivate.

Writer Cliff Hudder, a great friend of mine, built the first website for Nuestra Palabra. Alberto Diaz joined Us and worked with Us to create the updates of the website. I was always impressed when the folks who helped Us did not plan to read on Our stage. They helped just to help others, and that help branded Us High Tech Aztecs.

The next evolution of Our website came from Chicano writer Orlando Lara who was an undergraduate student at Stanford at the time. He would go on to earn his MFA and then his PhD.

The entire Guillermo familia gave Us the poetry of Yoli, but also donated their time, energy, good will setting up chairs, printing flyers, fundraising for banners and putting up those banners.

Marc-Antony Piñón is Chicano legacy. His mother is amazing poet Evangelina Vigil-Piñón and his father is brilliant visual artist Marc Piñón, who both inspired and edified Our movement and cultivated their son who would design the logo for Librotraficante and the update for Nuestra Palabra.

Carlos Cisneros was a founding member of Nuestra Palabra who donated so much time to help organize Our first readings, including getting donated in-kind color programs for Our early events. This included just up and designing the first logo We had, since the program needed to have some image to ground it. You will see those programs in the Nuestra Palabra Archives, the black and white flyer that was designed on my computer.

Thank you to Mrs. Fernandez. She took the elder writing class I led through Arte Público Press (APP), with funding from the Cultural Arts Council of Houston/Harris County. Mrs. Fernandez's son Fernando worked at Talento Bilingue de Houston, at that time run by Richard Reyes aka Pancho Claus, which is where I held the class for Latina Elders. Fernando also recruited Alvaro Saar Rios, who would take the class, make his literary debut, and go on to change the world. Of course, Alvaro also epitomized Librotraficante tendencies, as he was neither Latina nor an elder, but he got past the Cultural Border Patrol to take the class, and We gave him safe harbor.

This was the first writing workshop offered at TBH. This was the first writing workshop any of the participants had ever . . . heard of, let alone enrolled in. And this was my and Houston's Modus Ope-

randi, one first, after another, after another, after another. I was the
first Chicano to earn an MFA from the UH Creative Writing Program; I was on the way to creating Houston's first Latino reading
series, and so on, and so on, and so on.

Part of the workshop, as became Our pattern, included creating a chapbook of the students' work. This particular class would
also lead up to what would become the first monthly showcase of
Nuestra Palabra: Latino Writers Having Their Say, in which some
of the elder students read.

CCC shatters barriers.

Richard and Fernando got Mrs. Fernandez to take the class. From
the funds for the workshop, I created a chapbook of the writing
from the class and Community voices. She wrote an amazing essay
about her childhood that a young actor read for her at Our showcase, as the event would be held too late at night for her to attend
and read at herself.

But first, the piece had to be born.

APP did get a grant for that workshop, and after they got their
money, I got paid some money, which was more than I would have
gotten paid hourly or as an adjunct professor, so that was fair—but
it was still not completely what I was worth. I took the gig because
I was also Cultivating CCC, although I did not have the words for
that at the time. I also want to make clear that the Cultural Arts
Council of Houston/Harris County did not fund Nuestra Palabra
itself. Prior to teaching the Arte Público Press class, I had applied
for a grant from them to do a one-time showcase that I called
Nuestra Palabra: Latino Writers Having Their Say, describing in my
application what has become a national force.

Because CACHH was, as most arts granting orgs and governmental institutions are, illiterate about Latinos, they rejected my
grant application. This pissed me off. I vowed to engender Nuestra
Palabra on Our own, with the Community. That was the advent of
CCC.

I also need to add that teaching college courses adjunct was also
a racket. The pay was abysmal, so I did not do it. Instead, my work

with the Community was subsidized by the Center for Mexican American Studies (CMAS), where I was a visiting scholar. Typically, those spots go to PhDs, as in scholars/academics who are invested completely in the ivory tower/academic capital. But Dr. Tatcho Mindiola created a lane for writers who were working with the Community. The pay was less than the PhDs got for the formal fellowship, but way better than adjuncts got paid, and I got an office and an assistant. I hired Alvaro to work part time to help get NP off the ground, and CMAS would run copies of Our flyers.

In the class, I would share poems, essays, short prose in english, Spanish, and Spanglish with the students. We would talk about their lives, and I would talk to them about writing techniques. For a talk about concrete details, I had them describe a pencil. We passed it around and everyone had to describe one concrete detail from it without repeating anyone. At first my students were hesitant. Slowly but surely, as We do, We began picking away at it, layer by layer, by layer. By the end of the exercise, they were pinpointing precise, beautiful details about that writing instrument.

At first Mrs. Fernandez only shared her stories verbally in the class; subsequently she would write a few sentences, then a few more. She wrote a few sentences the day of the pencil. The rest of Le Gente shared their descriptions, then added some. We laughed a lot, they sometimes cried. It was a good day.

Mrs. Fernandez returned the following class with a beautiful piece about the days when she used to be a migrant worker as a child. She included a powerful, precise description of waking up in the morning to go pick blueberries. After she shared, We all applauded in class.

We asked her to talk about it, she said, "I didn't say anything that time you had Us all stare at that pencil, but I was watching. And I will never see the world the same way again."

The Crooked "E"

I remember the day I met with Enron.

In those days, the company had a huge, glass office building downtown, before downtown was a Houston destination to go to. You knew you were passing it because you could see the huge, crooked, capital "E" in front. Even if you were not Downtown enough or well-educated enough or corporate enough to have been inside the headquarters or at least even drive by it, the logo was branded onto your central nervous system in Houston.

The crooked "E" was a moral compass for Houston. It stood for and fell for the name "Enron." It was a for profit pyramid scheme responsible for billions of dollars that shaped The Level Playing Field of Houston and shaped the business mind of Texas, the US, and even the world. All down the street from Us. It was the center of their universe.

Luckily, as a Mexica, I know there are many universes. If you are Dante, many circles of hell; as a Chicano, many realities, some of which you are welcome in, some ignored, some barred from.

I was excited when I checked the Nuestra Palabra voicemail to find a message from the Enron Community Affairs Department, inquiring about possibly supporting Our Latino Book and Family Festival. The current that buzzed through the city caused by Enron was hard to resist, if not impossible.

Before it imploded, it branded jobs, futures, and even went backwards to re-engineer the past.

That is the metaphor for the Latino experience in Houston.

I am being imprecise to be polite, using that genteel discrimination that has shaped Texas. It seems rude, once you're friendly with them, to point out that someone's dear father is a racist son of a bitch.

But here, I must say that your father Enron, Houston, was a colonizing thief in the long line of pirates from the spanish in Mexico, the crockets in Texania, up to the delays in Enron.

Yet Enron formed every fantasy of the Houston American Dream. Worse, Enron was this force that killed logical discourse. Just saying "Enron" killed conversations, bent words.

Yet if you pointed this out, you were thought to not make sense.

Enron converted Rice University, on the outskirts of Houston's downtown, in the shadow of the Medical Center, into the Harvard of the South.

Even the British, the oldest of colonizers, fell for Enron's bullshit: I remember an *Economist* cover story on the wild success story of the US company . . . Enron.

But Enron never did shit for me.

I founded Nuestra Palabra: Latino Writers Having Their Say in April of 1998, just a few years before the Enron ponzi scheme crumbled on international TV.

I write this to you with some of the dust from the implosion still stuck in the rafters, still floating, looking for niches to find a footing, to hide, to be expunged, to finally die—or worse, to come back to life.

As Our movement ascended, We moved in tune with Our Community's natural resources on the ground, on Our stage, in front of my eyes. And We never registered a blip on the radar of Enron.

I knew the Mexican American, Mexican, Salvadoran, Guatemalan, Honduran, Chilean, Dominican niches of Art and Culture and Houston, all untouched by the mountains of capital, real or imagined, amassed and disappeared at Enron.

I also don't want to offend. There were people who believed they had a million dollars in their retirement fund who found the next morning that they were broke. There were mid-level administrators, among whom you typically find the few Latinos who do exist at such corporations, now out of work and competing with each other, scrambling for jobs to pay the bills of the lifestyle they had been lulled into by Enron.

Across the city nonprofit boards were shaken up: every large non-profit racket wanted to have someone from Enron on theirs in the hopes of accessing the company's largesse.

This was the Houston American Dream. The Houston Delusion.

The story went: A kid from the barrio, Manchester, the East End, Magnolia or Denver Harbor would get straight As at Milby or Davis High School, and then get a scholarship or take out loans to attend Rice University by the Medical Center and Herman Park. They would study engineering or accounting, and then they would graduate and get a job at either Enron or working for Enron's accountant, Arthur Andersen.

Of course, La Gente did benefit from the crumbs. With so much capital floating—as in hard to touch—around, the excess, the tax write-offs found their way to smaller nonprofits: a check or two to Talento Bilingue de Houston or MECA—Multicultural Education and Counseling Through The Arts.

This was nothing new to Us.

Enron's energy pyramid scheme was built to steal capital forged through previous schemes. The nationally recognized accounting firm of Arthur Andersen would soon be disbanded after being implicated in cooking the books for Enron.

I remember mediocre professionals telling me and other artists at the time that We must run Our nonprofits like a business. They had it backwards. Evidently, Arthur Andersen was writing fiction.

And Andersen's fiction was engendered by the natural gas and energy rackets that just this year, the week before I typed these words, caused the Texas power grid to shut down during a winter freeze under republican texas governor greg abbot.

Texans froze to death.

The curse that keeps on giving.

Those players, that money, led to the largess that spilled over to create The University of Houston, that led to the desire to be re-

183

spectable, perceived as intellectual, creative, and perhaps even a bit progressive. That led to the funds that became grants, fellowships, teaching fellowships. That money lured me. I would not have come to write in Houston unless I were paid. I was. It was with blood money.

As a Chicano, I know it is all blood money.

I would return to the land where right-wingers were vilifying people like me at the same time as they were looking for people like me to work on their land, their homes, to care for their young kids or elder parents, still. I was returning to the land where residents seceded from the Union to fight for the South in the Civil War, as slaves fled to Mexico for freedom. I returned to the land where the indigenous were wiped out, enslaved, or removed. I returned to the land that is occupied Mexico.

I came back a writer because Texas was so illiterate about Latinos that it could not find the intellectuals, the writers, all the Mexicans who could imagine and create right under their noses.

I came back to the land where my mother and father had been pickers, moving farm to farm, homeless, following the crops to make a living.

They are all rackets.

I was paid to come write in Houston. I was given a grant for tuition, cash which is called a fellowship in the Lit racket, a paid post as a teaching assistant, and an extra scholarship—just in case.

I took the blood money.

The difference is We know it is all blood money.

I could see how the "E" was crooked. It was no moral compass. It was a map. You had to hack it to see what Capone was thinking.

Still, in Houston, you saw their name everywhere, and I was not immune to the lure.

Besides their downtown flagship, if you attended any of the mainstream arts or cultural venues, you saw their logos. The older and whiter the group, the larger and brighter the crooked "E" appeared on a group's program. The larger mainstream nonprofits received so much money they included large pictures of the soon to be deposed Enron CEO and founder ken lay, or some other lieutenant of the corporate cult.

I remember, too, seeing the logo and the name ken lay on the Boys & Girls Club located off Navigation, on the East End, not far from the Talento Bilingue de Houston Theater.

I knew of a few Latinos who worked there because they were quick to tell you they did, just as relatives were quick to let you know if they knew someone who worked at Enron.

I was certain that ken lay had taken a photo op at the Boys & Girls Club, but I also knew he had not really done shit for Latino Art and Culture.

Of course, to say this was to speak ill of a religious leader.

When I started planning the Latino Book and Family Festival for the first time, Our organizing committee tried to get Enron to become a sponsor. Of course, every Latino professional in Houston at the time wanted to bring aboard their friend or colleague or sister or comadre from Enron.

The company didn't get back to Us then.

Still, We created the Book Fair. We studied the tropes. By the time We got a meeting with the Community Affairs Department, I was ready.

I don't remember the young woman's name. I do remember she dressed as if straight out of the luxury magazines dropped in high end restaurants, clothiers, and lounges. She wore floral printed high heels and a slickly cut modern suit, a $300 haircut with just the hint of highlights in her brown hair. She was super cool and polite. I sat in her office looking over Houston, a large, expensive-looking abstract painting on the wall, and she told me to aim big.

I described Our Book Fair, which would turn out to be as big as I pitched, drawing over thirty thousand people to the George R. Brown Convention Center, over one hundred writers, and media support from english and Spanish radio, including Our radio show, to english and Spanish newspapers—they still existed, in abundance, at the time—to english and Spanish TV.

She said think bigger.

At that point it was crystal clear to me she had no idea what the Latino Art and Culture situation looked like on the ground.

I have an internal gyroscope, radar, detector that gauges and then guides me. I asked her to tell me what she had in mind.

She said, "We just bought the baseball field. We now own Enron Field. We don't need more visibility. Let's do something big."

She was pleasant and polite. I imagined the meeting she thought she was in: a room of her fellow executives preaching this mantra, none of them sure what it meant.

The entire company was unsure of what it did. There were so many generalizations to add to generalizations. And I needed to get shit done.

We chatted. I left her information about NP and Our Latino Book and Family Festival. I didn't have time or energy to move the huge project of Our massive Book Fair off of Our plane of reality and try to find the frequency of Enron's definition of "big."

Of course I was not impressed. Our algorithms did not match.

When I first founded Nuestra Palabra: Latino Writers Having Their Say, "professionals" told me that I should run it like a business. Once Enron collapsed, I realized businesses should run more like a nonprofit for prophets. Today, it is clear that it is best to run on CCC to create more Culture.

Enron's massive words were part of a pyramid scheme to create a mountain of capital to steal more and more capital.

Our Pyramid, built on CCC, was intended to create more and more Culture. And never the twain would meet.

Then again, I'm not stupid. To organize the largest Book Fair in Texas at the time, you need sponsors, so on my list of calls was a follow-up with Enron. I left a message the week after Our meeting.

Months later Enron imploded, and shortly after that Enron charged the Houston Astros $2.1 million to buy back the naming rights.

To tell the story of NP, Houston, and Our CCC, I may have to tell you who Enron was.

But I tell you in Our Book.

Houston's Community Cultural Capital

I'll begin with the University of Houston Creative Writing program, September 1995. Houston's Art cartel led by the Menils sparked an Art Community that fueled the imagination of this former swamp.

There was enough old money, oil money, excess wealth, and interest in becoming a modern city with Art, theater, ballet, and music halls, major ones, or at least the entry-level major ones, so that the interest spilled over to other city institutions and the public.

The UH CWP had enough money to pay for former New Yorkers to come write, and teach writing while they complained about no longer being in New York.

And there was enough success after thirteen years that the program was making national news. At the time, The Level Playing Field of the media gained readers and ad sales by creating and publishing lists of the top Level Playing Fields, aka Universities. corporate media meets corporate education. Houston's Creative Writing Program regularly made that list.

I had heard about it in Chicago, in my research to pursue a Master of Fine Arts. Houston also was making more and more noise nationally. In terms of CCC, my compadres Miguel Delgado and Virgie Delgado, who worked for AT&T, had relocated to Houston to follow their jobs South. If you ever attend an Astros game and they play either the White Sox or the Cubs, you will see a packed house with just as many former Chicagoans wearing Cubs jerseys as Houstonians in Astros gear.

Also, the population of Latinos was being recorded, archived, and noticed as swelling on the news, via the Census. Never mind

187

that Texas is occupied Mexico, so of course Mexicans were always there—the numbers I'm referring to just mean they were being noticed, counted at dots on the Census and on corporate graphs for sales and profits.

And the University of Houston had enough leftover money to spend.

I am Unearthing the CCC at the base of my moving to Texas, because to both Chicagoans and Houstonians, the move did not make sense.

After I was admitted into the program, I formed ties with Arte Público Press, founded and run by Dr. Nicolás Kanellos. It was the oldest and largest Latino nonprofit publisher in the nation. He would be on my MFA thesis committee. I had also heard great things about the University of Houston's Center for Mexican American Studies, under the leadership of Dr. Tatcho Mindiola. After my book *The Aztec Love God* was published, I was a visiting scholar at the UH CMAS. I was paid a stipend, had an office, and had an assistant, Alvaro Saar Rios, who would be a founding member of Nuestra Palabra: Latino Writers Having Their Say. The first year of Nuestra Palabra was unofficially underwritten by the UH CMAS.

Lorenzo Cano was also part of the UH CMAS administration, and he too was very active in Cultivating CCC and would be a friend and ally for the cause who helped me figure out more ways for UH to subsidize NP.

I had also heard of poet Evangelina Vigil-Piñón before coming to Houston. She was a badass poet, published through Arte Público Press, who had also edited the anthology *Woman of Her Word: Hispanic Woman Write*. She was the host of the local ABC station's Community Affairs Talk Show, *Viva Houston*. I thought, *Damn, poets are on TV in Houston. Badass.* (Of course, I would wind up on TV, too. But I'm not a poet.)

This was more Art, literary, and Chicano historical action than I had access to in Chicago. I thought Houston would have a Latino poet on every corner. That was not quite the case, but it was the case that Chicago was not eager to create another writer.

A little later, I would find out that Sandra Cisneros was from Chicago. I had just missed her. Also, Denise Chavez and Lorna Dee Cervantes has been Visiting Scholars at the UH CMAS; I had just missed them. Either my timing was wrong—or US cities could only imagine one Chicana or Chicano writer at a time.

When my courses ended for the day, I left the ivory tower right away, crossing the moat and dodging the Cultural Border Patrol to dive into my Community.

There I found MECA, Multicultural Education and Counseling Through the Arts, founded and operated by Alice Valdez. She would produce a stage version of an early version of *The Aztec Love God*, which was awesome to see on stage. MECA is over forty years old, providing music and arts to generations. MECA is also the site for the Houston Librotraficante Under Ground Library.

I also met the late Macario Ramirez who, with his wife Chrissie Ramirez, was an owner and founder of Casa Ramirez FOLKART Gallery. He marched with Cesar Chavez. He was a hardcore activist. And he was able to stay independent because of his business, the gallery. He helped Us with so many initiatives. I had the honor of reading from my novel in his space during my Book tour. That was also first time I read in front of My Gente, including my mom.

That reading was the advent of Nuestra Palabra, which Macario fully supported. Later, this new beginning came full circle because when my mom died, he would let me heal by building an altar in her honor during his annual observations and display of altares for Day of the Dead.

Macario and Chrissie's gallery was also the site where We launched the 2012 Librotraficante Caravan. It had to be.

Richard Reyes, aka Pancho Claus, was the director of Talento Bilingue de Houston. This was a theater converted from a former supermarket called Sam's. Richard has now been in the Houston arts scene for four decades. He would invite me to move Nuestra Palabra from the Party Hall of Chapultepec Restaurant to TBH, where We then held Our monthly encuentros, readings, and showcases.

I would also partner with him to organize the Houston Latino Book and Family Festival. Richard had access to booking the George R. Brown Convention Center for free. He agreed to secure the site, as long as NP did all the organizing and conducting of the Book Fair. We gave him display space, and he put on a great show, bringing in lowrider cars and bikes and promoting Pancho Claus. And We split the profits.

I want to put into words some aspects of a Fair Exchange of Cultural Capital. And I also want to provide tactics on building on these foundations. Again, Our CCC, the base of Our Pyramid of CCC, runs thousands of years deep. For this Book, I want to model how I mapped, or quantified these assets as a CA, humanized them as familia, friends, and artists, and then learned from them and, I hope, added to their cause, too.

Every other writer in the program stayed in the ivory tower because none of them were from Houston. I'm sorry, I ran into two writers from Houston during my three years in the program. The rest were from all over. So evidently, they were good at finding neither Mexicans nor white potential writers from Houston.

They did not speak Spanish. They were not used to humanizing Mexicans, so plainly, it was harder for them to cross the moat. Also, Houston is sprawling. It is a hot, wet octopus. You had to figure out the city's pulse on your own, on its terms, and frankly, that might not add to your writing, or might take time away, or might not be as interesting, to you, as the shit you are writing.

This was a chance to invent myself. I pursued the next phase of my self-determination, my personal Tip of The Pyramid. I did not submit to the MFA to learn how to write. I didn't come to learn grammar. I came to learn the grammar of the ivory tower's racket. I know who I am. I know My Community. I unearth My Story.

I arrived to the ivory tower to get my papers. I came to the MFA to get my literary citizenship. I needed a license to create to get past the Cultural Border Patrol in order to shatter the next border. And I would spread the guarded knowledge to the rest of the city.

My summer before graduate school began, I joined a local tae kwon do school to continue studying martial arts, toward my goal of having a black belt, an MFA, and a book. Broad shoulders and a broader imagination.

I hung out at a comedy club, and joined a workshop they had to develop your routine. I did stand-up that summer because it was something I always wanted to do. I performed in front of strangers. I bombed on stage in front of strangers. Which is the shittiest feeling ever.

I also rocked on stage, which is the most thrilling feeling ever.

I quit at the end of summer, as I realized I could not do both stand-up and get an MFA. But I did learn a lot about writing, performing, and having balls. Pinche Houston, swamp of opportunities.

I also become a stringer, freelance journalist for the newspaper *The Advocate* covering Sugar Land and Stafford city council meetings. I learned to get paid to write. I learned to pitch stories. All of that would help me because my creative writing program taught me none of that.

I also quit that job once the program year started.

Again, these items are all the CCC that is the Base of The Pyramid. I began to learn to move these forces. corporate rules do not rule CCC. Instead, these forces were looking to be inspired to reach common goals, and Art, Culture, and History can embody that.

You Didn't Build That

In July of 2012, just shortly after the launch of the Librotraficante Caravan, then-President Obama sparked a controversy with a few lines from a campaign speech he delivered in Roanoke, Virginia: "Somebody helped to create this unbelievable American system that We have that allowed you to thrive. Somebody invested in roads and bridges. If you've got a business, you didn't build that." Opponents were furious at this so-called attack on American entrepreneurs, misinterpreting Obama's message for maximal offense.

Well, the far right, and then soon most republicans, opposed the clothes he wore, the clothes his wife wore, any policy he proposed—so there is that context. However, this particular moment strikes a chord because it parallels a line in the law banning Mexican American Studies. In that long speech that he often gave regarding how We must all work together in different ways, Obama was talking about CCC.

The enacted law—as in, this was officially on the books—mandated four points, one of which clearly harkens to Obama's speech:

> Arizona House Bill 2281 prohibits a school district or charter school from including in its program of instruction any courses or classes that:
>
> Advocate ethnic solidarity instead of the treatment of pupils as individuals.

This is plainly an attack on Group Identity, and so on CCC.

That attack, in so many words, was not litigated in court. It was not the focus of the court case. Even right now, as I write this,

this is not an issue that is a household topic such as immigration. It is not as salacious a topic for clickbait as anti-immigrant topics or book banning. However, this prong is akin to the debate that Obama's line sparked.

CAs can note the parallels.

Mainstream society wants Us to compete as individuals. We know that puts Us at a disadvantage. At the time, however, We did not have too much time to lean into this provision because it was not the most salacious prong of the law. The first line of the law took that prize:

> HB 2281 prohibits a school district or charter school from including in its program of instruction any courses or classes that:
> Promote the overthrow of the United States government.

This oppression of Our People was unleashed during Our lifetimes.

We used Our ethnic solidarity to Accelerate the Librotraficantes, fight against the most egregious line. Nuances don't Accelerate. We leaned into the middle of the sparks and flight of Our rocket and attending to the questions and issues in Our lane, fueling the air under Our trajectory to push harder, to lift higher, to shake up things towards The Tip of The Pyramid—overturning this racist law.

There is always the overall goal of attracting energy and attention to Our cause, but the strategy then was to stop the spread of the racist law to other states, especially Our home state of Texas, which was, at the time, the second most racist state in the Union, just behind Arizona—which took the lead as the most racist state of the union by becoming the poster child for the far right movement by passing two terrible laws targeting Latinos:

a. SB 1070 Arizona's "Show Me Your Papers" Law

b. HB 2810 Arizona's ban on Mexican American Studies

Arizona first made Our bodies illegal, then they went after Our minds by making Our History and Culture illegal. To clarify, SB 1070 attacked the undocumented Community in Arizona and profiled Latinos in general. A few years later, racist sheriff joe arpaio would get convicted for continuing to profile Latinos despite a court order to stop it. He would get pardoned later by donald trump.

Some republicans would argue, at the time, that SB 1070 did not mention Latinos and was therefore not racist or discriminatory, was only trying to fix the broken immigration system. They'd then claim they are for "legal immigration." However, to shatter that argument, then-governor jan brewer, a republican, would go on to sign HB 2281, the law banning Mexican American Studies. That clearly went after US citizens of Mexican descent.

Identity terms can play a role in the evolution of CCC if the terms are used on Our Terms. However, they are typically manipulated. Right-wing Arizona republicans manipulated the vagueness of the term "Hispanic" by attacking Latino immigrants through the "show me your papers" law. The general term Latino was posed as part of several identity terms to gain Our Community power nationwide. It has not accomplished that. It has gotten Us to this point. The power of this approach has, at the very least, plateaued. Meanwhile, those who oppose the basic premise of Ethnic Studies will claim that advocating for Mexican American Studies cuts out non-Mexican people. I know this from years of struggles at the Texas State Board of Education, where a board member once claimed the term "Mexican American Studies" was divisive. Another speculated that Mexican American Literature may not be as rigorous as British Lit. And so on.

At any rate, The Level Playing Field of corporate media could barely wrap its head around these issues. I should add that ten years prior to this Book being published, no media outlet or publisher on The Level Playing Field wanted to hear a Mexican's take on the "Group vs. Individual" question, as republican right-wing legislators wanted to take the right to Group Identity away from Us. We fought that. We won. I'm here to break it down in the aftermath.

This incident also shows how the rulers create the rules for The Level Playing Field to maintain their rule, as they rain down attacks on The Base of The Pyramid. They are attacking several fronts at once. They do so by creating separate lanes, using the blinders forced on Us to train Us every day to see just a slice of the world. How are We trained to use the blinders? Through the norms and enforcement of various Level Playing Fields, including mainstream, corporate media.

The fact that Obama's republican opponent, mitt romney, focused on one line of the speech—even creating a whole campaign video attacking him for it—is telling, because that one line is a border. It is a line in the sand, the same way all lines are arbitrary, all drawn lines are made up.

This backlash began a discussion, as best as can be had via media, via classrooms, over time. Obama was arguing that of course it takes a person to act, work, and deliver; however, We must not forget that We as individuals benefit from the work We do together as a society. Romney pushed back by promoting individualism, which harkens back to the old cliché about Americans pulling themselves up by their bootstraps. Ironically, mainstream society, the rulers, get to create the rules for creating groups. On one hand the republican party presidential candidate will point out that you must succeed on your own. However, the fact that he is the head of a group formed by rulers goes unacknowledged.

I don't want to dive too far into that old Obama vs romney debate. You can google that. What you couldn't google up to now, and what I could not dig into at the time, was the role this baggage played in the law banning Mexican American Studies.

The name "Librotraficante" dramatized the sophistry used against Us. But this time, We had weaponized it.

And We humanized the cause with Our bodies. We showed up on your doorstep. We were not just online, but We were happy to occupy your inbox. We were also even happier partying on your front lawn. Chicano civil rights lawyer Richard Martinez organized the legal dream team to attack the rest of the words in the statute in court. We pounced on this law's one line about "overthrowing the government" and all of its ramifications in the court of public opinion.

We Authored Our Authority.

The Obama-romney argument epitomized the edges of the argument. It did not directly state that Our CCC was at stake; however, that line vilifying Group Identity made it into the books—only to reappear as a keystone of the 2012 Texas republican platform.

Here is why Our movement is powerful, important, and vital.

I saw that line in Texas after We returned from Arizona. In the past, I would not read the republican platform because I was not republican. But because I now knew the gop was capable of banning Us, and that We did not want this to spread to Texas, I read it. I would not have profoundly understood what that line portended if I had not studied the law banning Mexican American Studies in Arizona. This and other actions by Texas gop right wing members made it clear that Texas was testing the waters for a ban. This was proof that Texas was looking to Arizona to lead the way in attacks on CCC, and the Librotraficantes were not going to stand for it.

Of course, some Tejanos didn't need this much proof to know that this was the case. In 2010, the republican-dominated Texas State Board of Education famously called Dolores Huerta, co-founder of the United Farm Workers movement with Cesar Chavez, a communist, in an effort to prevent her inclusion in Texas history courses and textbooks.

I pounced on this on my own, separate from Our movement, though I kept the Librotraficante crew up to date. I had the Cultural Capital to invest in this campaign. They supported my efforts on social media and with their networks; I shared, vetted, discussed this with Community members—but this was not a Tip of The Pyramid. In this case, this issue did not animate. Mi Gente were interested, but interest is not the frequency that forms a Tip of The Pyramid. This was indirect oppression. It would not animate, but it also could not stand.

The Texas gop did not fight this pushback head on, mention Our names, or respond directly to these critiques. But, that line disappeared from the Texas gop platform.

This was a lesson in fighting, and winning, a cold war—and yet another way to Cultivate, Quantify, and Accelerate CCC.

This example of a CA acting on their own is also an example of the legal "I" vs. the ego "I." Someone had to have the base knowledge to link the ink from AZ's racist laws to TX racist pontifications. Someone had to point it out. Someone had to write the op-ed. A voice must speak out on the radio.

Fine.

That is the terrain of the legal "I." the kings english creates the legal "I"—the individual who has copyright, who has the byline—and it creates The Level Playing Field of the media where the legal "I" holds the copyright, is the one spokesperson who speaks for the group. The doorway to The Level Playing Field is built to fit one person at a time: the legal "I."

Conversely, I am a CA because I am in touch with my Community. That skill, power, ability is what the corporate world covets. They don't want to know how to do that. They want to *own* how to do that. They can't.

But CAs must also resist giving in to the ego "I." That op-ed about Dolores Huerta bears my name because the editors demanded such; they don't even take open letters or anonymous letters. And I am not creating to advance my individual career, or status as a writer. Of course, all that is bolstered. And of course, corporate hacks would pay money for some of that.

Still, I must translate the legal "I" into the Community "I" as I fight against the possible legislation striving to erase Our ability to unite as a Community.

The ego "I" wants to be a great white writer, wants to dominate the ivory tower, wants to be published by corporate publishing, wants money, fame, power rained on it by the bastard sons of the king, the enrons of media. The ego "I" was trained at the UH CWP to tell my story, in the templates enforced by the kings english, for The Level Playing Field of corporate publishing for the trinkets, one tenth of the dimes they budget for mid-level writers, for diversity.

The legal "I," as the Community "I," invests my time and energy writing an op-ed, a genre ignored in MFA programs, for the *Houston Chronicle*, a local newspaper.

At some point CAs must reduce themselves to the legal "I" to puncture The Level Playing Field and champion Us at The Tip of The Pyramid. Our Own Gente may see only the ego "I," mistaking Our efforts for self-aggrandizement—or perhaps they are right and it really is self-aggrandizement, because We were lured by the ego "I," as the system wants.

We must navigate this. We vet "I" with Our Gente, crew, familia, team. We read the History coded in Our Words, We talk to Our intelligentsia.

We are vetted.

They give Us blessings.

We dive in. Alone.

It took all the capacity of Our CAs to unite and to topple that racist ban, If another state, especially Texas, had adopted the ban before it was overturned, it would have not just doubled the amount of work We had to muster, it would have exponentially multiplied the threat.

Likewise, Arizona's "Show Me Your Papers" law fueled an anti-immigrant movement, spreading similar laws to other states. Those laws were attacked in courts, but vestiges remained and grew into the anti-immigrant wave that donald trump would manipulate to ride into office. The mainstream media carved out a lane for Latinos in their coverage that was and is (perhaps it won't always be) about immigration. We are not perceived as intellectuals, so more lanes are not dedicated to Latinos issue or views.

Mainstream media is illiterate about Latinos. So they think We are illiterate. Or they fill in the void with stereotypes or generalizations. So, there were also not a lot of experts to understand how the banning of Mexican American Studies was a major attack on Our CCC.

This was a lane We had to fight for. Worse, it ran counter to the "immigration" issue. The ban attacked Mexican Americans, citizens of the US. For the media to address the erasure of Our History and Culture would also call to mind the erasure of Our History and Culture by the media. This reckoning flew in the face of all the easy to spot stereotypes the far-right wing of republicans lobbed at Our undocumented brothers and sisters, while also digging into the generalizations the media adhered to and had to shatter to cover Us properly.

Arizona's attack on the humanities forced media to examine—or at least face, even for a brief moment—how it dehumanizes Us, too. This would be the case again in 2019, when a white supremacist killed Mexicans and Mexican Americans in cold blood, and again in the 2020 presidential campaign as non-Latinos tried to figure out "The Latino Vote," and so on, and so on, and so on.

So, yes, I was complicit: We, too, bore out a lane for Our Community to stop the spread of the ban of Mexican American Studies. We co-opted the tactics of the mainstream to bore that lane deeper and deeper and deeper. We burned their stereotypes and generalizations to fuel Our trajectory to fly higher and longer, for as long as possible. And We did it with Art. We co-opted their imaginations and machines through the Art of the phrase: Librotraficante. That word pierced the stereotypes and generalizations in their mind, and Our caravan barreled through that crack.

And We reached The Tip of The Pyramid. We stopped right-wing republicans in Texas from adopting the same law.

Then the next Tip of The Pyramid to build on that foundation was to overturn that racist law and to tell more and more and more of the nation to support the legal team that would overturn this, and the plaintiffs who were fighting this in court, giving their time, energy, their youth, to this cause.

There was a strategy: Stop the spread of this racism. Then overturn the racist law. And then spread Mexican American Studies.

As I am revealing in this Book, the overnight success of the Librotraficantes was laid in place by fourteen years of work of Nuestra Palabra: Latino Writers Having Their Say. I would risk my skin, my time, my energy, my youth on this cause, because, as I am dramatizing in this Book, I found the frequency, I weighed the risks, I measured my and Our capacity, I knew the costs. I knew my and Our strengths and limits. Yes, I would have to benefit. I would not benefit by creating only more capital—the goal was not to create more and more mindless capital. The goal was and is to create more Cultural Capital.

I knew I was there fourteen years earlier, summoning the poets to the party hall of Chapultepec when the rest of Tejanos thought We did not exist.

And I knew I would be there ten years later, writing about how to Cultivate CCC and looking back on it all. And looking forward.

MFA: Mighty Fine Aztec

Creative Writing Programs captivate you in the ivory tower. You believe the scribbling and rants beyond the pale pale will never amount. You benefit from the crumbs of the racket. You are brought in to silence. You are cloistered to not speak about money. And you wait for one of your professors from New York to open some mysterious door for you in New York—either by telling a publisher about you, which they are doing for themselves and can barely cling to—or by teaching the mystical arts of writing. Never mind that they are not editors and can't publish you, so it is just their cool working theory about writing which they can form based loosely on the mysterious Art of Art they engender and resent you taking them away from. Or perhaps they can somehow give you one hint about the nebulous publishing world—through one of its derivative indy arms, also lieutenants of the racket, or through some of the other layers you suspect that they may know of.

But most likely they do not, or they would not be damned to this creative outpost in the swamplands of Texas, where they try everything to create a snow globe of New York, or try to incant a spell by constantly reciting how much they miss NY, how much better it is, how that is the cultural world.

All third grade-level shit. Pretty straightforward.

If it's so great, why are you stuck out here with Us?

If it is a science, how come no one is getting book contracts when they graduate?

If We are open-minded about Art, why are We bullied, seduced, lulled into the ivory tower?

If We are supposed to get published some day, why is it bad to talk about the business of writing, getting published, making money? A vato has got to eat.

But yeah, just like third grade, except the nuns were writers, poets, administrators from New York. Alcoholic nuns with thin books read by a few folks like psalms, in expensive horn-rimmed glasses, who perhaps had homes in NY.

But this is who I had to get through to get the paper.

Once again, my family was in line for Our papers.

Once again, my family was in Texas. This time We were not picking crops. I was picking brains. I had to get through them to get my advanced degree.

That parchment was a license to write.

I had gotten my bachelor's and that did not open doors to jobs. It opened doors to shitty jobs. Not as bad as picking, but mind-numbing, hourly, dismal.

I quit all that.

I was a citizen. I had a bachelor's degree. I had no student debt. I had no kids. No wife. I had a badass Buick LeSabre. At my age, my father was a father responsible for other lives, and had dived into a new country where he was not sure of where or how he would find work and he could not speak the language.

Me, I now had my papers. I had my high school diploma. I was the first male to graduate high school. My two sisters had graduated before me. That was a big milestone. And then they were married off. I was the first to even dream of and then to actually go to college.

I had the parchment from my bachelor's degree. I had three grand saved in the bank from my bullshit jobs. I had a midnight blue Buick LeSabre. No student debt. I not only spoke english, and Spanish, I had words.

Fuck it. I would go back to Texas to avenge My Gente.

My parents came to El Norte, but first landed in Texas—the South of El Norte. They eventually travelled to Chicago, the North of El Norte. But my father bought a house in a neighborhood called Bridgeport. Yeah, We were on the South Side of the North of El Norte. The American Dream was always fucking with Us.

I was happy to graduate from El Norte. I took Our Gente back to Texas to exact revenge.

The Pale Pale

By submitting to the master's master of fine arts program
you are signing a user agreement that there are masters.
The fine print of the fine art reveals you will never be master.

I liberated myself from the pale pale of the ivory tower I'd been working toward since before I was even born.

My early training as a Librotraficante took place in grammar school as I translated english with Italian, Polish, and Mexican accents into Spanish on the South Side of Chicago.

I knew that in class words stood still so you could identify them in the lineups called quizzes the teachers forced on you. You were a straight-A student if you repeated what the teacher said, even if you didn't understand it, agree with it, or believe it.

I attended a catholic school, the lower-class equivalent of a private school for Us. The nuns told Us that swearing was wrong, and gave Us a list of actions that were sins, or could cause you to go to hell.

Of course, once I was on the way home from school, I tested the theories. I swore the apostles up and down as I walked down Emerald Avenue, waiting for lightning to strike me down or for Joe "Bag of Donuts" to come out and try to steal my pens.

No lightning.

I kept my pens.

And I figured that was yet one more racket I was surrounded by. They meant well. I needed to deal with the nuns and priests to earn my eighth grade diploma one day, and my real mission was to learn english, fast, well, and use it to stick up for my mother, father, and family.

My father was no saint, so I could trust him. And I would do anything for him and my mom, since I could see they would do anything for me.

I was scared of Jesus's lighting and Jesus Cerda down the block, but neither of them could land a punch on me.

I was more scared of the shitty jobs my dad had. I grew up with my mom as a housewife. She, and even my sisters, when they were kids, as in my age, had been pickers when they were damned to Texas.

I wasn't scared to risk or hand out an ass beating, but that life . . . that was some scary shit.

I was not exactly sure what Education entailed, but my father was adamant that it would prevent me from working breaking my back like he did, and it would lead to me working with my mind.

That was my calling.

And every day I imagined my father and mother stooped over some godforsaken Texas field at 5 a.m. in the morning, the girls stumbling along, wiping off the dew from the side of the truck where they sat to get ready to pick the crops.

I imagined my father, every day, with the lazy sun rising slowly, him stooped over that godforsaken Texas field owned by some hillbilly; I imagine his arms flailing up and down, ripping out the guts of the earth, into buckets, to feed Our family, to feed his dreams of me, some day. I picture him stooped over the earth, his arms flailing hard, fast, and precise like he was punching the earth, making it cough up what We wanted, needed, demanded.

Like that I would crack the spines of books, tempted to crack open skulls, but aiming higher to open minds.

My parent's field of study was a field.

I carry their trauma, pride, and dreams on my broad shoulders and broader imagination.

My mother and father took jobs no one else wanted.

I create works no one imagined.

My mother and father believed in the American Dream. I am blessed to shape it.

CULTURAL ACCELERATION ESSAYS

Hacking France: Reading Latinos

First published March 19, 2019 on TonyDiaz.net. Broadcast on the radio show Nuestra Palabra: Latino Writers Having Their Say, *90.1 FM, KPFT, Houston.*

The good news is that I was right.

The bad news is structural oppression.

I hacked the imagination of French sociologist Pierre Bourdieu.

I think all of us Chicanos did. I was doing it since I was a child, from the first moment I began translating for my parents.

That was my first job—translating the outside world into Spanish for my mom and dad.

I don't even remember when I began doing it. I simply remember language as that power. It made me equal to adults.

And there was something wrong with that. Yet, I could not put that into words. And I did not have time to put it into words because I had to act. If I did not act, my family did not act.

We were one of the first Mexican—and I suppose I made us Mexican American—families in our neighborhood on the South Side of Chicago. And I knew if we did not take action, we would be crushed. I was not going to let us get crushed.

If I could pull my weight, and then some, just a little more, my dad easily carried the rest, and my mom smoothed out the rough edges. We would survive, and some day, and some days, or at least for a few hours, thrive.

I was a Cultural Accelerator. I had not coined the phrase for it yet. But it was formulating inside me, through me, because of me. And it helped me survive until I could thrive by uttering the phrase.

Chicana, Chicano, and Latino authors helped me survive the educational, work, and political system to get me to the exact wording of my struggle. They lived it and described and discussed it is so clearly to me.

Yet, other folks still did not understand.

Again, it was like translating. You can convey some literal explanations, but there are more profound ones that will escape the target of your words. The persons you are speaking to might even ignore the profound message even when it registers. Or, most likely, they have turned their minds off to you saying, thinking, or imagining, anything of importance except to report if you will or have fulfilled their desires.

Of course, they would listen to a white man, especially if he spoke French.

When I first read Pierre Bourdieu's work, I was as thrilled as when I first read Gloria Anzaldua's work, or Dagoberto Gilb's fiction, or Piri Thomas's novel *Down These Mean Streets*.

They struck a profound tuning fork. I felt that intellectual buzz of matching profound deep ideas.

The first novel written by a Latino that I read was *Down These Mean Streets* by Piri Thomas, a Puerto Rican writer from NYC. I was a Chicano on the South Side of Chicago, but I could relate to the chaos, violence, the Spanglish, the cursing, the struggle, the writing. It boggled my mind. Finally, as a Junior in college, I was reading sentences that worked at a literal level, a social level, a cultural, spiritual level.

My Creative Writing teacher had turned me on to it. No one else read it. When I read it to others, they did not get it. It was not taught at my college, my high school, and well, it was probably too intense for middle school.

I was a one-man island of the literature of one man from The Island. But that was more, because before that I was the only one in my head.

I was not a nobody. I was only body.

Now, I was mind and imagination. I was not crazy to think. My body carried a brain, and that brain was calling the shots. That brain was the boss. Not my fist or my kick.

35 years later, I would have the same experience reading Pierre Bourdieu's *Distinction: A Social Critique of the Judgement of Taste* finding his work on my own, then more, then more.

His breakdown of the sociology of cultural breakdown and buildup was the stuff of Chicana, Chicano, and Latinx fiction, poetry, and memoir and our own sociologists.

Again, his translated French was saying in english what we had been saying slightly differently in Spanglish.

I remember his discussion of the structural oppression of Moroccans in France. Their plight was familiar. It dawned on me that everything he observed about Moroccans in France could be applied to Chicanos in the US. And then it struck me.

Here's the bad news.

He studied structural oppression.

My family dramatized it.

He conducted surveys to quantify it.

We conducted protests.

He summarized.

We survived.

The rage is that we are saying the same thing. To our ears. Seems obvious. But his work puts it in terms Anglo folks understand from a white fellow who speaks French.

Don't stereotype me as bitter. Because now, because of him, we are allies.

He quantified in numbers.

We quantified in blood.

So, I was right. When I was a kid on the south side of Chicago, I knew I was surrounded by rackets, at every level, but I could not put it into words. However, I could find the words to act. I had to. That was my job.

Again, my first job was translating the outside world into Spanish for my parents. That made me equal to adults.

Now as an adult, as a Cultural Accelerator I translate our world into english, so others can understand us. That makes us equal to you.

I may have gotten to the books at a disadvantage, but my family's Cultural Capital multiplied the power of the educational capital they helped me obtain. And I was delivered to this era of upheaval by a community used to upheaval, so that everything that once simply helped us survive will now help us thrive. And I can act on that knowledge.

And I can finally put into words the blessing that will benefit my community and unite us with your community—I am a Cultural Accelerator.

The Era of Cultural Accelerators

First published December 4, 2018 on TonyDiaz.net and on December 6, 2018 on LatinoRebels.com.

"the elegant self-assurance of inherited wealth . . ." —Pierre Bourdieu

"Knowing hurts." —Gloria Anzaldua

"Only Art can save us." —Tony Diaz

"It's clear to me that our intellectual advancement is a threat to some people, because they tried to make it illegal." —Tony Diaz

If moving stairs are escalators, then elevators are accelerators.

And there we were, Summer 2017, taking a metaphor to the 3rd floor of the Arizona Supreme Court in Tucson. The Librotraficantes were on board with civil rights lawyer Richard Martinez and the legal team he assembled to overturn Arizona's ban of Mexican American Studies.

Closest to the buttons for the floors stood Stephen Weiss, a partner at Weil, Gotshal & Manges, LLP, who had taken on the case pro bono, as in free. It took millions of dollars in legal fees to fight the case.

I was nervous. The fate of freedom of speech was at stake, and it was friggin' hot like only a Tucson summer can be.

Stephen was not even breaking a sweat.

Of course, it's hard to stay nervous with Richard Martinez around. He's this tall Chicano who is always joking in english, Spanish, and Spanglish, and he has this huge laugh that makes you forget he's earned his massive, white mop of hair from battling dragons in the belly of the beast. His name will go down in history long after his far-right nemeses have been voted out of office.

My heart was racing because we could lose.

This could be the most glorious moment in our community's history when we defend freedom of speech, intellectual freedom for the entire nation.

Or it could be the advent of the Dark Ages where our history and culture is banned, and yours is next, then the next one, then the next one.

We sure as hell were not going to tolerate that. I would quit my job, we would organize Librotraficante Caravans in every state, every month, chain ourselves to school board seats like the students of Tucson did at TUSD meetings, hunger strikes like Cesar did, walkouts like Sal did.

History can be cruel. Our people have suffered. Democracy is fragile.

I told Stephen, "My heart is racing. I feel as if I'm about to watch Brown v. Board of Education."

Stephen said, "Be careful with that. "Brown v. Board of Education took over 14 years to fight right."

That made me think of *Brown, Not White* by Dr. Guadalupe San Miguel.

Brown v. Board of Education took place in the 50s, but even into the 70s, Houston was grappling with the issue of segregation, as documented by *Brown, Not White*. Officials called Mexican and Mexican American students White in order to trick the government into believing Houston schools were complying with segregation laws. In fact, as the book chronicles, the poorest students from Mexican American communities were put into schools with the poorest Black students to create the poorest school districts. Of course, that was not the intent of the law.

However, this time we were destined to win, and Arizona's ban of Mexican American Studies would be overturned later that year.

I got to see with my very eyes the advent of the enforcement of the banning of Mexican American Studies in Arizona in 2012 to the courtroom drama that overturned it in 2017.

We are a generation of Cultural Accelerators.

Just in that elevator, rode millions of dollars' worth of intellectual legal capital.

They called on leading Chicana and Chicano scholars, Dr. Angela Valenzuela, Dr. Stephen Pitti, Dr. Nolan Cabrera, who would provide bulletproof evidence that Mexican American Studies edified students.

And we mounted publicity campaigns for our community that Madison Avenue might match only with a budget of tens of millions of dollars. And across the southwest, all of Aztlan, all of the US, allies and community, united from the classroom, to the boardroom, to the courtroom, we had unleashed the era of Cultural Accelerators.

Cultural Capital transforms us to many things like standing up for our rights, voting, writing.

Arizona's ban of Mexican American Studies was intended to debilitate our community.

If it had happened just a decade, or a generation or two earlier, it would have.

In Texas, we would have known about the ban of our history and culture only after it would have been implemented, and when it would have been enforced in Texas, too.

We would be fighting bans of our history and culture in several states, instead of uniting attention and forces on one.

Of course, make no mistake—damage was done.

The TUSD MAS curriculum should have been extolled. Instead, it was dismantled and the teachers who engendered it were maligned, sued, or fired. Many students were not exposed to MAS during the ban. And worse, TUSD has yet to re-instate the original curriculum.

TUSD officials claim they do have culturally relevant courses, but they should implement the same curriculum that the courts proved advanced the intellectual progress of students.

I tell you that to clarify that History is cruel.

But I also bring it up to emphasize how strong our community is. We don't hear enough about that.

We are Cultural Accelerators. This is our era. We must quantify, cultivate, and accelerate our community's cultural capital.

Today, when our community is told we do not count, I can write, post, and email this essay. I will talk about it on the NP Radio show at one hundred thousand watts in the 4th largest city in America. We are making history on our terms. Our radio broadcasts are archived at the University of Houston Digital Archives. The radio broadcast will be saved to a podcast then shared through social media. I will talk about this essay on commercial TV. I will teach this to my Mexican American Literature courses. I will donate a hard copy version of this to the Houston Public Library which houses our hard copy history in its Hispanic Collections.

I am a cultural accelerator. I am blessed because my instinct has always been to stay connected to my community. At first, I thought that meant only my family. However, I realized as early as high school that if I was going to navigate the halls of education, I was going to need my community's support.

I have lived the power of writing.

I am blessed to have seen my theories about the power of writing come to pass.

I am blessed to get to articulate for my community how this works.

Only art can save us. I have lived this through my own eyes. And now, I will write a testament to that for our community.

Don't worry. I will provide a formal definition of Cultural Accelerators, soon. That's easy.

Right now, I want to enjoy the intellectual adrenaline of imposing our will on the universe and changing the world.

The courts are stifling, especially the Arizona Supreme Court, especially during a Tucson summer.

I knew we would win before I knew we would win.

And you can't confine me to that elevator, that court, or one narrative. My muses must be constantly amused.

I am also privileged to intellectual Oases, as in more than one oasis. I would soon be in San Antonio for Macondo, the writer's retreat founded by Chicana writer Sandra Cisneros.

You know it's a Chicano Renaissance when a kid from the South Side of Chicago, whose parents were migrant workers, the first of the family to go to college, can read the work of a bestselling author, relate, then soon connect, then host her on his radio show, at his reading series, and then smuggle her books across state lines. But that elevator kept going up. Macondo, her retreat, would soon be umbrellaed under my 501(c)(3) nonprofit organization Nuestra Palabra: Latino Writers Having Their Say.

What does it mean to be a cultural accelerator? I am riding the elevator to the Arizona Supreme court with a million bucks of legal eagles for a case where I have smuggled the contraband prose of writing pros who I know, making national news about views from my community, then detoxing from the racist bile that woulda shamed, discombobulated, and deported my predecessors, at a writing retreat, thinking and writing my ass off, hanging with Genius MacArthur Grant winners, and brilliant and beautiful poets and writers from all over the nation but really from my block.

Macondo takes place in San Antonio, Texas. Sandra Cisneros founded it decades ago around her kitchen table.

At the closing dinner, Sandra told us that Macondo had been in a coma, but this year was a Renaissance. It was that strong.

But to hear Sandra say this also added the urgency of quantifying and harnessing this power we have. It is now crystal clear to me that our community's cultural capital is under attack. And there are forces at work to see it whither or stamp it out. They will not succeed.

Macondo is more evidence of this.

Macondo's rampaging rebirth happened the first full year after Arizona's racist ban of Mexican American Studies was overturned. This also happened the year that the Texas State Board of Education unanimously endorsed Mexican American Studies statewide.

Those are just two powerful examples that prove that policy change is The Tip of The Pyramid and our community's cultural capital is the base.

The most famous line in the Arizona Republican law banning Mexican American Studies prohibited courses that promoted the overthrow of the government. Of course, the 80+ books in the curriculum were works of poetry and fiction, none of which even contained the word "overthrow" or "the government" in the same line, if they contained those words at all.

Sandra's *House on Mango Street* was on that list. I made my FBI file thicker by re-reading it to find the secret anti-government formula. Was it in the name of the main character "Esperanza"? Is "Hope" the threat to the government that the Arizona Republicans were legislating against?

On the other hand, Macondo is its own literary nation.

I nominate Sandra Cisneros King of Macondo.

We recognize no limits to our imaginations.

And in turn the state does not recognize us. I'm not playing. This is the case because Macondo is not a 501(c)(3) not for profit organization, which is what artists are economically bullied into believing they should become.

We, the literary community, invested our cultural capital to organize and conduct the most powerful Latinx literary workshop, program, school, party in the Southwest and possibly the nation.

Macondo is a potent example of our cultural capital.

That is the threat that Arizona Republicans really feared.

They were scared of the advancement of our intellectual base. They feared the moment we would not only think for ourselves but act in ways to cultivate and increase our cultural capital.

Too late, Arizona GOP.

Sandra told us, "I didn't create Macondo to start a literary movement. I started it because I was alone. I wanted familia." Those are the exact principles and ethos of cultural capital. We are blessed to be formed by them.

And now have coined new terms: Macondo.

Librotraficantes.

Cultural Capital.

For many of us, our first job was as translator. We knew the power of words because heavy responsibility passed through us. Back then our job was to translate the outside world into Spanish for our parents, our community. Now our job is to translate our community for the rest of the world.

We have been delivered to the Latinx Renaissance.

Long live Macondo.

Librotraficantes. Latino Rebels.
Zapata's Disciples.

First published November 15, 2012 on LatinoRebels.com.

I was recently knighted.

I didn't fully understand what was happening at the time as I flew to New York. But I did know that we were making history.

All around the nation Librotraficantes convened, on the same day, at the same time, to take a stand against Arizona House Bill 2281 passed to prohibit courses that promote the overthrow of the government. This was the legal trigger that Tucson Unified School District pointed at Mexican American Studies to force teachers to walk into classrooms and in front of our young confiscate and box up books by our most beloved authors—all accused of promoting the overthrow of the government.

I arrived in East Harlem, to the packed Casa Azul bookstore, to convene with banned prose kingpin Luis Alberto Urrea and banned iconic poet Martin Espada and other book traffickers. It was there that Martin read from and then handed to me his contraband book *Zapata's Disciple.*

Here are some of the words that an entire state did not want our people to hear: *"Some day, my son will be called a spic for the first time . . . I hope that I can help him handle the glowing toxic waste of rage . . . I keep it between the covers of the books I write."*

After he read more from the work, he formally handed the book to me.

On the title page, he wrote: *"Para Tony—Librotraficante y discípulo de Zapata. Un abrazo de Martin Espada, banned author Sept. 21, 2012."*

I wear those words like a tattoo on my broad back and broader imagination.

I open the book to read about Frank Espada, pictured on the front of cover, and his son writes, *"He was the most dangerous of creatures, a working class radical. James Graham in* The Enemies of the Poor, *compared my father to a guerrilla-disciple of Emiliano Zapata, the Mexican Revolutionary."*

No, this was not an instruction manual on how to overthrow the government.

This is a manual on how to save a people.

And to jaded eyes and ears it will seem I mean only a few people. I mean us all, all of the people. But I can't slow down to explain because right now we are making History and changing the world so fast that english has to catch up—on its own time.

I always knew we needed to tell our stories. That's why I earned a Master of Fine Arts Degree in Creative Writing from the University of Houston Creative Whitening Program. And then I wrote my novel *The Aztec Love God*, published at a university press. So we also needed to publish our own work.

Then I realized we had to promote our own work, too. So 14 years ago I founded Nuestra Palabra: Latino Writers Having Their Say, in the fourth largest city in America, with one of the highest dropout rates in the nation, with person after person even our own people telling me there was no interest, there was no audience. We went on to organize the largest book events in Houston, in Texas for all demographics.

And then six years ago, our *familia* in Tucson devised the Mexican American Studies program to teach our own stories to our youth from Kindergarten all the way to Senior year in High School.

And yes, I too, thought, that was enough. We had arrived at the promised land of the American Dream.

But this year Arizona officials prohibited that curriculum. They yanked now sacred books out of the hands of our young, they banned our history, they made our culture contraband.

We had to join our brothers and sisters fighting for our culture in Tucson, so Nuestra Palabra: Latino Writers Having Their Say organized the Librotraficante Caravan to Smuggle the Wetbooks back into Arizona in March of 2012, getting thousands of books donated from across the country. I thought that we would return to our old lives the Monday after. Instead, we had unleashed a national movement.

On September 21, 2012, thousands of us convened to honor the books banned in Arizona, and all our lost histories. We extolled the young students still protesting in the streets of Tucson, arguing in the Arizona Supreme Court, and still studying to earn their diplomas, degrees. We reminded America that everyone's Freedom of Speech rested on the backs of young Chican@s suing the state of Arizona. We raised funds for the Raza Defense Fund for heroes like Sean Arce, former Director of Mexican American Studies, and Jose Gonzalez, former Mexican American Studies teacher at Tucson Unified School District who were being sued as a result of their activism. That's like the grape companies suing Cesar Chavez for picketing them.

We united to make our literature go viral the old-fashioned way: one person at a time, from Librotraficantes in New York, including Ivy League Tejano Sergio Troncoso; Chicago; the Bay Area; Librotraficantes in San Francisco with Super poeta/organizer Naomi Quiñonez and La Mera Mera banned poeta Lorna Dee Cervantes; the City of Angeles, Librotraficantes at banned author Luis Rodriguez's awesome spot in LA, Tia Chucha Cultural Center, featuring El Padrino of Contraband prose, Dr. Rodolfo Acuña; in Iowa City, Boston, Milwaukee, Manhattan, Kansas; Kansas City, Lincoln, Nebraska; San Antonio, Texas; Minnesota, and more— thousands of us, across the country.

But in New York, in the confines of a bookstore owned by a Latina, in the barrio of the largest city in America, our mission became even more clear.

We also had to buy our own bookstores, too as Aurora Anaya-Cerda did with Casa Azul bookstore, so we could meet there on that night.

We had to promote our own events.

We had to report our own news.

We had to create ceremonies, initiations, readers, and we have to not only make history, but record it, spread it, and then repeat it.

That magical night of the written word when we were inducted into the sanctum of Protectors of The Word we were assembled by the concerted efforts of Nuestra Palabra: Latino Writers Having Their Say, The Librotraficante Movement, The Latino Rebels, poeta extradionaire Charlie Vazquez, Sangre Viva Alliance, Hostos CC, John Jay College, Fordham U., Casa Azul, Rich Villar with Accentos, Universalist Unitarian Assembly HUManists, Dreamers across the nation, The Southwest Workers Union, and more, so many more.

The blessing is that we are poised in a moment in history, when all of that is within our reach, within our grace, within our ability to put it into words.

And now these movements too delivered an election.

Arizona officials knew that we would never overthrow the government through violence. They knew we would overhaul the government by voting them out of office. And by banning our literature, they created that which they feared the most: An Army of Zapata's Disciples knighted Protectors of the Word.

America, I give you the dawning of the Librotraficante Nation.

Yes, the essay is over.

But since we are smugglers, here are some more words.

If it were a sheet of paper, they would slide off; since it's the internet, we can just sneak more in.

If the Librotraficantes were a band, I'm the lead singer, and my co-founders are dear friends who have been with Nuestra Palabra for over a decade each: Librotraficante HighTechAztec Bryan Parras, Librotraficante Lilo Liana Lopez, Librotraficante La Laura-Laura Acosta, Librotraficante Lips Mendez-Lupe Mendez.

I also got to flow in NYC with poets Bonafide Rojas, Miguel Ángel Ángeles and John Murillo; representing the NYC Latina Writers' Group Peggy Robles-Alvarado, María Rodríguez, and Nancy Arroyo-Ruffin reading from

The House on Mango Street; *representing the Capicu Cultural Show-case, Juan "Papo Swiggity" Santiago, Mark Anthony Vigo, and José Vilson reading from* Always Running; *and John Rodríguez, Grisel Acosta, Isabel Martínez, Elizabeth Calixto, and Vincent Toro reading from* Occupied America; *and Anamaría Flores, Jani Rose, Kim Possible, and so many others!*

PART IV: FINDING FREQUENCY: THE NEXT TIP OF THE PYRAMID

Rubble

Scholars chip off The Tip of The Pyramid they can reach, hustle it back to the basement of the ivory tower, turning Us into rubble.

You write in the basement of the ivory tower.

Your findings . . . are never found.

Your research must be in the code of the ivory tower. Something the world outside of these walls, let alone beyond the moat, would never understand. Yours is the only serious work in the whole damn place.

You must stay cloistered inside those walls. Across the moat that surrounds the tower, you have heard is a barren wasteland of cantinas, taco shops, country western bars, and . . . a bookstore or two . . . an art gallery . . . one cool *avant-garde* art space. You have a little map drawn on a napkin, blotted with spilled red wine, to guide you there the first time.

Afterwards you stumble back to the basement of the ivory tower, memorizing the path so that you can make the trip drunk.

And you plan to drink again.

Unfortunately, though, you sometimes run into the poets and writers from the PhD in Poetry program. What the hell is that? Is there a PhD in Prose Writing? Is that a PhD in Literature? No, a PhD in Literature is the Truth. A PhD in Fiction would be based on . . . lies. It says it in the title. The entire idea of Doctorates in Poetry is ridiculous. Only Doctors of Literature make sense. Yet, you run into them at the few bars that are refuges in this swampland. Worse, if you are not careful, you may wind up at a reading you thought was for serious work and find out there are slam poets slamming their lips to "spit" words—those are their words, not yours. They are proud to spit with no notion of the true syntax, form, etymology, sources.

Sure, they revel in the large, boisterous audiences they might gather, the adulation, the free drinks of that open mike night. But can they stand up on the page, the lonely pale pale of the white page? They reveal themselves by what they call themselves, the genre they destroy—no, they are not that powerful, unlike you who can truly dismantle and deconstruct a genre—they simply color outside of the lines.

How can three minutes of spitting have anything to do with pursuing a doctorate in the field of english, where you spend hours upon hours conducting your research on the use of diphthongs in altered meters in two continents across two eras?

And then one day, as you decide to come outside of the stacks, in the six-foot section near the loading dock with a steel ashtray and a white outline forming a one-foot boundary around a green bench where you can smoke, someone from the department walks up to you, strikes up polite conversation, and three sentences in asks you if you speak Spanish.

We appear as dots on The Level Playing Field of the university department. We are constricted to the dot that engenders the box We must jump in, so the university can check off the law, policy, donor requirement, progressive credential it pursues.

They expect the dot, a blip, a generalized person. We have to stay inside the dot. We sign user agreements every day, from Our forms to submit, to Our course schedules shaping time, to limiting Our imagination to the "correct" templates and using the words that conform to the standard.

That is the standard.

That is what is expected of a candidate.

However, if a CA pierces through the barriers to gain admission into The Level Playing Field of corporate education, a CA strives to force The Tip of The Pyramid through the space they are allotted. They have to in order to survive. They do not have the generational wealth or generational power to compete in the racket of The Level Playing Field of the ivory tower under rules created by the rulers to maintain their rules.

At the same time, if We arrive and begin to occupy more space than that afforded to Our dot, the Cultural Border Patrol will strive to put Us in Our place.

Let me provide you with the quick proofs of this structural discrimination before getting to the business of breaking down how university capital grinds Our scholars' research into rubble—a deteriorative process that opposes the way CAs invest in Cultivating CCC to survive and thrive and create more culture, even from within the University.

I want this proof not to be static: Write down the names of five universities that are closest to where you are right now.

Look up their upper administration. How many folks are from the Community? How many are Latino?

How many folks from Our Community are tenured professors?

How many folks from Our Community are enrolled as graduate students with scholarships, fellowships, or other benefits? How many are Latino?

Now look up the University of Texas at Austin. How have they profoundly addressed the structural discrimination revealed by the report of discrimination created in 2020 by Latino scholars who are full professors and tenured at their institution?

How was I the first Chicano to earn a Master of Fine Arts in Creative Writing from the University of Houston Creative Writing Program when it is located in Occupied Mexico?

Is CCC still ignored or simply given lip service on the mythical Level Playing Field of academic capital?

There is more, but this proof is enough for CAs. The books that matter in the university racket are not about Us or by Us. Those works do not unearth Our profound CCC, Our History, Our Art, Our Culture. The rulers who create the rules to maintain their rule are illiterate about Us. They forge a literacy devoid of Us, having erased Us so long ago that Our erasure has been erased.

I remember sitting in the University of Houston english department, like sitting at customs and border patrol having my papers checked, and the Cultural Border Patrol checking off my submission as I submitted to them, as they checked their forms to make me conform.

There is no record of the Chicano who got that far before me; they are undocumented. You become documented once you earn your literary citizenship, in my case, an MFA, which, of course, because Mi Gente are always going to El Norte and winding up on the South Side of El Norte, is looked down upon by PhDs as Not-A-Terminal Degree—even though it must be terminal, since I will surely starve to death once I earn it, and, technically, in writing, by their own policies, it says on the dotted line that it is a terminal degree.

To settle the issue, the UH CWP created a PhD in Poetry that poets could pursue after completing their terminal MFA in Poetry. Thus the confusion for them.

This is exactly how english works. *I'm perfect for this place,* I thought then.

In the english department office, the nice Cultural Border Patrol agent who has taken the Texas Genteel Oppression lessons since she was a child—so it would be rude of *me* to point out all the things that seem rude—asks which Foreign Language I will take for my required Foreign Language credits.

Well-versed in the racket of the school industry, I say "Spanish" because I already speak it, but I also know not to point out the obvious or explain my hand to the dealer. That's just not cool.

She pauses.

It's an interruptive pause, forcing her to turn away from the form she was squeezing me into, obviously struggling to make me fit the boxes, in a nice way, 'cause clearly, I don't quite fit. "Would you prefer to choose French?" she tells me, pretending to ask.

The question, as many do, caught me off guard, but it's like catching a punch, maybe an odd-angled hook you didn't see coming, just glancing off your forehead, not enough to buzz ya, but you still have to roll with it.

"The foreign language requirement is clear," I answer, "but is it required to be French?"

"No," she says politely, "but there is not a lot of serious criticism in Spanish?"

This punch lands a bit more squarely.

And I'm still learning the Texas polite fight. "Well, then I suppose I can do a lot with Pablo Neruda's work here. Spanish."

She pauses, looks at me. It is just another short pause, but it is meant to speak volumes if you let it.

But I learn a new trick, too. And at that moment I'm certain that I am the first Chicano to earn a Master of Fine Arts in Creative Writing from the University of Houston because no other Chicanos coulda put up with this shit.

Me, I knew a racket when I saw it. And I could tell there was enough of a gain for me to gain, too. Everybody wins, Capone.

Counter polite pauses with impolite pauses. I can just wait. I'll wait a friggin' hour, a day, a year, a lifetime.

Looking back, I have words for it now.

It explains why I was the first Chicano in that room if they don't even let Pablo Neruda in.

Now, Pierre Bourdieu's views finally came to life: You exist by merely being a player and existing on the field, which is presumed to be level.

At that moment, I was admitted onto the field.

The Theory of the Dialect is a similar racket. We do not fit into the dot begrudgingly assigned to Us on The Level Playing Field, the graph, the theory. If you are offered the spot, the powers that be literally mean a dot. You typically only have a few moments to decide. You are not given the user agreement or all the fine print in the gentleman's agreement. But, I am a translator trained on the South Side of Chicago since my infancy, armed with Books and deep ties of Family, Knowledge, more Books. I'm used to navigating these rackets.

It takes generational work for one of Us to stand on The Level Playing Field. That is erased from the theory, from the equation, just like Our Art, History, and Culture are erased.

Only Art can save Us. I was imported across state lines in order to shatter other borders and claim more firsts.

What I realize now is that the system quickly assesses and moves the goalposts. They watch you at first. Then they go back and seal the leaks. There can't be too many of You at once.

I decide to keep track, keep a long memory, and return with dynamite, send coded messages, books of poetry, fiction, prose, radio broadcasts, readings, emissaries, tweets on how to follow through, where the holes were, where I planted shovels and picks to hack your way through the ivory tower. That way, more and more Librotraficantes could liberate themselves, even if they did not know they were Librotraficantes.

Sometimes, it is best if they don't know they are Librotraficantes, or their family does not know, or their co-workers, or their judges, until it is too late, and We are inside runnin' shit.

And it is like a life of crime, this doing time behind books: once you break into one vault, you want to break into the next, and you become more and more and more brazen.

Of course, The System does not give up the fight easy.

They have generations of experience oppressing, bullying, forcing the submission of many minds, even great minds, in the mines.

How far down the mind mine will you go?

We Build Our Own Cells

Is it in a mine of your mind that you mine? Is it part of a Pyramid?

The Level Playing Field encourages you, forces you to stay in your cubicle, alone, a long time—the longer, the better. Turns your office into a cubicle.

The ivory tower is an academic cubicle.

The boss does not stand over you, but lords over you and empowers you to keep yourself in line.

In the case of the ivory tower, in the case of pursuing academic capital, you are trained and promised rewards if you think, write, research according to the rules the rulers create to maintain their rules.

Again, this is not to look down upon any of Our scholars, any one from Our Community who pursues those avenues. They are important. However, I write this to remind you that the ivory tower can and most likely will abandon you.

The liberal University of Texas at Austin in the liberal city of Austin, Texas, has quantifiably underpaid, overworked, and under-delivered scholars from Our Community. Even if, the day after this is published, UT receives a multi-million dollar donation and dedicates that money to address these quantifiable wrongs, an essential question would still remain: will the university institute long-term, innovative ways to stop the, at best, ignoring of Our CCC and, at worst, the oppression of it?

And if they did, would every other university in the city, the state, the region, and the nation, and then every college and community college likewise adapt?

The entire notion of "Hispanic-Serving Institutions" was supposed to address some of these issues. This term refers to institutions that have at least 25 percent "Hispanic" enrollment. That's it. The rulers who create the rules to maintain their rule do not acknowledge CCC, as reflected in their use of the term "Hispanic." The lords of academic capital took the sentiment, reduced it to Our Terms on their terms, and then created a policy that pandered to Our Community.

The designation of Hispanic-Serving Institute has become a method for universities to Quantify CCC on their limited terms, to comply with federal policies vaguely about inclusion, which are minimal compared to genuine concerns regarding CCC. This creates a pool of applicants who will submit to their forms of "Hispanic" in order to gain funds to pander to Our Community themselves, and in turn devise ineffectual ways to dress up the mythical Level Playing Field of the university, where in reality We may be allowed to prosper but never rule.

This is how governmental institutions use the term coined by the Nixon administration to reduce Our Community to dots on their forms to comply with bare governmental policies, such as admitting students from Our Communities into their schools, as opposed to the generation of exclusion. The oppression has been so bad that this seems like progress. That's an age-old trick: Oppress so much for so long that the slightest relenting seems like progress.

To deserve a legal designation for serving Our Community, an institution of higher education should have several of Us, more than half, in upper administration, on the board of trustees, as tenured professors, as endowed chairs of departments, as deans, and chairs with budgets, as graduate students with fellowships, as undergraduate students with scholarships, forming an abundance for the student body. Their curriculum should be teaching Our Art, History, and Culture at the undergraduate level, researching Our Art, History, and Culture at the graduate level, forming student groups and extracurriculuar activities that support those aspects and also build real bridges into Our Communites—to start with.

I am writing this to convey to CAs the tactics the ivory tower employs against Us and how to navigate and survive them: We are paid off or bought off to become dots on graphs of institutions that need Us as proof they are not discriminating against all the other folks who resemble Us—as they have done for decades if not generations.

Those same institutions won't read to Us the fine print on their user agreement. The UH Creative Writing Program never told me that I was the first Chicano to earn an MFA. Years later when I tried to quantify this, another alum helped me by looking through all the thesis dissertations to exactly prove that I was right. Yet, the institution has never yet acknowledged this, perhaps because they fear that this naming would bring up so many other historical travesties against Our Communities.

The system never says, "Give up your CCC." They simply ignore, erase, or co-opt it.

They persuade you that it is much easier to successfully complete their program by spending more time in the ivory tower—their books, their perspective, their rules. And then they will give you a cool title, the parchment that documents you as scholarly and opportunities for fellowships and publications; they talk you up, give you job leads. Maybe they even hang or post your picture.

This picture of prosperity is powerful in complicating arguments for dismantling the structural discrimination that is prevalent at the university level.

The university reduces your CCC to rubble when it breaks you off from the base of CCC. This act is cloaked in a graduation gown.

First, you submit as a student. To earn As, you repeat what the educators tell you regarding history, art, culture, which is not your History, Art, or Culture. You are given the message that your CCC should not cross the border of school or you will fail.

The fact that the health of your Community impedes your ability to regurgitate the oppressive classroom's notions, complete assignments that teach the notions, or even show up to hear the notions is ignored.

This is also why the banning of Mexican American Studies by Arizona right-wing republicans is a travesty. Our Community Cultural Capital was woven into the Academic Playing Field at the Tucson

Unified School District, resulting in major increases in student success. Thus, it was banned.

Students who drop out of high school drop off the radar and are cut from the cattle call to compete on the mythical Level Playing Field.

Those students who represent generations of how Our Gente have been treated are profoundly part of Our CCC. However, the high school diploma is one more piece of paper in the vast set of papers individuals need to be documented to compete on the mythical Level Playing Field, which has smaller sub-fields, including, in this case, the Academic Level Playing Field.

Of course, as this is not discussed in the very school that chews Us up and spits Us out, and as Our Gente have little time to sift through the levels of rhetoric, Our Gente have to act quickly to fight to survive, and hope to thrive.

The question of who is allowed to exist on the field is an ongoing one. As treacherous as it is, those who can should and must continue to compete on the mythical Academic Level Playing Field.

It appears that high school tests which of Us can shift and shape into the templates and forms they create to form Us. This continues at the undergraduate level. Again, the rulers who create the rules to maintain their rule pandered to Our Community by adding "community" to the brand of "community colleges." However, you need only to study the enrollment rates, graduation rates, and transfer rates to see that these institutions do not profoundly engage CCC—and I'll bet that is the case right now as I write this and for decades after this is published.

However, right now, I want to focus on those of Us who enter the graduate level.

We know how the system thinks. We have become experts on them. We have been rewarded to not be an expert on Us. As such, we will conduct research coded for them. We will gamble and invest in academic capital. The odds are against Us.

However, some scholars also invest in CCC. They are Cultivating CCC through their academic pursuits. I would argue doing so mitigates their personal risk if they are not rewarded as they see fit by the university system. Additionally, that funneling of work, energy, and resources can help Us reach The Tip of The Pyramid.

Now I'm going to be very specific and bring it back to the banning of Mexican American Studies.

I would not typically broadcast the findings of PhDs or scholars, even if I am fascinated by their work. I am thrilled and informed by the work of Pierre Bourdieu, but I do not cite him extensively. Typically, scholarly work is rubble, debris from The Level Playing Field that is discarded in the ivory tower. It moves on a parallel line that crawls up the ivory tower with little interaction with the outside world.

However, in The Pyramid of the fight against the MAS ban, the work of Dr. Nolan Cabrera from the University of Arizona and the team he led quantified the success of the outlawed curriculum. This scholarly evidence was conveyed via Our Media to other media. So here We have the rare occurrence where scholarly research in general, let alone from Our Community, makes it to radio, TV, print, social media, and then courts or legislatures.

Dr. Cabrera's work, as well as that of Dr. Angela Valenzuela, helped to move Us to that Tip of The Pyramid: overturning the racist ban. These scholars researched and wrote about CCC, including Dr. Valenzuela's book *Subtractive Schooling: U.S.-Mexican Youth and the Politics of Caring*, which featured findings about the education of Houston Raza Youth. This scholarship was also cited in court as evidence to overturn the racist Arizona law.

Of course, We need CAs to receive PhDs. CAs Cultivate links to CCC.

There were many lists circulating of the Books banned by the AZ politicians. They were fine, but they did not gain steam on their own. Chicana activist Elaine Romero, PhD, created an annotated bibliography of the outlawed curriculum and that registered with more professors, more students, more educators, and then more Community. That bibliography is included on the Librotraficante website and in the resources listed in this Book.

Claire Massey PhD, aka Librotraficante La Gringa earned her PhD in Germany and wrote her dissertation on The Librotraficante Caravan. She tweeted the following:

> the Librotraficantes seek to develop connections often neglected in the telling of the Civil Rights Movement; bridges built yet often rendered invisible in media representations of twenty-first century social protest against nativism, anti-immigration, and police brutality…

NP alum poet Icess Fernandez, aka Librotraficante La Chapina Cubana earned her MFA as part of the NP MFA Initiative. She is Afro Latina, bilingual, Cuban and Guatemalan, teaches Mexican American Studies in college, and created a directory of Mexican American writers as a resource for educators.

Stay in school, kids. Get that parchment and smash borders.

As Librotraficantes, We build The Pyramid via broadcasts: Media that is tuned into to Our Gente's Hearts, Imaginations, Visions. The corporate world reduces all of Us to simple terms. They see Our Work, Our Art shatter barriers, tear up The Level Playing Field. Our packages, segments, Voices appear on corporate media after rising through indy media, social media, grassroots campaigns. corporate media constrict prose to copy for thirty-second packages. We expand. Our Messages transmit. We inspire Others, so they will unearth more and more about Us. We are broadcasting The Tip of The Pyramid to more of Our Community.

Mainstream news hears only part of the message. They only see Us as dots on their demographic and ratings charts. They constrict language into the kings corporate english. We broadcast contraband prose that defies their Cultural Border Patrol. Our Words, like Our Art, like the Books the oppressors burn, also transmit Our People's History, Culture, Visions, Hopes. We also inform Others about the other ways to build toward The Tip of The Pyramid.

In the case of the modern Texas fight for Mexican American Studies, which the Texas State Board of Education first endorsed in 2019, one arm of The Pyramid was an updated version of the plan We developed during the fight in Arizona. In this style of campaign, the other two sides of The Pyramid are evidence, especially scholarly research, and then the government. In the case of AZ, that included the Ninth Circuit Court of Appeals. In Texas, this included The Texas State Board of Education. I write more about this specifically in the Quantifying CCC phase of this Series, with charts, and legal, media, scholarly, and Activist receipts. I provide only an overview right now.

I type this as the National Ethnic Studies Movement has been disappointed by both Democrat- and republican-elected officials. In California, a Democrat governor first vetoed a state-wide bill for Ethnic Studies. He finally signed the bill into law during a later legislative session. Yet, the latest version of the anti-Ethnic Studies and anti-Critical Thinking movement has stolen the headlines of corporate media with the latest version of its clickbait anti-intellectual campaign, so this news did not become household information discussed over dinner tables across the nation.

Here in Texas, the republican lieutenant governor suffocated House Bill 1504, which passed the Texas House of Representatives. This bill, sponsored by Texas State Representative Christina Morales, would have made Mexican American History and African American History count towards high school graduation requirements in Texas high schools. It was unanimously voted for in the Texas House of Representatives Special Education Committee. It was supported by both republicans and Democrats and even had a republican State Representative as co-author. It also passed the Texas Senate Education Committee. I thought it would receive enough votes from both parties to pass out of the Texas Senate and then head to the tx governor's desk.

That was not to be.

The republican lt. gov killed the bill. That body is rigged so that only he decides. After that, the tx governor called a special session to force the body to pass voter suppression laws, a bill to allow gun purchases without licenses, and anti-Critical Race Theory bills that will AGAIN constrict critical thinking and Our Community's History and Culture—and then passed the law that torpedoed Roe v. Wade, among a slew of even MORE repressive laws. It's clear that the republican governor will never sign HB 1504.

The National Ethnic Studies movement focused on political capital, and corporate politicos revealed their . . . limitations. That is the bad news.

Here is the good news.

We can count on only CCC to demand change.

This is Our Time.

I write this Book to not simply respond to another right-wing attack against Our Community.

I write this for more CAs to reveal.

I write this for more CAs to realize.

I write this to unite more CAs.

Our Words Were Often Attacked

Juan González, in his book *News for All The People: The Epic Story of Race and the American Media*, writes about how Spanish language newspapers in Texas were burned down for publishing pieces the white establishment disapproved of.

There have been waves of "english-only" campaigns to undermine Our cultural asset of speaking more than one language.

You can, of course, link this to the anti-immigrant, anti-Mexican, and anti-Mexican American campaigns that led to Arizona's "show me your papers" law and their banning of Mexican American Studies.

Closer to home, I know writers who have been subjected to court over their writing. In the late 1980s Chicana poet and writer Demetria Martinez was put on trial for her writing during the government's attack on the Sanctuary Movement in . . . Tucson. She is a friend and activist ally, working with the Librotraficante Under Ground Library at the Jardines Institute in ABQ.

Curtis Acosta, one of the founders of the prohibited MAS curriculum at TUSD, was grilled during the final series of hearings overturning the MAS ban at the Arizona Supreme Court. Arizona lawyers attacked him on the stand for reading in public a poem he wrote in which he called Arizona officials names and chided them. It was unpublished; he did not read it in class as a teacher.

Librotraficantes have the imagination, skill, and audacity because We are in tune with Our Community and link the base of CCC with The Tip of The Pyramid. We also create forums, platforms, events, works, writings, Art to convey and instruct and edify.

I knew Dr. Angela Valenzuela when she taught at Rice University in Houston, Texas. That is an expensive private institution, with hedges and policies to keep out Community. As I write this, I know two of the six tenured Latinos on the staff. Both are dear friends, Dr. José Aranda and Dr. Richard Tapia, who are both Chicano. Jose is on the board of the nonprofit version of Nuestra Palabra: Latino Writers Having Their Say. I am also good friends with David Medina, also Chicano, who works in Rice's marketing department. I serve with him on the Mayor's Hispanic Advisory Board. He is co-chair for the Art Committee, which I founded.

I just recently had lunch with Dr. Valenzuela when We both testified at the Texas House of Representatives Public Education Committee hearings for Texas House Bill 1504. Before she wrote the book that would help overthrow Arizona's racist ban, Dr. Valenzuela was denied tenure at Rice University. Her official credentials, which she has earned:

Dr. Angela Valenzuela is a professor in both the Educational Policy and Planning Program Area within the Department of Educational Administration and the Cultural Studies in Education Program within the Department of Curriculum & Instruction at the University of Texas at Austin.

Yet her research was considered rubble by Rice University.

She did receive tenure at the University of Texas, in acknowledgement of her research. Of course, as mentioned, UT at Austin is also the subject of a report where the Latinx tenured professors Quantified how they are underpaid and unfairly worked.

This provides a glimpse of the number of risks there are in investing in academic capital.

Thus, as Librotraficantes, it is wise to invest in Cultivating CCC along the way.

Here, if this were just a book to Quantify Our Community for those who are illiterate and frankly want to stay as such about Us, I would stick to the numbers, these dots on the graph of "diversity" for a corporate university striving to gain enrollment from students with Spanish surnames to satisfy the boxes on policies, institutional grants, or "progressive" credentials. Instead, I will point out it is better and more thrilling to profoundly invest in CCC.

In the case of scholars who break their connection with Community, they learn the academic rules and then become experts about them. They are lured further and further into the silos of the ivory tower. CAs figure out the rules of The Level Playing Field of Education, too, which are pretty easy. Then they devise a way forward, work hard within the ivory tower while also Cultivating CCC and working to link the Community and the academy.

Cultural Acceleration occurs when a CA moves CCC toward The Tip of The Pyramid on The Level Playing Field. But every second on that ride is based on years of work in the Community.

Fireworks On The Level Playing Field

We pay the price of admission with Our skin.

The price is set on Our back. We make minimum wage to work The Level Playing Field. We hold up the entire structure. We break Our backs raising the rafters, pounding the nails, planting the sod. We fight to make minimum wage and are thrilled with time and a half for overtime as We construct the seats We will never occupy.

And when We do appear on the field, We have paid for it with Our youth, Our health, Our mind, Our imagination. And then, We are asked to pay for it with Our CCC.

There are other costs to being the meteor of Cultural Acceleration.

This is not to discourage you. This is to prepare you. This Book creates the bridge between Cultural Acceleration and Cultivating CCC.

No one pays you for this.

And you don't want a corporate sponsor.

Yes, folks donate time, in-kind as they are kind enough to donate food, books; some folks make monetary donations.

But you will not be paid direct capital for this. Most likely you'll spend your own money. And you're consuming up hours that you would spend working hourly or for a salary.

We're not talking about a weekend.

Fourteen years is a grind. I founded Nuestra Palabra in 1998. The Librotraficante Caravan first rode in 2012. I'm writing this book in 2022.

Yeah. It is thrilling to Accelerate CCC. And, after years of seeing your People ignored, exploited, punished, it's badass to see Them rise.

That does not happen without fourteen years of work—for starters.

The writers you meet and know are despite years of college.

Every second of Cultural Acceleration builds on years of Cultivating CCC. Few know that. Most don't appreciate it. And even after you thrill millions on The Level Playing Field of corporate and national media, We are still not considered experts—about anything, let alone experts about Ourselves.

This expertise is hard to unearth.

A bachelor's degree takes four years of school. An MFA takes an additional three years. Some candidates hide and milk it for five years.

Most students in the US won't read any works written by or about Mexican Americans or Latinos in that time. Some might read one or two if they are lucky. They might meet one Latino writer one of those years who is visiting the campus—during Hispanic Heritage Month.

I'm always ready to speak in public. And I'm great at it because I have decades of practice. That's one of those corporate english sentences that I have to break down. 'Cause for Chicanos, We hate braggarts, especially Chicanos bragging. But as a Chicano, when I interact with corporate folks, esp. non-Latinx corporate corps, all they do is brag, even if it is in their lingo.

We have to talk Ourselves up, which We are taught not to do as little kids. But if We don't, no one else will.

Most Americans can't name five Latino writers, let alone humanize decades of Latino Art and Culture that We don't "find"—we Cultivate. That means Americans can't imagine twenty or thirty years of grinding work in the Latino Art Field. Of course, it ain't as hard as picking alfalfa in a field like my mom and dad used to do. So I have to be grateful that I'm not breaking my back as I rack my brain.

I have been in front of an audience one to three hundred times a year, since 1998.

This means readings of poets and writers ranging from nationally published novelists to an abuelita who wrote a poem on the drive over.

This also means driving an hour for a "literature" talk at a League of United Latin American Citizens (LULAC) meeting in a restaurant, or a patio, or a bar. Ya show up and maybe most of the folks have no idea you were showing up, for folks who are not the intended audience for the books you read in graduate school, in a garage or basement. You have a few minutes to summon the words, images, narrative to reveal the frequency that turns them into your intended audience.

Do I add every class I have taught, in person, to this list of public speaking events? 'Cause I don't play when I teach. I perform.

And, every week I host Our radio show Nuestra Palabra: Latino Writers Having Their Say. We have a badass team of volunteers: Rodrigo Bravo, who mixes Our sounds; Bryan Parras, aka Librotraficante HighTech Aztec, aka Music Director Emeritus, who helps Us pick tunes; Roxana Guzman, who develops Our multi-platform broadcasts on social media and streaming. Marc-Antony Piñón, who creates Our graphics. Liana Lopez, aka Librotrafciante Lilo and Producer Emeritus, who inspires Our research; Leti Lopez, who shapes Our infrastructure; Lupe Mendez, aka Librotraficante Lips Mendez, co-host Emeritus; and Laura Razo, aka Librotraficante La Laura, Education Consultant Emeritus—and there are even more volunteers who have put in under a decade. We each put in so many hours a week preparing for the one hour broadcast of Nuestra Palabra: Latino Writers Having Their Say.

Do We add all the hours We spend reading the Books of the poets and writers We interview, the music of the musicians, the research on visual and performing artists?

In order to squeeze Ourselves into the radio, We have to get used to people saying Our name wrong. In corporate english folks keep demoting Nuestra Palabra: Latino Writers Having Their Say to just a reading series, just a radio show.

We are a Movement.

That's cool, tho. No hate. Call Us by the slice of Us that caught your attention, the last thing ya heard about Us, and let's see how We occupy your imagination and then grow.

Then add how folks pronounce and define poetry with a corporate english accent. They prefer not to believe poetry and politics are synonyms.

So We added another radio show. Another. Radio. Show: Latino Politics and News. Don't double the effort, multiply exponentially. And, if this was a Book in the Quantifying CCC portion of this Series, I would explain all the differences, similarities, nuances. But this is not.

In a city, state, and nation that says there are no Latino writers, We find them every week. And We grow them. And just as folks think they have figured Us out, We burst into a harvest they never imagined.

Political parties and politicians seek out these skills.

corporate media seeks out these skills.

corporate education seeks out these skills.

To profoundly succeed the grind of decades of free work in a society that values only work that generates money, even if it is only minimum wage, you must get used to a pace that slowly Cultivates CCC.

And then you experience the roller coaster of Cultural Acceleration.

We are born translators. We can shape Our Story for corporate media to understand enough to convey, to reach more people, to move Our Community towards The Tip of The Pyramid.

A Movement flows as a group. corporate media reduces you to one person.

corporate media also overlooks. I've had to argue with some corporate media broadcasters who claimed that Arizona officials were not banning books.

They argue there is no book ban; you become a lawyer for the Books. Others claim Our Movement is only marketing. You have seconds to argue these points. Believe it or not, this is progress since others ignore the issue entirely, as the industry ignores Our Art, History, and Culture. They become apologists for the anti-Ethnic Studies Movement. They are not defying as vociferously the erasure of Our Art, Culture, History.

They relent.

And the next moment, corporate media casts you broadly, and breakfast will never be the same again. Barrios busting borders and barriers boggles breakfast. It's hard to contain yourself once you have burst through the membranes that are the work of the understaffed, simple, and petty Cultural Border Patrol. But you have to slow down. There is no such thing as perpetual energy, but there are perpetual borders. Huevos rancheros, tortillas, and coffee at your home begin to taste slightly different, like a compromise.

Even if you are experienced conducting interviews, being interviewed on corporate tv is like a street fight with hosts paid to kidnap your message for their boss viewers. Even if you have a black belt, it's a blur, time is compressed and intensified; your body resorts to moves you've memorized as you also have to improvise. You have to swing, you have to strike, you have to land. You're fighting for language. You have to free language even as you communicate in the eighth grade-level corporate words media makes its dime on.

And then it's over. But it's not over. It's rising.

You go from not-existing to being the embodiment, for those viewers, of the entire Community, Culture, all Latinos, or whatever they call Us if they think of Us. They don't want to hear if that is right or wrong. They have their narrative they want to express, things they want to get off their chest.

There are some things We are just not ready for, that We as A Gente are not trained for.

As a writer, the ultimate experience is to sit, alone, think, read, and the best is to write. Essentially, We spend hours upon hours alone.

All the other activity I have described is with other folks. I happen to also be an extrovert, but few things get you ready for the joy, the intensity, the bursting of energy when Our Gente get together.

This began with hundreds of folks at the first NP showcase. As in hundreds of folks that Houston tried to tell Us did not exist. And you, as the person at the mic, as the founder, become the symbol of NP. For better or for worse, You are slammed with a wave of energy.

This increases when you are transmitted via radio, print, social media, live events, and then you add corporate tv.

And then you feel the power of television. You are in the spotlight.

Television viewers imagine it is heaven to be in the spotlight. But the spotlight freezes slices. It shines for a long time, for a lot of people, one small part, reduced for mass consumption. It deals in images first, quick. For Activists it is a curse to stand still for so long. For Artists it is death to trap words for so long. It is made for reducing, smaller, and smaller, to cast Us as broadly as possible, into the nooks and crannies of the American imagination.

Remember: Cultural Acceleration occurs when a CA moves CCC towards The Tip of The Pyramid on The Level Playing Field. But every second on that ride is forged by years of work in the Community.

If you make it look easy, folks forget you are an expert.

If you make it look too easy, your Own Gente think they can do what you do and do a better job.

You wish someone would sometimes, so you would not have to do this.

Of course, there are wonderful moments. You are in the midst of The Community. Writers, visual artists, scholars, intellectuals, Community members seek out NP, the Librotraficantes. It is great be appreciated. It is great to help others. It is great to learn from others and help others learn.

But there is more, way more.

Gaining their attention is powerful. Having them see Us, just you, is thrilling. Finally, We are seen, in you. You are We. But they see You.

Finally.

That is addictive. That is alluring. That is distracting.

For brief moments at a time, We are stars, over the life of the campaign—not all of Our lives, and not profoundly in their lives.

There are fans. That sounds nice, but fans is shorthand for fanatics. There are fans who are the opposite of the people who ignore Us. These folks pay too much attention to Us, while still dehumanizing Us, not quite imagining Us as persons.

You also get haters.

Haters send you emails, make phone calls, give you dirty looks, call shows when you are on the air. They leave racist messages. They say they want to fight you.

You will also have groupies. You will have volunteers. People will expect you to lead them, to tell what to do, to pay them, to pay attention to them if you can't pay them, to love them.

You will be envied. Those who look at you, can relate to you, will wonder why they were not picked. If they are spurned long enough or resent you enough because they suspect they could have been picked, they will begin to pick at you, drag you.

You will be second-guessed. You will be misunderstood. When that does not work, there will be a mini-movement that rides the coattails of your movement by simply being against you. That is how desperate We get. That is how the rulers set up the rules to work.

Fanatics say wonderful things about me. Haters say terrible things about me. I don't believe either.

I never feel unsafe. I know how to handle myself. I have a great Crew. I have a large crew. My wife reminds me this is also male privilege.

When I present to an audience, it is a performance. I give all my energy and then some. I revel in it. I feed off their energy. I cause more energy.

It is exhausting. And then you have the next event of three or four or five that day, with interviews in between with hours of driving, as Your Crew makes calls, talks to folks, rides social media to create news. The rest of Your Crew is as invested, as exhausted, but not in the limelight. Our Crew, Familia, is key. In the case of the

Librotraficante Caravan it was the other co-founders, Bryan Parras, Liana Lopez, Laura Razo, Lupe Mendez.

We have gone over Our game plan. We have talked extensively. Each of Us brings decades of experience to the table. Yes, We are a group. Yes, We are dealing with corporate media. Yes, I will lean into the spotlight. Yes, here are all of Our roles. We are a Team. On the bus, We convene as We did in Bryan's lving room, as We convened in the lobby of the KPFT lobby, as We did at the George R. Brown Convention Center, as We did at Talento Bilingue de Houston, as We did at the party hall of Chapultepec Restaurant.

We found out that Arizona banned Mexican American Studies through Nuestra Palabra: Latino Writers Having Their Say. NP provided the foundation to organize the 2012 Librotraficante Caravan. We organized a six-city caravan in eight weeks by Investing and Accelerating the Culture We had created through Nuestra Palabra: Latino Writers Having Their Say. There were other caravans, for other campaign, but for this specific caravan for this specific campaign, We were the only ones in the nation able to organize this. Just like the CCC in Tucson was the only site that could develop that brilliant Mexican American Studies curriculum they devised and conducted.

In the case of an emergency, you can count on families, friends, allies who you have met and developed relationships with over fourteen years. Counting on the generosity of strangers is risky. And they are not likely to commit to too much.

So, We have created that thing We have critiqued: an inner circle. We have made a deal with the devil. But the devil is also banning Our Art, History, and Culture.

We have a few moments to squeeze into the tube of corporate tv to Accelerate CCC towards The Tip of The Pyramid to contain AZ's racist ban of Our Art, History, and Culture. And We don't have time to explain to the others on the bus, to devise words We've forged over decades of working together, or to the folks who support Us at each spot, each new Librotraficante Under Ground Library, each Banned Book Bash. We must Act.

And then it is over.

Cultural Acceleration is short, sweet, but followed by the grind of Cultivating CCC.

Does it pay off? Of course, but not in cash only. And society is not structured to analyze this type of pay.

And then, when it's over, and you get the peace you were whining for, you see your car payment is late, your light bill is past due, your fridge is empty.

It makes your adrenaline hangover that much worse.

Your Cultural Acceleration is fireworks over The Level Playing Field. The day after, ripped, burned paper lies strewn in odd places, thin sticks with heads burned off. The bright morning that you knew would come dissipates any bursts, presides over the mess, the tiny flags of paper, the whiff of sulfur.

The day after is hard.

Are you alone? Are you spent? Where do you wake up? What do you eat? What do you do next? What have you left? What is in your future?

My wife, who was there for the launch of NP, Our massive Book Fairs, and the Librotraficante Caravan—all of it—tells me that is not right for me compare this feeling to post-partum depression. My body does not create actual life. But this figurative life still costs me. It is delivered, beautifully. And then, as must be the with something so beautiful, it is out of my hands.

The cost dawns on me. The risks come to fruition. The tiny gratitudes you expected, lost. Resentment grows in its place. The parochial world, mundane, banal world, exacts its revenge: late bills, missed payments, deadlines.

How much of you is consumed as you reach the high? How high do you get? Do you reach The Tip of The Pyramid?

Who is there for you when you come down? As you plateau, it will dawn on you that there is only one way to go after that. Do you lean in? Do you flap your arms? Do you burn more of yourself to squeeze one more glimmer?

Do you muster more of you to burn, to bask in the glare a moment more?

Whatever you do, your Cultural Acceleration evaporates. What is consumed is your Cultural Capital, your youth, your time, your energy, your family—their future?

Do you have kids? That's an entirely different Book, Activist Parents.

The costs in just dollars do not add up. You have to Quantify your own CCC before you step up, as your ride, so you can survive the steep plateaus.

Still, there is a bounty, not a scarcity. This nation teaches you, forces you, tricks you into not counting CCC. We must hack that rigged system for more Advanced Degrees earned in the classrooms of Our Community, Our Culture, Our Terms on Our Terms.

Oh, yeah—and aren't you supposed to be a writer? What fiction did you invent as you rode around smuggling books? How many words did you advance on a novel, a collection of short stories? Can you count the pages you did not make up as you invested your time in the Cause?

Back then, language could not rise to that task, to instruct, edify, educate. But now, ten years later, here is This Book.

Supremacy

Who has the power to create words?

In english, the power of this act is revealed by the metaphor of "coining a phrase." This is like printing money. We become intellectual mints.

Let's study a word We are working together to forge: BIPOC.

The word that this term seeks to be is still in its nascent stages, so it is currently known as an acronym that stands for Black, Indigenous, and People of Color. This word is a rational attempt to convey the desire of CAs to unite across the identity labels imposed on Us nationally, historically, officially.

This desire is beautiful.

It is also not how We Americans work.

Each letter represents a different group rewarded and taught to work within its own identity label for scholarships, jobs, political representation, and so on, in a system that finds its easier to deal with Us one group at a time if at all, each group in its lane, preferably with just a few appointed leaders.

That is the grammar of corporate english.

We CAs know We are more powerful Together, and when We define Our Community, We do not employ the Cultural Border Patrol. Community is expansive.

But, I am not writing a poem about this. I am writing about how We shape meaning.

So I'll get more basic, concrete.

*   *   *

The official press release read as follows:

On January 26, 2022, The BIPOC Art Network Fund (BANF) announced that 120 Greater Houston Area arts organizations and artist collectives serving Black, Latinx, Indigenous, Asian American, Pacific Islander, Middle Eastern and other important communities of color received a combined $2 million in grants from its inaugural round of funding!

The handsomely paid-for website for the BANF reveals Our leadership:

Sixto Wagan, Project Director; Patra Brannon-Isaac, Director of Education and Community Projects, Kinder Foundation; Bao-Long Chu, Senior Program Officer, Houston Endowment. Tony Diaz, Writer, Activist and Political Analyst. Adán Medrano, Chef, Food Writer and Filmmaker; Deidre Thomas, Senior Advisor, Mattison Advisors; Frances Valdez, Executive Director, Houston In Action; Kheli Willetts, Principal, Dira Professional Development.

This group resembled organizations I'd worked with previously, comprising Artists, Activists, Community Leaders—CAs who did not know they are CAs. But there were also some mind-blowing differences. I have never seen a board with this broad a spectrum of folks, from Grassroots Crews to more formal entities, including representatives from philanthropic organizations. The board is set up for the Community to outvote the formal.

And, as was never the case in the past, We had funding. Lots of funding.

Three years earlier, my 2019 State of Latinx Art Report about Houston detailed how a Latino Legacy nonprofit organization had folded. The fate of the Talento Bilingue de Houston Theater where the group was housed, an important structure in the Latino Art Ecosystem, was now up for grabs due to a historical lack of fair and sustainable funding.

Now, as We strove to recover from the COVID-19 shutdown and navigated its iterations, the organization BANF is born with $12.5 million in funding.

I'll explain this capital. As CAs, Artists, We must put into words, images, convey the changes We witness.

Things were so bad for Art in Our city, that every other large Texas city, *except* Houston possessed a new, state-of-the-art Latino Cultural Center. Our cultural centers were not new. MECA, Multicultural Education and Counseling for the Arts, founded by Alice Valdez in 1997, does brilliant work, but it is housed in a repurposed grammar school built in 1912. The TBH Theater building was repurposed in 1995 from an abandoned supermarket named Sams and was owned by the city, only operated by Latino Cultural Legacy Arts Groups—who never received the operating funds needed to operate.

After the advent of the George Floyd Era and just after the coronavirus shutdown, the Ford Foundation launched ACT, as defined by their website: "America's Cultural Treasures is a two-pronged national and regional initiative to acknowledge and honor the diversity of artistic expression and excellence in America and provide critical funding to organizations that have made a significant impact on America's cultural landscape, despite historically limited resources."

This is an example of corporate english with good intentions. However, this is also an example of abstract terms having to gain specific meaning in Segundo Barrio, on Navigation Avenue, 333 S. Jensen.

The website goes on to explain how funds from that campaign worked their way to Houston: "As the second component of America's Cultural Treasures, numerous foundations will drive fundraising and design for individually-tailored regional grantmaking initiatives, which will be seeded by an initial $35 million in support from the Ford Foundation."

Those millions were divided into different regions, with $5 million allocated to Houston Endowment, which is "a private foundation that partners with others in the nonprofit, public and private sectors to improve quality of life for the residents of greater Houston" that responded to the initial Ford Foundation ACT invitation. BANF Executive Director Sixto Wagan conveyed BANF in a presentation prepared for a Q & A session for potential applicants for an RFP. RFP is corporate english for Request For Proposal for a Developmental Evaluation Partner for the BIPOC Arts Network And Fund. (And now I have to explain what an Evaluation Partner is: We don't know yet. That will be more defined after We hire that crew for five years and invent new methods to convey the Work, Art, Culture We are guiding, which is also what I've been doing with this Book and Our Movement.)

> Houston Endowment engaged a coalition of local foundations to join in on ACT. BANF's current $12.4 M initiative also includes investments from Brown Foundation and Cullen Foundation who have historically supported the arts, The Powell Foundation who has supported arts education, and the Kinder Foundation who is new to arts-sector funding.

Here is more proof from the universe that We are CAs:

Houston Endowment has guided the work in Houston by placing the governance and leadership of BANF in the hands, hearts, and imaginations of The Community. I am proud to serve on the founding board. I see my role, as a CA, as infusing Our Work with the Imagination, Words, and Acts of the Community, to combine these funds with CCC to devise methods of Fair Exchanges of CCC to empower more and more People through Art, Culture, and History. Our Terms on Our Terms.

These are new manifestations for the tactics We have employed to navigate systems that ignored Us that now, all of a sudden, seem to be looking to Us. I'm thrilled because We, not just as BANF, but Our Generation of CAs, get to see how Our Art shapes cities.

I am typing this after We gave two million dollars to one hundred and twenty BIPOC Community Arts Groups in grants ranging from five to fifty thousand dollars. That equals one hundred and twenty facets of the definition of BIPOC, including The Ensemble Theatre, with its own building, founded in 1976 by the late George Hawkins to preserve African American artistic expression and enlighten, entertain and enrich a diverse Community; to Museo Guadalupe Aztlan, founded in March 1994 by Jesus Cantu Medel to promote indigenous folk art of the Americas, whose artifacts are stored in his home; to Sur Fest, founded by Pablo Devera in 2013, focusing on Rock en Español concerts showcasing South American bands, and one hundred and seventeen more profound facets of acronyms.

These groups also become part of Our larger discussion of how to employ the remaining money, and additional funds that will follow, to empower Community Art for the long run, to create more Culture, for the good of Community, Art, Philanthropy, The City, The Nation, The World.

Of course, this is not just about the money. Our Intellect, Wisdom, Knowledge, CCC must be Cultivated, along with any investments. Otherwise, there would be an adrenaline rush for one year or two, and then afterwards, We would be abandoned and back to the operating budgets that don't operate for Us.

Which is to say, We must infuse the capital with CCC. corporate english has a way of thwarting that. I return to the challenges posed in "AztecMuse: Preface on the Precipice." How do We shape words to speak clearly to people, yet defy the Cultural Border Patrol of corporate english?

Sixto was in charge of creating the portal for all grant applications, creating the nonprofit infrastructure, organizing the steering committee, hiring and directing the communications team, creating a panel of judges of Community Artists to review looming applications in conjunction with creating an advisory committee. At the same time, he still had to convey this work in terms that Our philanthropic funders understand. And We must convey this work in languages other than english.

The communications team tackled translating the grant application and then the press release announcing the grant opportunity into Spanish. As a member of the steering committee, as a Community organizer, I serve as the Spanish language spokesperson working with Trill, the Latinx-owned communications company We contracted. I am one of three Latinos on the steering committee. The others are Adán Medrano, who is a chef and writer, and Frances Valdez, who is a musician, lawyer, and the director of a nonprofit org. Adán and I navigate the translations.

We soon discovered, revealed, encountered a clear border of the kings english: We had a very difficult time perfectly translating the term BIPOC into Spanish. The easiest response is to simply literally translate word for word. This is typical of corporate english. The resulting words would be completely wrong.

CAs who delve into Identity are working on the equivalent of Multi Variable Calculus. Meanwhile corporate media is still on basic math—so a literal translation of corporate english into the kings spanish makes sense to corporate, and corporate only.

In reality, translating BIPOC from corporate english into corporate spanish is difficult because We are translating from a language that forged a direct caste system into a language that forged an indirect caste system, one that nonetheless encompassed the owning and commodifying of people.

Five hundred years ago as they crashed into the shores of Abya Yala, the spanish pirates were white people who subjugated Indigenous People of Color. kings of spain created their caste system to impose on the Indigenous Peoples in Abya Yala, whose land they stole, whose minerals they extracted, and whose bodies they put in chains.

Caste systems are simple. The king is supreme, at the top. Every other person is below. Those furthest down the caste run the risk of falling off the chart—which leads to dehumanization. The closer you are to the king, the more power and privileges you have. Indigenous Peoples were cast(e) at the bottom, so as to serve, in chains, at the risk of violence and starvation, those above them.

the kings and Indigenous People would never be on the same level, or caste.

This question is tangible every time Latinos fill out the US Census and must report their race. Do they identify as "Black" or "White"? The government's instructions are not very instructive. The 2020 Census form reads: "Note: Please answer BOTH Questions 6 about Hispanic origin and Question 7 about race. For this census, Hispanic origins are not races."

To further complicate this seemingly simple question, I will point out that through legal precedents We are a protected class. But I won't engage in the clickbait tactic of corporate media and cram over five hundred years of ignored History into five hundred words. For those who have sincere questions about Our Identity, they should read several books from the Mexican American Studies curriculum banned in Arizona. They should also read the chapter titled: "Legally White, Socially Brown" in the book *U.S. Latinos and Criminal Injustice (Latinos in the United States)* by Lupe Salinas, retired judge of the 351st Criminal District Court in Houston, Texas, a Professor of Law at Thurgood Marshall School of Law of Texas Southern University.

Our Community has to consider similar questions to understand the term BIPOC. There is not an "L" for Latinos or an "H" for Hispanics in the acronym.

As a Chicano, We are born Mexican American. We must choose to be Chicano. We study Our History, Art, and Culture. We know Our ancestors are Indigenous to Abya Yala from over five hundred years ago. I am at home in the "I" of "BIPOC" for my Indigenous roots, and I am proud to be Brown.

That's here in the US.

As We translate BIPOC into the kings spanish, We can't simply literally transpose all the History of an Indigenous identity from Mexico into the corporate english version of the word, which has its own issues in the USA. Add to that the Indigenous Histories of El Salvador, Guatemala, Chile, and other nations, and then add the facets of the Afro Latino experience for each of those nations—for starters.

America is illiterate about Latinos. Individual letters implode.

This leads giant corporations to do things like hire white folks from spain to fulfill their diversity goals on the southwest side of Houston, which a large majority of Central Americans call home, some of whom have Indigenous roots. If the true purpose of such programs is to empower and build Our CCC, hiring individuals who are illiterate to the struggles Our People will not achieve that.

The question remains, do We use language, or does language use Us?

Centers are figurative spots on your papers, points in your plan, a thesis statement. You can build your center and other forces will relegate it to the periphery of an orbit you missed, feared, or ignored altogether.

Centering is a metaphor. Metaphors are forced confessions. When they strike a chord, they reveal Our hearts, or they appease Our hearts, until the user agreement the metaphor signs is revealed. Call something the center all you want, shout it, pay for it. There is still another center over there, and over there, and over there.

America loves the idea of centering because it creates a fiction of order.

the kings english upholds the informal caste system of dethroned, decapitated kings—after all, this nation sprang forth from deposing a monarch. supremacists populate the caste castle around him, reviving the informal caste system with layers and layers of user agreements buried into perspectives and language.

corporate english aspires to fill the void of the headless monarch. The corp, after all, forms a body, a legal body. It has a head. It creates a center of power.

This is why CAs are vital to this era. We must liberate language to convey Us instead of letting corporate english limit all of Our imaginations, and therefore limit power. It is up to Us to change the default setting, to revise the user agreements that shape society.

I am on the board of BANF because I believe BANF will help Us.

By the way, I am a writer. You know this, all of this, because I am writing this. However, this is not the stuff of the corporate publishing world. In most circumstances, this Work would typically take time away from my precious writing. That's not the case for me. I live My Writing.

But you should be reminded that We do not have the luxury of only writing. We don't have the luxury of creating Art for Art's sake. And, of course, as We unite to render BIPOC, We have a lot of work to do with Our immediate Community.

I am also on the board of Advocates of a Latino Museum of Cultural and Visual Arts & Archive Complex in Houston, Harris County (ALMAAHH). I wrote their grant that, in 2020, was awarded $1 million from Houston Endowment to plan, over the course of two years, to create a Latino Arts Complex that is fueled by and also sustains Houston's entire Latino Art Ecosystem. The first funds We received were through the help of City Council District H representative Karla Cisneros for $40,000. City councilman of District I Robert Gallegos followed with $110,000 in funding. Additionally, 2021's Cien Latinos por la Cultura consisted of one hundred Latinos who donated $1,000 each to raise $100,000. The co-chairs for the initiative were lawyer Wendy Montoya Cloonan, who served as a Port Commissioner on the Port of Houston Authority Port Commission, and Paula Mendoza, CEO of Possible Missions, Inc., former University of Houston System Board of Regents.

The advocates in ALMAAHH span a similar range of folks, but this time focused on the Latino Community, business folks, activists, artists, CEO's, nonprofit directors, Democratic, Republican, Socialists, entrepreneurs, former elected officials. They are:

Geraldina Interiano Wise, Board Chair; David Contreras, Treasurer; Norma Torres Mendoza, Secretary; and board members Sofia Adrogué, Nory Angel, myself, Tony Diaz, former Texas Supreme Court Justice David M. Medina, Massey Villarreal, and emeritus members Dr. Dorothy Caram and Nelly Fraga.

Because I have been writing the Annual State of Latinx Art Report in Houston since 2018, I know that ALMAAHH was born with the largest operating budget for any Latinx-run Arts nonprofit, ever. This is a big deal, but should not be because the number is actually low.

In a city of over two million people that is at least 45% Latino, MECA previously had the largest operating budget at just over $1 million. Other non-Latinx arts nonprofits needed budgets of $3 million and above to work at their full capacity. This is not just a challenge for the Latino Arts Community. Proof that the nonprofit racket is not built for Us is the fact that even the non-art-related Hispanic Chamber of Commerce, whose president and CEO is Dr. Laura Murillo, reported an income of about three million dollars. Of course, both of these organizations possess large amounts of Cultural Capital. MECA is one of the few Legacy Latinx Arts Orgs that owns its building, but that does not count towards operating budget figures when grants are doled out. And of course, the Hispanic Chamber of Commerce has a massive economic impact with its annual report on Latino buying power, its access to Latino professionals, and all of its media resources.

As a board member of ALMAAHH, I see my role as guiding the group's language to document the Latinx Art Ecosystem, to de-center fundraising so that We seek sustainable and equitable funding, devise Fair Exchanges of CCC, and create new ways to deliver Art to Our Community. De-centering means ceasing to imagine the Latino Community as just the two legacy Mexican American Houston City Council districts of District H and I, which are both over 70% Latino in population. The last Census revealed that every Houston City Council District is Latino. The lowest Latino representation is in City Council District G, which is 20% Latino—in other words, one out of every five residents there is Latino. And the numbers just go up from there.

Also, We have to de-center because if ALMAAHH follows the old pattern of opening merely a center, funding will drift to it instead of MECA or TBH and the other smaller Latinx Nonprofits. No: We must pool Our genius to humanize Our Community and to convey Our CCC, to Cultivate CCC, and to Quantify CCC for fair and sustainable funding for an abundance of organizations.

Lastly, We must not build just a big, square box and try to shape Our Gente to fit into the box.

These approaches touch on some of the issues that CAs have brought up, but which can evaporate in a haze of corporate english or spanish. Now, We must document them transparently in order to build on them, and We must unearth the Art, History, and Culture of Our People.

Yes, capital is important, but is also not enough in and of itself. Just as importantly, Houston Endowment is investing in Our CCC, Our Intellect. They had never previously invested a million dollars in a plan for any group. And Our Community has not had the chance to address issues about Our Art, History, and Culture, let alone have a place to store those answers.

Perhaps the AztecMuse has found a home: the new, state-of-the-art Latino Arts Complex in Houston, Texas, that will be built with CCC to empower the city's Latino Art Ecosystem.

It is powerful to see Us Unite to shape Our City, Our Communities. Finding the Frequency of the next Tip of The Pyramid is a process that is organic to a time, a place, a People. Perhaps, for this era, rendering the perfect metaphor for BIPOC is Our next Tip of The Pyramid?

Bao-Long Chu is a poet. I met him at the UH CWP. He is the first Vietnamese American poet to earn an MFA from the program. For that to occur during the same time that I became the first Chicano to earn an MFA from the UH CWP reveals that there was probably a corporate diversity program in effect. People in the ivory tower with power moved bricks to help Us, allow Us, pull Us, imagine Us through. Someone invested in Us. I was paid to leave Chicago: a scholarship, a fellowship, a stipend, a post as a teaching assistant, and I occupied a slot that other writers coveted.

There were no strings or parachutes attached. Neither the institution nor I quite knew how to act with each other. I didn't know who to blame for all the injustices surrounding the ivory tower. But I got to roam its halls. I thank all those who paved the way for me by paying it forward. That younger version of me was looking for the folks who kept others like me out. Older now, I realize there are many who want Our Communities to succeed.

Long now works for Houston Endowment. He is also on the board of BANF. We have graduated from workshopping poems to workshopping cities.

Our Crew will devise the potent metaphor, a new term that conveys Our desire to melt borders and Unite the Houston Art ecosystem across boundaries: Plur.

That is what AztecMuse demands. It will occur on Our Watch, and Our generation will yet again reach a Tip of The Pyramid so long elusive.

*   *   *

Other CAs warn me that instead of profound assistance, the surge of support from mainstream philanthropists marks only that We are in the Latino Decade. I say if We are "the flavor of the decade," then We have to advance fifty years towards The Tip of The Pyramid during those ten.

Ten years ago, Our Crew was on a bus delivering contraband prose to Librotraficante Under Ground Libraries. In the decade after that, We continued to invest in CCC, Reading, Writing, Thinking. We grow into spaces, partnerships, and conversations previously unimagined.

We are the translators.

It would be pleasant, perhaps, to sit back. To organize this way. Sign user agreement after user agreement to attempt to ring in this latest attempt at equity and sustainability. And if I, myself, did give in, to rest, We would have still made gains. These papers have engendered more. We are farther along . . . some path.

That sounds nice.

That's because corporate english casts spells. It builds ivory towers that are easy to enjoy. It turns mundane tasks into well-paying jobs, with guaranteed vacations. It leads to folks specializing in tasks that typically drown Community Organizers. In a room, on a high floor, with a view of the city, with snacks and validated parking, corporate english casts the spell that perhaps you have contained social ills to your fine sheets of paper. They can be fixed from there, the center of the universe.

No.

There's the illusion that on any given Tuesday, especially a beautiful afternoon, with the right twelve people in the room, maybe thirteen, you can sentence social ills to paper. Meanwhile, down there in that view obscured by distance are so many people who will never walk into that room, sit at that table. The base of The Pyramid could never fit into one room of the ivory tower. There's not one clever meeting that can deliver the voice of the people.

On a nice Tuesday afternoon, after great conversational synergy with polite, smart people, you might sign the user agreement that erases a Community.

This is how corporate english works.

There is the threat of a hidden agreement in the term BIPOC, if carelessly deployed: the collapse of the experiences of many into one, vaguely defined signifier; a view that maintains the supremacy of the kings whiteness as filtered through the perspective of the kings english. The corporate body, corporate english, the wonderful view from twenty-three floors up.

We as CAs must translate the needs of Our Gente again, and again. The Tip of The Pyramid begins with the people you look down on from the thirtieth floor of the ivory tower.

CAs must again immerse themselves into that view with these ideas. The way to do this can't be reduced to one sentence or one marketing campaign; it cannot be reduced to a dot on a corporate graph for profit forecasts, investment, diversity.

Here is what it starts to mean on the ground.

Nuestra Palabra is a Movement. But, We also had to get Our papers. NP is a 501(c)(3) nonprofit; however, because the nonprofit system was created by folks who are illiterate about Us, the forms do not form profoundly around Us. We discovered this quickly and began shattering the established forms for conveying Art, Culture, and History. This led to Our monthly literary showcases in a city where no one thought Our Gente appreciated lit or had stories to tell. This led to Our massive Latino Book and Family Festival, creating the largest Book Fairs in the city where book deserts ensconce Our Communities. These events were built on CCC and a lil capital. We organized $300,000 book fairs with $30,000 and a lot of CCC. We figured, having proven Ourselves, We would begin to receive funding from the city, state, nation.

However, We soon realized that the nonprofit sector was a racket. One quick reason is that typically, large philanthropic orgs and governmental arts funding orgs give grants based on a nonprofit's operating budget the previous year. This is an artistic poll tax. Our Community is not built for that game. That system does not count CCC. NP decided to invest in more CCC instead of chasing capital.

This included keeping Our annual budget under $50,000. If a nonprofit org makes less than $50,000 for its operating budget, it can fill out a short form for taxes annually which consists of a postcard. If a group raises more than $50K, it needs to fill out a more complicated form, and then things get more and more complicated. This demands more accounting work and less Art and Community Work. This forces more attention to numbers than people.

However, with the inception of BANF, We have re-calibrated. And I will break down some details, in order to demonstrate how corporate english must be shaped to cultivate CCC.

The BANF board had to vote to decide if NP could apply for a BANF grant as a nonprofit even though I sat on the board. The board unanimously voted that NP could apply. Thus, NP was not punished for my expertise.

Nuestra Palabra leaned into the mission of BANF. As such, We were ready to exceed Our $50K cap on Our operating budget.

Mainstream funders often resort to cliché by asking, "Why don't those small, underfunded groups just work together?" The answer is that working together takes money, just as any work takes money. And most of Our Crews are fighting for survival on Their own.

But now, NP also will serve as a fiscal sponsor for Community Arts Collectives who could not apply without an umbrella group, an established 501(c)(3). We were fiscal sponsors for eleven other collectives.

Again, the spell of corporate english conveys completion; it conveys the illusion of something concrete. Here is what the above sentences leave out:

The Latinx Art Collectives that applied through NP would never have applied had I not known them, worked with them, if they did not trust me and I did not trust them. That is how traumatized Our Community is from being ignored, erased, co-opted by the corporate, nonprofit system of funding.

BANF funded Our groups, and now the NP budget is boosted, not just through further grants, but also with BANF and its funders as resources for questions about tax issues, development, etc. NP will work with each group under Our umbrella to determine the best paths forward as individual Artists, Collectives, Nonprofits, or what other forms and services might serve Us best. In theory, that is the larger question that BANF will tackle: How can all of Us, as BIPOC Community Art Groups, work Together, with the rest of BANF funds, with Our funding partners, with Houston at large, to create and sustain more Art and Culture?

How close can We get to creating new structures? Rendering BIPOC plays a role in that.

Can BANF do that in five years?

Of course not. But We can go a long way in framing questions and possible answers that have so far defied Our Community.

NP and The Librotraficantes are Accelerating CCC with Our new Partners and always with Our Community.

With the BANF funds, NP is now edifying new chapters in every Houston City Council District, building Our multiplatform broadcasts to reach the upcoming NP chapters in every state of the union.

But don't get too happy.

As We ponder large, intellectual questions and disperse larger-than-ever funding allotments, We are under attack yet again.

To the untrained eye, their attack is new. We Librotraficantes recognize their old tricks. They are ancient. They have been updated. Their latest movement has been built for corporate media and the algorithms of social media.

corporate media has branded this iteration of their movement as anti-Critical Race Theory. That branding is perfect for corporate media, because the name is illogical: Critical Race Theory is an established field of study, in which some scholars have written about The Librotraficantes. It's typically taught in graduate school. There are no graduate school courses crossing the border into high school or kindergarten, unfortunately. That would be quite an influx of knowledge.

The more accurate name for the updated anti-Ethnic Studies movement would be the anti-Black Lives Matter movement because their campaign was created to stifle the success of BLM and to stifle the gains made during the George Floyd Era, when America was more deeply addressing structural discrimination. Civil War monuments were coming down.

This anti-reason campaign is also in response to the success of Our Ethnic Studies Movement.

At the peak of The Modern Ethnic Studies Movement, not only did We Unite to school right wing AZ republicans; Our fight fueled constant news about specific school districts across the nation implementing Ethnic Studies as a required course, universities requiring Ethnic Studies to graduate, even states passing laws implementing Ethnic Studies.

All that work was relegated to the sidelines and would not make news again once corporate media wrapped its ratings around and owned the new anti-reason, anti-intellectual, anti-Critical Thinking campaign instead.

As Culture Accelerators, We know not to respond to every single act that has evolved from this anti-intellectual campaign whose aim is distraction, disarray, dejection.

Instead, We're about to activate CCC to make sure that Our History and Culture are preserved and to make sure that Our Voices are edified.

We want to make sure Books get in the hands of the Community. Book banners will not dare ban Mexican American Studies again. They learned. Now they come after Our Brothers and Sisters who corporate marketing locks into their demographics that *other* Us.

This Book is part of a Movement. This Book morphs into an electronic version, into a live event, into remote events. This Book fuels more Voices which then define the Words in this Text. That is how language works. By day, lawyers contract language on the level court of The Level Playing Field. By night, poets liberate language among The People. La Raza. BIPOC.

I am writing ten years after an attack on Chicanos for reading Books. There are still many dangers. That perhaps indicates how powerful We have become. We survive the attacks. We address them. We thrive. We will unearth the metaphor that truly rings in Our Unity—and I trust that the Community Poet who does not yet know she is a poet is already shaping that name.

Every ivory tower is raised on Our razed temples, the rubble of Our Community Cultural Capital.

Do Not Mistake This For A Book Tour

A Book does not come to paper to die. It comes to thrive.

This Book is The Tip of The Pyramid.

CCC is the base.

The Tour for this Book will link the Tip to the Base.

On the tenth anniversary of the 2012 Librotraficante Caravan to smuggle back into Tucson the books banned by Arizona right wing republican legislators, We will follow that same route and visit anew the cities that form that legacy of Our Community's Literary Legacy in the Southwest.

You can track that path by visiting www.Librotraficante.com and clicking on "2012 Caravan." That outlines the outposts in Book deserts where Our Gente created places to showcase Our CCC from Houston, to San Antonio, to El Paso, to Mesilla, to ABQ, to Tucson, across the borders of Texas, New Mexico, and Arizona. And Our Cultura runs even deeper than that.

We will visit the Librotraficante Under Ground Libraries We established and replenish them.

I will launch this Book that breaks down for CAs how to Cultivate CCC. We will dramatize the work by promoting an anniversary, a Book, a Book Tour, a reading, a nonprofit, America to CCC.

Each Under Ground Library is a Book Oasis in a Book desert. Our Terms on Our Terms.

I flow from the prose in this Book, but I won't read alone. As before, We will spread the voices of the over eighty authors whose works were part of the Gold Standard for Ethnic Studies—the original Mexican American Studies curriculum banned by Arizona legislators.

And of course, as always, We will build on the foundation, unleashing readers' Librotraficante to engender an army of Poets, Writers, Intellectuals. This time The Tip of The Pyramid will be to create a national Voice for Writers from Our Community. At this time, there is not one.

We will launch a chapter of Nuestra Palabra: Latino Writers Having Their Say at each stop, each point on this new mapping of Our Literary Capital.

On the tenth anniversary of the Librotraficante Caravan, I will read from this Book at the sites We first visited.

Writers will read from the Books banned by Arizona legislators.

On the twenty-fourth anniversary of Nuestra Palabra: Latino Writers Having Their Say, new members of the new chapters of Nuestra Palabra, writers from the Community, will make their debut as We first did, unleashing Librotraficantes in the party hall of Chapultepec Restaurant in the Book desert of Houston, Texas in April of 1998, where We were told by one Texan after the other that We did not exist, that We did not have a voice to share or even interest in reading or writing. We are honored to have proven them wrong.

We will feature these new voices on the Nuestra Palabra Radio Show. Each chapter will have air time to showcase their writers. Voices from Tucson will share with The Gente of Houston, San Antonio, ABQ, Messilla, El Paso, Houston, the original stops for the 2012 Librotraficante Caravan. We will also broadcast Our radio show in other cities, too, and of course, as always, being the High Tech Aztecs that We are, We will use other platforms and networks to edify the Palabra of Our Gente. And of course, We are happy to work with any group, organization, or entity who respects Our CCCl with a Fair Exchange of CCCl. We will not tolerate colonizing, co-opting, oppressing, etc.

The new voices from the new cities in Our network will convene with Us remotely, via their Lit, and on Our radio show, where We will interview their leaders, their writers, their inspirations, their familias. And then We will visit them.

On the twenty-fifth anniversary of Nuestra Palabra: Latino Writers Having Their Say, We will return to replenish and bolster those new chapters as We launch the NP Anthology, marking the Renaissance of Our Community with even larger live readings, bolstering Our Community, Our Under Ground Libraries, the Book.

We will ring in the Renaissance with Our Books.

Let's make this clear. This is a rebirth, a Renaissance.

We did experience a death.

During Our lifetime, Our History, Culture, Literature were banned.

But We united to defy and overturn that oppression.

And now, We have united to free Our Voice.

My family had been chasing El Norte all their lives and always winding up on the South Side of El Norte.

You Want Real Life?

This morning I am typing this instead of what I wanted to type for this Book.

I was supposed to read through the second half of what you are reading right now.

Will this make it into the Book?

Will I finish the Book on time?

There is no timeline, but there is a timeline.

If I don't complete this Book in time, it will not be published by March 2022, the ten year anniversary of the Librotraficante Caravan.

Does it matter?

Does anything matter?

What could possibly throw my day, this Book, into upheaval? So much oppression, so little time.

It turns out the hearing for Texas House Bill 1504, the Texas Ethnic Studies Bill that will make Ethnic Studies count toward high school graduation is scheduled for tomorrow morning, Tuesday, April 6, 2021, after the Easter holiday weekend. No one is still answering phones at The Texas Capital to let me know how to tell people to testify.

State Representative Christina Morales's office has shared with me that We must prioritize in-person testimony, as online, remote testimony is complicated and challenging. This is Texas Code for "We don't want you foos testifying!"

Does this stay in the Book?

Do I finish the Book?

Of course, I will finish the Book. There is no scenario where I can tolerate any other reality. But as I type more, I know it will hurt more to reach the finish line. More work, more pressure, less sleep, more upheaval, more diving in. This is the life of a Mexican. Some of Us do it to survive, some to thrive. Some of Us do this to put food on the table. I have the privilege of doing this to change policy. This is what my father wanted. He broke his back all day, would go home and tell me he did that so I could work hard using my mind. Here you go, Dad.

I just got off the phone with Dr. Christopher Carmona, Chair of the K-12 Education Committee of the National Association for Chicana and Chicano Studies Tejas (NACCS Tejas) Foco, one of the other organizations that has helped to organize to spread Ethnic Studies through the tropes of academic capital, and Dr. Angela Valenzuela, whose research has paved the way for Ethnic Studies. She testified at the Arizona Supreme Court and shoved a dagger deep into the racist ban of Mexican American Studies. The dates We originally had for testimony were mixed up. Thanks, short notice.

I'm setting up a press conference in front of the south entrance to the capital, which I will find out is closed down due to COVID-19. Dr. Valenzuela plans to attend the press conference. She lives in Austin. She has to juggle class and preparing for a lecture she will give. I join her for lunch after still on the adrenaline rush from testifying before the Texas House of Representatives Public Education Committee regarding HB 1504, with two of her graduate students who testified and Lucero Saldana, a Community organizer and educational consultant who has been part of Our cause in Tejas since she was an undergraduate. We rocked the House.

Dr. Carmona can't attend. He lives in the Rio Grande Valley. He is preparing a press release to send to his media list for Our coalition and to Our network in the NACCS Tejas Foco.

I ask them to be part of a Facebook livestream tonight, as in a few hours from when I'm typing this. We can then give people the heads up about tomorrow. I will set up using Streamyard, which makes a Facebook Live broadcast look better than a corporate news broadcast.

I called Rep. Morales to see if she can be part of the FB Live broadcast. She will be driving back to Houston from Austin and suspects she can be part of it at 6:30 p.m. I list her as tentatively attending. I don't ask her about the fact that she will then have to drive back to Austin tomorrow morning, 6 a.m. at the latest.

We set up the press conference at 9:30 a.m. to fit her schedule. She will be on the Texas legislative floor at 10 a.m. This means she and the Rainbow Coalition of co-signers, State Representatives Gene Wu and Alma Allen, will have just enough time to say a few words then get to their committees.

I am pausing to write this, and think.

I am not looking forward to writing the email blast. I resent that it is taking time away from writing the Book. But I point out to myself that . . . well . . . this is what the Book is actually about . . .

I also only have this shot right now. I don't like to look back and regret. I never do. So I know I must do this right now. I will create the newsletter content and then send it Our list to reach over twenty thousand people. I already created and sent the press release to Our media list, created the FB event for the press conference, and posted info from and about both on the webpage I built previously.

I also posted on Facebook, Instagram, LinkedIn, and Twitter.

I have a call to one of Our interns, Gabriela Vasquez, who I will train at 2 p.m. today to follow up and call media for coverage tomorrow.

I am also about to fill out the forms for a personal day from the college, as I don't want haters to accuse me of lobbying on state time or money. Of course, I am not a registered lobbyist, and this is not for a candidate running for office, but haters are gonna hate.

I write this to also remind you that as activists no matter how badass you may be there are only so many minutes in an hour, and only so many hours in day. You have to pick.

I will not miss my deadline.

This bill will pass.

Each of these are lines drawn in the camino real.

All of these lines will vanish someday. Which lines do you follow, if any? Some of these lines you could not once see. There are long lines for some of these lines. Some are lonely.

No one owes me anything. I will not put my Book at risk. Of course, I won't write tomorrow either, not the stuff I was planning to write. But again, I would never complain that I did not finish the Book because of this. I won't blame anyone. There will be no resentment because I know I can do both. I know I can handle the pain, work, and stress to do both. And I have to. That is what the entire fucking Book is about. And I am blessed to have these problems.

Of course, I don't know if the bill will pass this May, as in before the ink dries on this Book. Or if it will pass in September of 2023 via the Texas State Board of Education. But I do know that this will come to pass. It will happen sooner than Our other policies have, and Our movement will be stronger because of it and this Book.

The Tip of The Pyramid shatters the calendar of The Level Playing Field. It will come to pass. In a month, a year, a decade, a lifetime, a generation, The Tip of The Pyramid will be achieved. And Our Generation is blessed to have reached several generational Tips of The Pyramid during Our lifetime.

Today, I will perhaps not work out, even though today is chest day, and I must to defy diabetes, to keep energy, to stay strong, to defy the COVID-19 shutdown.

When I say write, let me be clear. I must finish this Book by May, so that it can be published by March 2022, the tenth anniversary of the 2012 Librotraficante Caravan, which engendered the Librotraficante Movement.

As I write the Body, I write ten pages a day of new material.

I have delivered the first part of the Book. In my hubris, I sent an email yesterday to the publisher that I would send these one hundred and fifty pages of the second half this Friday, before I knew I'd have to scramble to live the Book in real time.

My pace prior to that was to proof and polish twenty pages a day. I have enough raw pages, not that raw, that I knew where they fell, that I can bring together, finesse and proof.

I have not heard yet about my publisher's take on the first half.

Let me know in the future if I did not fuck up, if I lived to my word and delivered the words on time. Is it two hundred pages long, three hundred? Did the Bill pass? Ever? Did I give up?

No. I never give up. Alone at this computer, alone in the gym, alone in the Book, I never give up for an audience of one and the universe.

Today, then instead of polishing my twenty pages, I write to this ten.

Do they help?

Are they tangents?

The pages make me feel stronger. I give a fuck if they are published or read. I care that they are uttered. I care that I have seen them, said them.

I began this Book two years ago. In 2018, my praxis was to write an essay a week for the entire year. I did that.

The year after, my praxis practice was to turn that into a Book.

I would write a Book.

I wrote Like this. And instead unleashed six Books.

2020: I bore down and began writing one Book. It became three books.

2021: I wrote this Book.

I stopped typing as I'm typing now, as my mind and fingers flail too fast and hard. I just cracked the "D" key, just like I previously cracked the "F" key. And I continue.

I spent the beginning of the year writing by hand in ledgers to slow down, focus my thoughts into the Book.

I began typing as the Book took form.

The Books now have this life.

This is the tenth Book. This is the version that lives.

I do not play.

I chop wood.

And what else are my muses fucking?

We must impose Our will on the universe.

This is a sign that a Book takes on its own life, a movement gains its own momentum, chaos and upheaval.

I organized a Facebook Live broadcast on short notice to promote the short notice testimony We must give in Austin.

But, to show the state of Our Community, even this, now packs a punch.

On air is Texas State Representative Christina Morales from Houston's Segundo Barrio, who is Chicana Legacy, as her family started the first Spanish language radio station on the Gulf Cost and opened the first Latino-owned funeral home. This is her pet project. She focused on presenting, but taking to the mat, just a few bills. TX HB1504 is one of them.

We were joined on FB by Texas State Board of Education Representative from the Rio Grande Valley Ruben Cortez, who has been in this battle from the first time We set foot at the TX State Board of Ed and has dived in, and Texas State Board of Education Representative from San Antonio Marissa Perez, who has been helping fight for these policies on the TX SBOE, also.

We were joined by Dr. Angela Valenzuela and her husband Dr. Emilio Zamora, one of the nation's leading Mexican American History scholars. They are both at UT Austin and pivotal in this battle.

Dr. Christopher Carmona is with Us, too. We also have educators such as Ron Castro from Project YES. He is creating their MAS curriculum for the entire district. He is so committed that he once lost his job because he drove his high school students to Austin to join Us to testify against a racist textbook, but he did not follow the rules completely. Of course, he was picked up by another school that could see how he is a brilliant teacher. He has full permission to attend tomorrow.

Also, Lucero Saldaña joins Us. The entire point of the talk was to help the next generation. Lucero brought one of her sixth grade students, Frida, who brilliantly discussed why she loves taking Mexican American Studies in grammar school!

There are more, there are others, but I do this to thank some folks in particular, and to map Our Cultural Capital, and to also let you see how thrilling my day was.

I worked over the weekend on my college course. I am teaching one class online, and I also mentor students, and I am faculty advisor for a student group.

My online class is flexible. But I spent the weekend tracking down mentees and students who were about to fall through the cracks. I had six students the system required me to drop because they had not completed an academic task by now. I tracked them all down. Zero students had to be dropped.

I did not have to attend to that on Monday.

I was paid to appear on the live, weekly political talk show *What's Your Point?* on Fox 26 Houston, again using my home studio setup.

I have two radio shows that will air tomorrow, Tuesday, as I am in Austin or driving back: *Latino Politics and News*, 2 p.m., and *Nuestra Palabra: Latino Writers Having Their Say*, which broadcast at one hundred thousand watts on the classic media platform of 90.1 FM, KPFT, Houston, Your Community Station.

And that happens every week.

I used my Nikon Z 50 for an industry-level, broadcast-clear camera shot, with a Shure mike for smooth, crystal clear sound, plus Streamyard to dress up the typical FB Live broadcast with nice effects.

Librotraficante High Tech Aztec Bryan Parras gave me the idea for this badass look, and he hooked me up and set it up. He wanted me to be a living, walking, broadcasting ad for his freelance business doing such things. I did give him $100, which is the friend's discounted price instead of the usual $500 an hour through his company, Lucas Digital Media Services.

Also, this takes money.

I make enough money where I can spend it on such things, and also invest my talents, my assets, my CCC to create more capital.

It will lead to money. A vato has to eat. And for me to rise above the borders of time, I need to understand my worth and invest.

I don't give time. I invest.

The camera costs money.

Streamyard costs money.

The ring light around the camera costs money. The beautiful Shure mike costs money. The Mac to broadcast with costs money. The iPhone costs money. The email blast service costs money. It costs money on FB to further promote an event.

It costs money to buy the Zoom H6 digital recorder to record the audio for the radio show.

I have learned to Quantify my Cultural Capital. I am donating a $50,000 media campaign to the office of Texas State Rep. Christina Morales to help spread the word for TX HB1504.

The website costs money. The domain name costs money. The website builder on the hosting service costs money.

It costs money to pay the visual artist who designed the graphics.

Rodrigo Bravo Jr. is donating his sound engineering expertise to mix the audio interviews I record with music, balanced for airing tomorrow.

It costs money to take a personal day from work.

It costs money to pay for the gas to get to Austin and back. It will cost food. I best buy some lunch for Our folks who testify tomorrow.

Raze their forms to raise Our voices.

Your Power: Nuestra Palabra

You are on your way to Nuestra Palabra.
Many have tried to take it away from you. Pero no nos dejamos.
Others have tried to hide it from you. Yet, We are everywhere.
Others have tried to erase it. Yet, there you are. Our Word.
You are the walking power of Our Community.

You pull into the parking lot. A lot of Raza has beaten you there.
Your heart races a bit. You hope you can find a spot and get in on
time to sign up for an open mic slot. You hope you haven't missed
any of the first writers.

You heard NP starts on time, even early, and created the new
definition of Raza Time/Chicano time: On time or early.

You're missing the bonus knowledge.

You recognized your friend's car, your neighbor's car. You find
what appears to be the last spot before Gente start parking on grass,
on the median, inventing spaces wherever there is room the architects didn't imagine.

Your cousin said she would never attend this NP-thing, whatever
it was. She said she was not a poet. Yet, here she is—well, her car
anyway. Or maybe a thief stole it to arrive at NP not just on time,
but early. A punctual pinche poet pilfered her purple ride.

No one whose car you recognized told you they would be here.
Yet, you are also not surprised they are the ones who are here. Next
time, you'll call or text more of the folks in your mind who you
know should be here, would love, or grow, or benefit from listening to this, from being around so many of Us—reading, flowing,
convening, not just listening to other poets and writers from . . .

279

here! from among Us!—but listening to Raza intellectuals, leaders, professors sharing their knowledge like We're neighbors and family.

You didn't tell them, not because you didn't want them to come or want them to benefit, but you were wrestling with your own muses, demons, spirits. Are you a writer? Are you a good writer? Will people get you? Will people judge you? Can you be honest? Will you stutter as you speak even though you've practiced and practiced and practiced silently and even out loud, alone?

There are forces actively at work to keep you from sharing your voice, planting that doubt in you.

You have already defied them by filling up the parking lot. By filling up that paper. By filing into the building, you defy the Cultural Border Patrol intent on stopping Our Voice. You shatter those barriers with your presence, and those words you have archived on paper, the legacy of Our Gente pouring through you, demanding to see the light of day and to continue.

Tonight you join a packed house, even if you are sitting alone reading this. You join a wide and deep base of CCC that is ancient, current, and the vision of the future. You are empowered by the wealth of this CCC, which is now richer with your intellect, vision, and voice. Stand with Us to listen to Our Word, Nuestra Palabra, Our Terms on Our Terms. You carry Our power with you, and today, We stand united, conveyed by the power of Our Art and Culture to change the world for the better. Unidos!

CULTURAL ACCELERATION ESSAYS

Million Dollar Grant

Excerpts from a grant for $1,000,000 for ALMAHH: Advocates of a Latino Museum of Cultural & Visual Arts and Archive Complex in Houston, Harris County, submitted to the Houston Endowment by invitation August 27, 2021. The grant was written by ALMAHH board chair Geraldina Wise and ALMAHH board member Tony Diaz.

Grant Question: Describe the organization's mission.

Response: We are uniting to plan and program the building and design of a sustainable, state-of-the-art Museum complex for Latino Art and Culture in Houston, Texas, in partnership with public entities. We aim to ensure equitable and authentic representation and access to the diverse Latino Culture and communities of Greater Houston. We will do so in an inclusive, grassroots way, by creating the intellectual and digital infrastructure to quantify, map, listen to and understand Houston's Latino Cultural Capital. The physical plant, intellectual infrastructure, and digital platform will support, connect, and grow Houston's Latino Art Eco System for the benefit of all Houstonians.

Grant question: Describe the project.

Response: ALMAAHH requests funding for a two-year project that will quantify the overlooked art resources in the Latino Community, chart the Latino Art Eco System and infuse those aspects of Latino Community Cultural Capital in a clear plan to build a state of the art Latino Museum Complex.

The culminating plan will articulate a Latino Museum complex that will be the physical and multi-sensory seat of Latino culture in Greater Houston and Harris County. This state of the art complex is not envisioned as a single large box, but as a set of facilities that will sit on a *zócalo* (plaza) that will encompass green space, community space, and additional facilities that will make the site multi-purpose.

The research for the building plans will involve a profound analysis of Houston's Latino Cultural Capital—art and cultural assets cultivated by Houstonians for decades, even generations, that have functioned outside of Houston's mainstream art infrastructures.

This research will create the intellectual infrastructure to empower Houston's Latino Art Community to gain additional support and work with more organizations. ALMAAHH will also provide a voice for the Latino Arts Community. This approach will create an arts complex that will address the articulated needs of the Latino Arts Community, involving it from the beginning.

Our board consists of former elected officials, former and current corporate executives, artists, activists, professors, community organizers, lawyers, community members. We intentionally embody both the grassroots and the grasstops of Houston's Latino Community. We will engage governmental agencies at the city, state, county, and federal levels.

These synergies will be the artistic and cultural basis for programming that will inspire local residents at the same time as drawing tourists from throughout the state, the nation, and the world. This will define Houston and Texas as leaders in cultivating Latino Art and Culture.

The East End is the most likely location for the complex given factors like the history of the area, availability of land—including city and county potential contributions to the project—proximity to Downtown and its amenities, proximity to Buffalo Bayou Park East End.

The most important urban concepts behind the vision are:

-organizing the anchor site around a *zócalo* (plaza) as a point of arrival and immersion into the culture. (Zócalos play a large role in everyday life in Mexico, for example, where families, kids, tourists congregate to socialize, rest, or in the vernacular of the youth "hang out." Visitors from Mexico or Latin America to Houston seek such a place, but there is currently not an equivalent.)

-connecting to Buffalo Bayou Park and using green space and the bayou as links to multiple sites.

-devising the multi-modal transportation scheme for the area to ensure accessibility to the complex, including planning for future boat transportation.

-potential for multi-site connected development for Houston's Latino Art Eco System

The salient architectural features of the project for Phase I are:

-a multi-functional *zócalo* (plaza)

-a new Museum building

-Cultural Center/theater complex

-a marketplace

-multimedia functions built into the infrastructure, indoors and outdoors, to house static visual art exhibits to virtual reality exhibits

-a complex planned to accommodate a wide range of programming: international art exhibits as well as after-school *Folklórico* dance classes

The central concepts that will be embodied in the complex are:

-Environmental sustainability

-Tech forward

-connectivity

-accessibility

-community

-authenticity

-excellence

-opportunity

-inclusivity

Grant question: Why is this something the community needs?

Response: Houston's population is at least 45% Latino; however, there is a major disconnect between the 900,000+ Latino community and the rest of the city. This disconnect, and its on-going effects on the quality of life of the entire city, have been recently clearly revealed by the effects of the COVID-19 epidemic.

Latino families were hit harder by COVID-19 than other groups; were harder to reach to get tested for COVID-19; were harder to reach for vaccinations and for reliable information about them. Latino families were harder to reach for online remote school access, and had less access to secure and stable Wi-Fi.

This disconnect is perennial in standard outreach regarding voter registration, voter participation, the Census; however, the

COVID-19 shutdown has marked the dangerous effects of this disconnect and puts into a new light the possible dangers to the Latino Community and to all of Houston if this persists.

Additionally, outreach attempts based on standard engagement have not had a profound impact for one simple reason that thwarts even planning meetings—what do you call us: Hispanic, Latinos, Chicanos, Latinx . . . ? If institutions don't know what to call us, how can they quantify us?

Although the sheer size of the Latino population is what brings us to the table, Latinos are dispersed in the region. The census shows that every Houston City Council District is a Latino district, and, as proven by the activism and grassroots campaign of our board members, the Latino Community could and does unite and build bridges to other communities through our Art, History, and Culture, on our terms.

To address the above-mentioned issues, ALMAAHH will perform the first ever quantification of Houston's Latino Community Cultural Capital and mapping of the Latino Art Eco System. This research will inform our plans for a state of the art arts complex that will serve the needs of Houston's Latino community, while gifting it to all Houstonians. We intend to connect Latinos physically and digitally and serve a centralized role for convening and disseminating reliable information pertinent to our community.

No institution has done this before.

These actions do not fall under the mandate of any single agency. Now, this is ALMAAHH's business.

666 Laws

Published September 4, 2021 on the Ethnic Studies Interactive Website at Sacramento State University. Broadcast on the radio show Nuestra Palabra: Latino Writers Having Their Say, *90.1 FM, KPFT, Houston.*

I am writing this the day 666 laws go into effect in Texas—giving it the title of the most far-right state of the Union.

Of course, metaphors are forced confessions. So the number 666 is appropriate. Some of the laws are so evil that I suspect the devil has self-deported from Texas. Of course, we activists are used to the heat. So although some of this may seem new, it is clear to we community organizers on the ground that this is a reboot of past oppression. Texas is always behind the times. Retro-fashion is cool, retro-racism is not cool.

I'm not going to go over every single one of these laws. I don't even have time to provide a "top ten worst laws" list. There is one specific law that demands our attention.

Texas's right wing Republicans, as in other states, have implemented their own "Anti-Critical Race Theory Law." I hate to repeat that name because it plays into the right-wing strategy of misinformation. This law should be called the "Anti-Black Lives Matter Law" or the "Anti-George Floyd Era Law" because this law is intended to prevent and intimidate educators from talking about the structural racism exposed during that movement. Notice that news about the anti-Critical Race Theory campaigns picked up steam as more and more confederate statues were being taken down across the country. CRT misinformation has now dominated the news.

The Anti-CRT movement is a repurposing of past oppression. I don't mean in general. I have receipts.

You see, I am a Librotraficante. You can translate that into english as Book Trafficker.

I clearly remember when Arizona right-wing Republicans banned Mexican American Studies. They enforced the law in 2012, forcing administrators to walk into classrooms during class time and box up books by some of our most beloved authors in front of our youth. There were 80+ works on what should have been extolled as the gold standard of Ethnic Studies Courses. This curriculum raised the graduation rate to 98% for the predominantly Mexican American student population of the Tucson Unified School District.

Instead of celebrating our art, history, and culture, reactionary Republicans banned it.

When I and 4 other veteran members of Nuestra Palabra: Latino Writers Having Their Say heard about this attack on our familia in Tucson, we were enraged.

If Arizona officials were going to ban our history, we would make more.

We organized the 2012 Librotraficante Caravan to smuggle back into Tucson the books that formed the brilliant Mexican American Studies Curriculum that Arizona right-wing Republicans banned.

We mobilized Houston's Community Cultural Capital, then linked with Communities across Texas to unite with our Gente from Arizona. Soon the entire Southwest galvanized Calfornia, then other states. We united to overturn that racist law.

Each member of our crew had over 10 years experience (at least) organizing our community through Nuestra Palabra. I founded Nuestra Palabra: Latino Writers Having Their Say in April of 1998. It would become the first regular Latino reading series in a city where we formed over 45% of the population. Librotraficante High Tech Aztec, aka Bryan Parras; Librotraficante Lips Mendez, aka Lupe Mendez—recently named Texas Poet Laureate; Librotraficante La Laura, aka Laura Razo; and Librotraficante Lilo, aka Liana Lopez.

We are approaching the ten-year anniversary of the 2012 Librotraficante Caravan, and it is clear that right wing Republicans have re-purposed that attack on our community, our imaginations, our history, our culture. They have changed the details, but the overall attack plan is the same. And this time, it has spread.

But we are experts at thwarting oppressors. We are fueling the bus, re-stocking the contraband prose, and alerting all our Librotraficante Under Ground Libraries.

Let us know if you are ready to ride.

Latinx vs. Community Disorganizers

Originally published September 23, 2020 on www.LatinoRebels.com. Broadcast on the radio show Nuestra Palabra: Latino Writers Having Their Say, *90.1 FM, KPFT, Houston.*

I named my project LatinxIcons precisely because there's been pushback against the term "Latinx" and the younger generation that identifies with it. Let me make something clear: our community does not need to pick one identity label so that others can more easily Google us. Society must profoundly imagine us more.

The tragedy is that all the bickering about our identity labels can be addressed by taking just one Ethnic Studies course.

When I teach Mexican American Literature, I dedicate only one week to two dozen of the possible identity terms. More exist and so many more will exist. The rest of the semester, we profoundly examine the manifestations of those terms generation by generation through the poetry, plays, essays, corridos, and other works our community created to navigate a system that some days ignored us and other days actively tried to erase us.

I have an affinity for the term "Latinx" because it is organic to our community. Our youth coined it. Additionally, all the pushback against the term gives me an insight into the pushback against the youth who first identified with the term "Chicano" during the Civil Rights Movement.

This is dramatized in the play *Zoot Suit* by Luis Valdez when the main character Henry Reyna is criticized for and warned against hanging out with, belonging to, or acting like a "Chicano."

I, like all Mexican Americans, was not born Chicano. My parents were migrant workers in Texas who then settled in Chicago. They handed down to me rich cultural traditions and values, but I had

289

to discover our role in history on my own, through books that crossed my paths, through research I had to struggle to find and understand.

I chose to be Chicano after immersing myself in our history, art, culture and understanding the role of self-empowerment.

It is unethical for community organizers to sabotage a person's path to self-empowerment.

Community *disorganizers* revel in the bickering over identity they produce or recycle as clickbait.

Our culture is worthy of more than merely clickbait.

Every publication that posts a piece on this-term-vs-that-term should also publish 10 pieces about Ethnic Studies and figures important to our history, written by our intellectuals profoundly navigating the terms our identity is built upon.

Identity labels are The Tip of The Pyramid. We must unearth our community's culture and history.

That is the role of writers and other artists. We must clear the dust to re-invent language so that we can find ourselves.

Happy Ultimate Hispanic Heritage Month.

The American Dream Through Our Books

Originally published April 13, 2014 on www.nbcnews.com. Broadcast on the radio show Nuestra Palabra: Latino Writers Having Their Say, *90.1 FM, KPFT, Houston.*

People often ask me why I'm so passionate about books and education. I am usually shocked that more people aren't.

I have to keep in mind that not everyone has had their life changed through education, and not everyone has had to fight tooth and nail for it.

In my case, books have made the American Dream a reality.

My parents were migrant workers. I'm the first of my family to not only go to college but to attend graduate school. In one generation—through books and education—my family has gone from the farm fields to the national stage, where I have had the honor of representing my community and advocating for Latino literature and history in our classrooms.

I have a gift for language. I get it from my mom. She never went to school, but she taught herself how to read. She would keep all of our family spellbound when she told stories about her life in Mexico or in the fields, or about the misadventures of family members navigating their new life in Chicago.

I knew language was powerful, because as early as third grade I was translating english into Spanish for my father. I remember salesmen looking down at him, judging him because he needed me to understand. That's when I learned. I would remind a clerk that he didn't speak Spanish, so he too needed me to make a sale.

Language helped me protect my family. Language helped me defend myself. Maybe that's why I always wanted to be a writer.

My first poem was published in sith grade, over the lunch hot menu touting "Sloppy Joe Burgers" at St. David's catholic school on the south side of Chicago. Overnight, teachers who had ignored me knew my name and would walk up to me to talk about my writing.

Same me, same school, different universe, all from one poem.

You would think that with this love and fascination for reading and writing I would have been reveling in books by and about Mexican Americans. The truth is I was never exposed to them.

I didn't read a novel written by a Latino until I was a junior at De Paul University, taking a Creative Writing Course with Professor Ted Anton, a graduate of the University of Iowa's Writers Workshop. He would ask me why I didn't write about my family, my story. I remember wondering if that was even allowed since I had never seen that in a book.

Professor Anton handed me *Down These Mean Streets* by Piri Tomas.

That was the first book I read that switched back and forth from english to Spanish, to Spanglish to slang, then back, in a fast, furious and poetic pace. It was set in the rough urban sprawl of New York that looked and smelled like the South Side of Chicago. It was packed with crazy confrontations and barriers. If we can just survive the weekend, the book showed, we can get to school on Monday to keep fighting.

Books are dangerous—and crucially important. They make us dream big and believe we can deliver.

It worked for me. In 1994 I became the first Chicano to earn a Master of Fine Arts in Creative Writing at the University of Houston's Creative Writing Program. It was there I first met in person and chilled with a real life Chicano author, Dagoberto Gilb, when he had become the first Chicano to win the PEN/Faulkner prize as well as a ton of other awards that year.

In 1998 my first novel, *The Aztec Love God*, was published. That same year I founded the group Nuestra Palabra: Latino Writers Having Their Say (NP), to promote Latino literature and foster literacy. NP would go on to host the release of Dagoberto's book, *Woodcuts of Women.*

But years later, in January of 2012, that book, along with Dagoberto's book *Magic of Blood,* was among the 84 works confiscated from classrooms in Tucson, Ariz., after Mexican American Studies had been prohibited in that state.

That's when I and other members of Nuestra Palabra first became Librotraficantes or book smugglers. During our March 2012 Librotraficante Caravan we took banned books back into Arizona.

This last week I was part of a statewide coalition that advocated for the Texas State Board of Education to implement a Mexican American Studies elective to get more books into the hands of our youth. There were many who shared stories about what our literature and history has meant to them, and how it has changed their lives.

And the first person to testify was—you guessed it—Dagoberto Gilb.

We went to Austin looking to implement Mexican American Studies. We came back with the Texas Plan that allows us to control the content of our courses, yet still have the courses recognized and advertised as electives by the state. It also allows us to get the textbooks needed for not just Mexican American Studies, but also African American, Asian, and Native American Studies.

I see this event in Texas as part of a journey, a direct route from our underground libraries in community centers to the upper echelons of the textbook publishing world, with hundreds of stops in classrooms along the way.

Why am I so passionate about education and books? Art changed my life. I believe that through broader imaginations, we can update the American Dream for everyone

Write. Buy Books. Part I

Originally published March 3, 2019 on TonyDiaz.net.

We have to tell our young 730 times that reading, writing, and culture matter.

That works out to 2 x a day in a year.

This means literally, at the most essential level, telling them exactly. Because on any given day, even before they walk out of the door for school, they have been told otherwise several times. By the time they get to sleep they have been flooded by messages that teach them that reading and writing do not matter. At the very least, they have not received any positive messages about culture, let alone their culture.

On a really bad day, they have seen or heard their culture denigrated.

Do I need to show you how? I will resist, in this essay, for the moment, breaking down how our culture is broken down by those who do not like us. I am writing a book about our Community's Cultural Capital. This essay and this part of the essay is about the exact opposite.

It's sinister and a lot harder to quantify the missing.

It's impossible to count the number of times our culture is not mentioned.

But I measure it the first day of my Mexican American Literature course. I give students a very straightforward Cultural Quiz.

I ask them 4 questions. I'll talk about each of the questions in later essays. I'm focusing on just one this time.

Question number one is: Name 5 Latino writers.

This is linked to my discussion of Community Cultural Capital because we are basically quantifying Community Cultural Capital.

Most students can't name one Latino writer.

Of course, by the end of the semester they can name many. On top of that, during an amazing semester, they will meet 5 Latino writers in person and participate in campaign to further Mexican American Studies. That's Cultural Acceleration.

But back to the bad news. The majority of them have not taken a single Mexican American Studies course, even as the entire public school system is now majority Brown. Latinos make up over 52% of over 5.2 million public school students. Yet, most will finish school never having read a book by or about Latinos. Of course, this is set to change Fall of 2019 since last year the Texas State Board of Education endorsed Mexican American Studies statewide. But it won't change fast enough.

I convey this to you to manifest omission.

We are talking about quantifying nothing. Our young believe there are no books by or about Latinos.

What does this tell our youth? They will think that:

We do not write.

We are not intellectual.

We do not have a voice.

We do not matter.

But that's okay because writing doesn't matter.

Poetry doesn't make money.

Who cares?

Mind you, these are students who have already graduated from high school. They have passed at least 2 english courses, Composition I and Composition II. They were the last generation to deal with Remedial english courses. Add english as a Second Language for some.

Additionally, they came looking for Mexican American Literature.

These are the motivated and interested students looking for culture in our system. They have been denied their literary culture in high school, middle school, and kindergarten.

As you can imagine, they are edified by the works in the class.

I want you to experience that.

Don't get scared. You won't have to pay a semester of tuition. You will get it for free.

But first, tell your youth our history, our culture, our books matter.

If you want to be more subtle. Read in front of them. That counts for 2 mentions.

If you want to be even more subtle, write in front of them, a letter to a relative, an email to a friend, a poem, a short story.

If you want to change the world, buy books. Dedicate a shelf where you live as your family library. On days you forget to tell them our voice matters, the books will say that for you.

Of course, we are Cultural Accelerators, so let's take this to the next levels.

This is good, but I want you to know what it feels like to earn an A in my Mexican American Literature course.

Don't worry, it won't cost you a semester of tuition. In fact, it's free.

Attend the 21st anniversary celebration of Nuestra Palabra: Latino Writers Having Their Say Wednesday, April 3, 2019, 6:30 pm–8:30 pm at the Brown Auditorium of the Museum of Fine Arts Houston. It's free. It seats 350. If you want to rsvp your seat, please visit www.NuestraPalabra.org and make a donation. Or just come. No one will be turned away.

That day you will meet in person 6 Latino writers.

But not just any 6 Latino writers.

You will meet the godfather of Chicano literature Dagoberto Gilb. He's is the author of nine books, including *The Magic of Blood*, *The Last Known Residence of Mickey Acuña*, *Woodcuts of Women*, *Gritos*, *The Flowers*, and *Before the End, After the Beginning*. He is also the editor of two canonical anthologies, *Hecho en Tejas: Texas Mexican Literature* and *Mexican American Literature*, and the founding editor of *Huizache*, the country's best Latino literary magazine.

He's also my mentor. And you know you are experiencing a Chicano Renaissance when a writer whose work you admire becomes your mentor and friend. You know he's good because 2 of his books were on the Mexican American Studies curriculum banned in Arizona. On top of that, he joined us on the 2012 Librotraficante Caravan to smuggle the books banned in Arizona back into Tucson.

Speaking of the ban of Ethnic Studies in Arizona, you will also meet *Huffington Post* reporter Roque Plana. He is the journalist who first wrote about the ban and the Librotraficantes and brought national attention.

You will also meet me, but you already know me, but if you're keeping score—that's three writers.

Our Nuestra Palabra Second Generation Writers round out the evening. These are some of the writers who first read in public with NP and began working with us to promote Latino literature and literacy, and now they have their own nationally published books and projects. They are spreading the word to the next generation.

They are:

Poet Lupe Mendez, with his new book *Why I Am Like Tequila.*

Poet Jasminne Mendez, with her new book *Night-Blooming Jasmin(n)e: Personal Essays and Poetry.*

Poet Leslie Contreras Schwartz will read from her book *Nightbloom & Cenote.*

As Nuestra Palabra enters its 3rd decade of work, we are also expanding how we approach culture and art.

The line-up that evening will also include Mari Carmen Ramirez, the MFAH Wortham Curator of Latin American Art. She will discuss the MFAH's holdings of Chicano and Latino art.

But don't mistake this evening for simply an anniversary.

This is a living narrative.

We are experiencing a Renaissance.

Never forget that in 2012 Arizona banned our history and culture.

Community Cultural Capital overturned that ban.

Nuestra Palabra: Latino Writers Having Their Say played a role in that story by creating the Librotraficantes and fighting for MAS in Arizona and Texas. Nuestra Palabra has gone from its first reading at the party hall of Chapultepec Restaurant to drawing thirty thousand people when we organized Houston's largest book fairs, to creating underground libraries as Librotraficantes, to the main-stream as we celebrate in the Museum of Fine Arts and in official buildings throughout the county and beyond.

If you join us, if you buy the writers' books that night and have them sign them, you won't just have 6 books to begin or to add to your family library, you will have a story to share with your kids, your students, your friends about celebrating our culture, which you will be reminded about every time you see those books and which others will retell. Those books tell a generation that our voice, nuestra palabra, matters.

This is the most advanced way to convey to others that reading and writing are essential.

Read. Write. Buy books.

Community Cultural Capital in Action: NP, Macondo, and TAMUSA

Originally published May 7, 2019 on TonyDiaz.net.

The era of old-fashioned nonprofits and educational institutions is over. In order to fully serve our community and create structural change, we must quantify, cultivate, and accelerate Community Cultural Capital. Nuestra Palabra is honored to unite Macondo, the writers retreat Sandra Cisneros founded decades ago and the University of Texas A&M San Antonio via our Cultural Acceleration program.

Several strands of this union are traditional. Workshops are fundamental to the writing community as are 4-year educational institutions. In fact, a nonprofit acting as an umbrella group or a fiduciary agent is not that uncommon, especially for Anglo, mainstream groups.

However, none of these entities is interested in becoming a typical nonprofit or mainstream organization. All three entities are successes in their own right and strive to have a profound influence on our community and create structural changes that will ensure that our community will thrive.

Nuestra Palabra has built and helped maintain the Macondo Writers Workshop website. This included facilitating Macondo's ability to process applications online. Additionally, NP has helped promote the organization through mainstream media, social media, and via a grassroots campaign. More importantly, Nuestra Palabra is helping Macondo and its ad hoc advisory board to position itself to get to the next level.

Nuestra Palabra's goal is help organizations that serve our community achieve in one or two years what would take 5 to ten years to achieve in the past. And then we keep pushing ourselves and each other to get to the next level. Within the next 5 years, we will help achieve enough structural changes to make Texas, especially Houston, the leader for delivering our community's art and culture, and we will shape the way the entire nation imagines us and deals with us. Stay tuned for updates on this potent movement.

Here is how the press release conveyed the signing of the Macondo, NP, TAMUSA pact.

On Monday, April 22, Nuestra Palabra and Texas A&M University-San Antonio (A&M-SA) signed a memorandum of understanding, bringing the nationally renowned, culturally creative Macondo Writers Workshop to A&M-SA's campus for the next three years. A&M-SA will host the exclusive workshop during the week of July 23–28, 2019.

The agreement between A&M-SA and Nuestra Palabra essentially establishes a a partnership in which A&M-SA hosts the Macondo Writers Workshop, while Nuestra Palabra, working with the Macondo Ad Hoc Advisory Board, organizes and sponsors the workshop's independent study retreat, seminars and faculty.

"This agreement marks a pivotal time for the Macondo Writers Workshop and its relationship with A&M-San Antonio and we are thrilled to bring this creative collaborative back to A&M-San Antonio," Dr. Cynthia Teniente-Matson, A&M-SA president said. "This is A&M-San Antonio's second consecutive year hosting the Macondo Writers Workshop, and we are hopeful this agreement lays a strong foundation for building a permanent home for Macondo. A&M-SA is honored to be hosting the workshop and we are proud to be a part of the vibrant and socially engaged creative arts community in San Antonio," she added.

Tony Diaz, founder and director of Nuestra Palabra, said, "Nuestra Palabra is thrilled to link Macondo and Texas A&M University-San Antonio under our Cultural Acceleration Program to take this cultural capital to even more people. Texas will be known as the leader for delivering our community's art at the highest level and for the greatest good. We are honored to unite to change the world."

The Macondo Writers Workshop, now in its 24th year, has been a transformational experience for many of its participants. An all-star faculty has been assembled to lead this year's session. Sherwin Bitsui will lead the poetry workshop; Helena Maria Viramontes will lead the fiction workshop; Joy Castro will lead the creative nonfiction/memoir workshop; and Cisneros returns to the faculty working with Ruth Behar to lead a special section.

The Macondo Writers Workshop is a master's level workshop, meaning that participants are expected to be established writers capable of reviewing each other's work with compassionate rigor and vision.

Cisneros, acclaimed writer, MacArthur Fellow and author of *The House on Mango Street*, founded the workshop in 1995. Macondo gathers writers from all genres, who work on geographic, cultural, economic, gender and spiritual borders. The program, named after the town in Columbian author Gabriel García Marquez's 1967 novel *One Hundred Years of Solitude* is an association of socially engaged writers working toward non-violent social change. They seek to advance creativity, foster generosity, and serve community.

About Texas A&M University-San Antonio

Established as a standalone university in 2009, Texas A&M University-San Antonio (A&M-SA) is a comprehensive four-year public university that reflects the culturally diverse, heritage-rich community it serves. Situated on nearly 700 acres in South San Antonio, A&M-SA is a Military EmbracingTM institution offering more than 40 undergraduate programs to 6,600 students. Visit tamusa.edu for more information.

Nuestra Palabra

Tony Diaz founded Nuestra Palabra: Latino Writers Having Their Say (NP) in April of 1998. NP's mission is to promote Latino literature and literacy. The group began as a monthly reading series featuring nationally published and community-based Latino writers performing their work live in english, Spanish, and Spanglish. NP went on to organize the largest books fairs in Houston and create the Nuestra Palabra weekly radio show on 90.1 FM, KPFT, Houston. During its second decade, NP organized the 2012 Librotraficante Caravan to Tucson to defy the state's banning of Mexican American Studies and also fueled the struggle for Mexican American Studies in Texas. As NP enters its third decade, its Cultural Accelerator Program will aggregate the efforts of organizations to create structural change through the arts. NP also is advocating for equitable and sustained funding for Latinx art groups. www.NuestraPalabra.org.

Macondo Writers Workshop and Ad Hoc Advisory Board

Founded in 1995 by writer Sandra Cisneros, the Macondo Writers Workshop is an association of socially-engaged writers working to advance creativity, foster generosity, and serve community. The Macondo Ad Hoc Advisory Board includes Pat Alderete, Miryam Bujanda, Alex Espinoza, Anel Flores, Natalia Treviño, Carla Trujillo, and Viktoria Valenzuela. This board primarily consists of long-time and new Macondo Members from Texas and California who volunteer to maintain the collective and produce this high caliber writer's workshop open to dedicated writers.

Can You Name 100 Latinx Artists?

First published February 28, 2019 on TonyDiaz.net.

- The names of 100 Latinx Artists.

- The works of 100 Latinx Artists.

- 7 art exhibits of Latinx Artists, poets, and writers.

There are 3 examples of our Community's Cultural Capital.
And today, 'cause I like ya, we're giving it away.
This is the Librotraficante style of creative nonfiction.
We ain't playin'.
But we are playing with reality, altering it to suit our imaginations.
And today you get to ride along because of the magic of www.MANTECAHTX.com, which is actually very good for your diet of fine art.

As Nuestra Palabra: Latino Writers Having Their Say turns 21, we are thrilled to step into our era of Cultural Acceleration.

MANTECAHTX is a potent example of quantifying our Community's Cultural Capital.

This is very different from the manifestation of our Community's Cultural Capital. Here's why. There has never been a lack of interest, talent, or artists in our community. Never.

I know this from working in this field for decades. Yes, it is rare for most folks to hear about them. Yes, many moved to other cities where they could not make a living off their art or their work might be more appreciated. Some moved to work with mentors or to study their craft.

And again, when I was organizing the first reading for Nuestra Palabra in 1998, many folks, even Latinos, said the same thing: There are not enough Latino writers, there is not enough interest, that's not what our community is into. We are honored that you have worked with us for over two decades to prove those folks wrong.

And we are proud that we can unite for our next decade of work as we enter the era of cultural accelerators. Don't worry, I'm writing an entire book on this, so if you want even more explanations for different aspects, they are either on my blog or they are coming.

But let me make this easy for you.

www.MANTECAHTX.com is great way to accelerate our Community's Cultural Capital.

If you could not name 100 Latinx artists, be they writers or visual artists, now you can.

All you have to do is visit the website, go to the artist profiles page and begin scrolling through.

Did I mention these are only artists from Houston?

The entire nation will now have to imagine Houston as a hotbed for Latinx art, artists, and innovation.

Are you thrilled yet?

Not only can you now name over 100 Houston Latinx artist, you can even visit their profile pages and see their work, or get links to their work.

Not only that, now you can also meet them in person. We have all united to organize 7 exhibits during this Spring of Latino Art. Wait, did you not know that Houston's Spring of Latino Art has started? You best join the email list to be kept up to date.

You best check out the events on MANTECAHTX created by MANTECA artists.

The exhibits will feature thrilling visual art, awesome poets and writers, and music.

But in order to be considered for these shows, artists, poets, writers, and musicians have to sign up and create profiles.

Response has been so great that we are creating even more ways to spread Latinx visual art and poetry. Of course, we'll feature

MANTECA folks and events on the *Nuestra Palabra* Radio Show with shout-outs and interviews. But we will also pitch them to other radio and TV shows.

Our 21st anniversary showcase takes place Wed. April 3, 2019, 6:30 pm at the Museum of Fine Arts Houston, Brown Auditorium.

Most nonprofits plateau after 20 years. NP is revving up to unite with more artists, activists, and leaders to shatter stereotypes and barriers.

We have to thank our partners. MANTECAHTX is made possible in part from a grant from City Initiatives.

We thank the Nuestra Palabra familia for spreading the word and committing to make sure you will be getting more and more MANTECA for years to come, as much MANTECA as you can handle.

And most importantly, we want to thank all the artists who have been so generous with their time, energy and genius: MantecaHTX is part of Nuestra Palabra's Cultural Acceleration Program, along with other projects such as the Macondo Writers Workshop founded by Sandra Cisneros. Cultural capital was provided by Delilah Montoya, Tina Hernandez, Moe Penders, Theresa Escobedo, Gabriel Martinez, Julia Barbosa Landois, Francis Almendárez, Yeiry Guevara.

And to demonstrate that we continue to change the world, here are 3 more examples of our Community's Cultural Capital that you will get to experience in Houston soon:

Central American Cultural Capital Wed. April 17, 6:30 pm – 8:30 pm at Yes College Prep.

Chicano Cultural Capital Wed. April 24, 6:30 pm – 8:30 pm at Marshall.

South American Cultural Capital Wed. May 1, 6:30 pm – 8:30 pm at the Institute of Hispanic Culture.

Happy Spring of Latino Art!
#LANHouston #LAN2019

Latino Legacy Arts Groups

Originally published September 10, 2019 on TonyDiaz.net.

As Cultural Accelerators it is our mission to quantify Community Cultural Capital.

In Houston, as we wrap our heads and hearts around the death of the nonprofit organization Talento Bilingue de Houston, it is vital to also take stock of the other Latino Legacy Arts Groups.

And even if you are not in Houston, there are at least two aspects of this that should be a wake-up call to other Latino arts organizations throughout Tejas and the nation.

1. Any one of us can cease to exist at any moment.

2. We must unite to Quantify, Cultivate, and Accelerate our Community Cultural Capital.

This can many things, but with the passing of a Legacy Latino Arts nonprofit this means we must quantify Houston's Latino Legacy Arts organizations.

Nuestra Palabra: Latino Writers Having Their Say and the Librotraficantes are spearheading this because we are Cultural Accelerators. Our work in art, civil rights, and social services has made us experts in Cultural Capital.

So, for the first step, we are creating, for the first time in Houston, Texas, and in Texas, the list of Houston Latino Legacy Arts groups.

They are Multicultural Education and Counseling through the Arts MECA, founded by Alice Valdez over 40 yrs ago; The Pancho Claus Foundation, founded by Richard Reyes, who has over

40 years of work in the community; Festival Chicano, founded by Daniel Bustamante; Ambassadors International Ballet Folklórico, founded over 40 years ago by Mr. and Mrs. Fraga; and Arte Público Press, founded over 40 years by Dr. Nicolás Kanellos.

Of course, because we are the writers of history, I am mustering the audacity of adding Nuestra Palabra: Latino Writers Having Their Say, which I founded in 1998, to the group. I do so because 21 years of survival is a major milestone for our community. NP, the Librotraficantes, and I have invested a lot of our Community Cultural Capital into this campaign for equitable and sustainable funding for Latino arts groups, and, as our actions and feats—which are beyond our years—testify to, we will see this campaign to fruition.

Discussing our fallen brother, the Latino Legacy Arts group Talento Bilingue de Houston was over 40 years old.

Also, to clarify, the former nonprofit is gone. However, the TBH Theater still exists. Houston Mayor Turner has met with us and made a commitment that the doors to the TBH Theater will not close and programming will not cease. He is working with us to devise a short-term plan and a long-term plan, and he has renewed his commitment to Latino arts and the future.

What this is we must now start elaborating.

Together we Latino Legacy Arts Groups represent over 260 years of community cultural capital.

Of course, even with this list, we are privileging those groups who attained 501(c)(3) nonprofit status. Can we even count all the arts groups who died at a younger age? What about all the artists who left or were so discouraged they never became a formal organization? Who have we forgotten?

We must also use this as a first step to devising a way to bolster the emerging Latinx groups and the new organizations as well.

This will be complicated.

Running a Latino Arts Nonprofit is very hard. You have to be part accountant, part lawyer, and part artist.

The rules for traditional nonprofits were cultivated by folks who had more resources and could tap into a network of experts, people with resources in the form of money, time, or connections or all three of these precious facets.

Latino Arts nonprofits tap into our community in order to also provide social services that are needed by our community.

So not only are the rules for nonprofits created without us in mind, our networks depend on us differently. And finally, at this moment, because of the shock of the loss of one us, we are trying to have a conversation that should have been going on for at least 42 years—the lifetime of the former nonprofit Talento Bilingue de Houston.

We must pause for our fallen brother. We must take stock of what happened, and we must unite to move forward.

That first step is naming our Latino Legacy Arts Groups.

Which are yours?
How are they?
What is in your future?

PART V: APPENDICES

The Librotraficante Dictionary

You're using Webster's Dictionary. *Give it back to him. Define with the Librotraficante Dictionary.*

Librotraficante Koan:

I. Learn the system.

II. Don't trust the system.

III. We are the system.

Accelerate Community Cultural Capital

Allowed to prosper but not rule

At some point, it seems plain rude for you to insist you exist after all those nice Texans said you do not.

Author Our Authority

Blur

Community Cultural Capital

Community Libraries

Cultivate Community Cultural Capital

Cultural Accelerators

Cultural Border Patrol

english is brutally honest about its oppression.

Every ivory tower is raised on Our razed temples, the rubble of Our Community Cultural Capital.

I am so glad Houston did not convince Us We did not exist.

In this day and age, a Latino can't be president. I hope one day this sentence will be defied with a sitting Chicana president. This sentence reveals that We are relegated to second-class citizenship, and We are oppressed. We are allowed to prosper but not rule.

Lawyers contract language.

Librotraficantes liberate words.

Librotraficante Underground Libraries

NotForProphets

Metaphors are forced confessions.

My family had been chasing El Norte all their lives and always winding up on the South Side of El Norte.

The North of El Norte

Only Art can save Us.

Our Community Cultural Capital was exploited, co-opted, colonized, erased, or, on a good day, simply ignored, neglected for so long that Our Art nonprofits must attend to many issues at once.

Our Terms on Our Terms

Plur

Quantify Community Cultural Capital

The Mythical Level Playing Field

Raze their forms to raise Our voices

Rubble

Rulers create rules to maintain their rule.

Under Ground Libraries

We are forced to buy metaphors without understanding the cost.

We cannot compete on The Level Playing Field because We do not have generational wealth and power. We can only compete on The Level Playing Field with Our generational wealth of Community Cultural Capital.

We do not have the luxury of Art for Art's sake.

We recreate Our power one sentence at a time, one original word after the other.

When We master language, We become masters of Our Own thoughts and liberate Our imagination.

Writers are capable of the unimaginable.

Original TUSD Teacher-Plaintiffs vs. Arizona

Curtis Acosta
Sean Arce
Maria Federico Brummer
Dolores Carrion
Alexandro "Salo" Escamilla
José Gonzalez
Norma Gonzalez
Lorenzo Lopez
Rene Martinez
Sally Rusk
Yolanda Sotelo

Librotraficante Caravanistas

This is a list of the caravanistas who rode the 2012 & 2017 Librotraficante Caravans to Tucson. The map of the six-city caravan is available at www.Librotraficante.com.

Belinda Acosta, Librotraficante "la prensa"
Cecilia Balli, Librotraficante "Texas Monthly"
Gabriel Carmona, Librotraficante "El Commandante"
Ruben Castilla Herrera, Librotraficante "Buddha-zas"
Dennis Castillo, Librotraficante "Youngblood"
Victoria Corona, Librotraficante "Hasta la Victoria"
Tony Diaz, "El Librotraficante"
Blas Espinosa, Librotraficante "Blaze"
Tony Garcia, Librotraficante "Crusher"
Augustin Laredo, Librotraficante "El Guti Q"
Adam Efren López, Librotraficante "Pancho Flópez"
Diana López, Librotraficante "DLO"
Liana López, Librotraficante "LiLó"
Claudia I. Macias, MS Ed., Librotraficante "La Comadre"
Antonio Maldonado, Librotraficante "Smokey"
Brandon McGaughey, Librotraficante "High-Tech Hybrid"
Lupe Méndez, Librotraficante "Lips Mendez"
Susie Moreno, Librotraficante "La Mom"
Paolo Mossetti, Librotraficante "El Italiano"
Bryan Parras, Librotraficante "HighTechAztec"
Delia Perez Meyer, Librotraficante "La Hashbrown"
Laura Razo, Librotraficante "La Laura"
Gloria Rubac, Librotraficante "La Gloria"

Branden Selman, Librotraficante "Pelo-Chin"
Jacob Shafer, Librotraficante "Sound"
Harbeer Singh Khabardaar, Librotraficante "Indio"
Zelene Suchil Pineda, Librotraficante "Rebelené"
Joceyln Viera, Librotraficante "yolibrotraficante"
Stalina Emmanuelle Villarreal, Librotraficante "La Lucha"
Citlahli I. Villegas, Librotraficante "La Sketches"